CATHERINE OF SIENA: TO PURIFY GOD'S CHURCH

Catherine of Siena:
To Purify *God's* Church

Catherine M. Meade, CSJ

ST PAULS

Verses excerpted from *The Letters of Catherine of Siena*, Vols. I and II, edited by Suzanne Noffke. Medieval Renaissance Texts and Studies, Tempe Arizona © Arizona Board of Regents. Reprinted with permission.

Excerpts from CATHERINE OF SIENA: *The Dialogue*, translation and introduction by Suzanne Noffke, O.P., from The Classics of Western Spirituality, Copyright © 1980 by Paulist Press, Inc., New York/Mahwah, N.J. Used with permission of Paulist Press. www.paulistpress.com

Excerpts from *I, Catherine: Selected Letters of Saint Catherine of Siena* by Kenelm Foster, O.P. and Mary John Ronayne, O.P., eds. & trs., Copyright © 1980 by Collins, London. Used with permission of Sr. Mary John Ronayne, O.P.

Library of Congress Cataloging-in-Publication Data

Meade, Catherine M.
    Catherine of Siena : to purify God's church / Catherine M. Meade.
        p. cm.
    Includes bibliographical references.
    ISBN 0-8189-1224-3
    1. Catherine, of Siena, Saint, 1347-1380. 2. Christian saints—Italy—
Biography. 3. Church renewal—Catholic Church—History—To 1500.
    I. Title.

    BX4700.C4M42 2006
    282.092—dc22
                                2005028045

Produced and designed in the United States of America by the
Fathers and Brothers of the Society of St. Paul,
2187 Victory Boulevard, Staten Island, New York 10314-6603,
as part of their communications apostolate.

ISBN 0-8189-1224-3
ISBN 978-0-8189-1224-5

Printing Information:

Current Printing - first digit   1   2   3   4   5   6   7   8   9   10

Year of Current Printing - first year shown

2006   2007   2008   2009   2010   2011   2012   2013   2014   2015

Dedicated
to the memory of
my sister and brother
Sister Maura Meade, SND
and
Peter John Meade
whose love and support nourished me
throughout my lifetime

Table of Contents

Preface

In close communion with God, obedient to divine impulses, Catherine of Siena lived an active public life sustained by a deeply spiritual personal one. From her earliest days, upholding the sanctity of God's church was her dominant concern, and her daily desire to achieve this goal came from the depths of that personal and intimate union with God. Throughout the ages, even to the present time, this dedication has been recognized and honored. Shortly after his accession to the papal throne, the late Pope John Paul II, as a demonstration of his gratitude to the people of Rome for their generous welcome to a foreigner, publicly honored the two patron saints of Italy, Francis of Assisi and Catherine of Siena. At his visit to Catherine's tomb in the Roman Basilica of Santa Maria sopra Minerva, he spoke these words:

> Here, beside the relics of St. Catherine of Siena, I wish once again to thank the Divine Wisdom for having made use of the heart of that woman, simple yet of profound character, to point the way in times of uncertainty to the Church and especially to the successor of St. Peter. What love, what courage, what magnificent simplicity, and at the same time what spiritual depth! A soul aware of its mission and open to every breath of Divine inspiration. St. Catherine has been recognized as a visible sign of women's mission in the Church. The Church of Jesus Christ and the Apostles

is also a Mother and a Bride. These biblical titles show how profoundly the mission of women is inscribed in the Mystery of the Church.... O that we may discover together the manifold significance of that mission, drawing strength from the qualities which the Creator from the beginning placed in the hearts of women and the wonderful wisdom with which, centuries ago, he endowed St. Catherine of Siena. As in those days she was a teacher and leader of Popes who were far from Rome, so may she be today the inspiration of a Pope who has come to Rome.[1]

It is the wealth of Catherine's own writings: her Letters, *The Dialogue*, and Prayers that allow us to follow the development of her role in the church of her day. Though written by the hands of loyal and learned scribes, in them we hear her own words, experience her joy and sorrow, her pain and exaltation. We come to realize the innate power of a woman's voice, yet feel its loving tenor, its gentle but firm dedication to truth and to those whom she loved and served. We discover that a woman of power can be brilliant and at the same time gentle and loving.

It is in these letters that our journey of understanding begins. She was still a young woman when she initiated her correspondence, at first of a local nature, but gradually expanding to encompass an ever-widening circle of followers. Increasingly their content evolved beyond the personal spirituality of her followers to include serious debates with important personages regarding the position of the church in the politics of the day. As her journeys brought her to Pisa, Florence, and Avignon, it was the issues of the seventy-year exile of the Pope in Avignon as well

---

[1] Mieczyslaw Malinski, *Pope John Paul II: The Life of Karol Wojtyla*, The Seabury Press, New York, 1979 (tr. by P.S. Falla; text provided to Malinski by Sister Jadwiga of the papal secretariat).

as the Tuscan League of cities formed in opposition to the Papacy that occupied her efforts. Then a new and more serious threat to the stability of the church appeared in the Schism that saw two popes reigning simultaneously in Rome and Avignon following the death of Pope Gregory XI.

It was during an interim period, while awaiting her official summons to Rome to participate in this grave crisis, that Catherine returned to Siena, where she gathered a small group of her most trusted scribes. In the quiet of the countryside outside of Siena, she spent hour after hour in ecstasy dictating her most precious work, *The Dialogue.* The title implies a conversational exchange of her questions, spoken in the third person, and God answering directly in words replete with symbolism, the language of mysticism. *The Dialogue* is perhaps the most intimate record of her relationship with God and her most valuable gift to society.

The third part of her written legacy is her Prayers. Her followers began to record these as she prayed aloud, at first in Avignon, then occasionally during her travels throughout Italy. The greater number date from the Roman days when the intense period of the Schism was disrupting the church and society and it was becoming clear to her followers that Catherine's health was failing, that her time was becoming limited. For a short period her letters continued, but then we are dependent on the language of her friends and followers as they share with one another her final words and actions.

Gratitudes

The lovely delicate painting that adorns the cover of this book was a surprise gift from one of my former students at Regis College, Sharl Heller. One could suspect that she had been frequently exposed to comments about the work in progress since she was so adept at selecting important images representative of

St. Catherine's life: the tree, the branch of lilies, her dress and veil, and the steeple of San Domenico in the background! Sharl commissioned this picture from a talented artist friend, Olga Bassine, living in Lincoln, MA, during January of 1998.

The framework and design surrounding the cover picture is the creative addition of a dear friend, a talented graphic designer, Anne Souza Martens of Amhert, MA. Anne also created the illustrations accompanying the selections from *The Dialogue* marking the chapter divisions of Catherine's life based on her tree symbolism.

Sister Marie Cicchese, CSJ carefully proofread the entire text and offered valuable comments.

A dear friend, Leo P. Brassard, A.A. donated hours of his time over the past several years to reading and commenting on the text, enriching it considerably with his wisdom and enthusiasm.

My immediate family has been and remains in every sense, a blessing and continuous joy in my life. My gratitude to my sister Cathleen and her deceased husband Richard Coté, for the gift of their four beautiful children is enormous. In turn, with their spouses, these children have gifted me with three grandnephews and a lovely grandniece whose lives bring blessings to us all.

Finally, I rejoice in my debt to my religious family, the Congregation of the Sisters of Saint Joseph of Boston. When, at the beginning of last year, the effort to complete this project appeared overwhelming, I turned to them for the opportunity to spend an extended period of time at Mercy Center at Madison Ct. Here, in an atmosphere of peaceful quiet, natural beauty, and sacred space, all came together—even the most delightful displays of trees clad in seasonal array. The sisters from all over the country, who were companions on this part of the journey, contributed their support and their joyful spirit as each invoked God's daily presence in their private search for the "holy" and the "blessed."

   To each and all of those mentioned above, I repeat my profound gratitude for the gift of your time and the quality that you have added to the manuscript.

Catherine M. Meade, CSJ
Regis College
Weston, Massachusetts
December, 2005

Introduction

An Obituary from the Medieval World

Catherine Benincasa, 33, beloved daughter of Lapa Piacenti Benincasa and the late Giacomo Benincasa. Formerly of Siena, she died in Rome on April 29, 1380. Survivor of three outbreaks of the Black Death, she was a spiritual icon in Siena, attracting a devoted following because of her tender care of the sick and needy and her work as a peacemaker among warring families. A member of the Dominican Third Order, popularly known as the Mantellate, her reputation for holiness quickly spread beyond the confines of Siena.

Her peacemaking efforts expanded with her attempts to diffuse a League of Tuscan States formed in opposition to the Papacy. Eventually, she journeyed to the Papal residence in Avignon to encourage Pope Gregory XI to return the Papal seat to Rome after an absence of seventy years. She continued her efforts to achieve peace between the Pope and the Tuscan city-states and worked tirelessly for the purification and internal reform of the Church and the appointment of worthy administrators. Finally, she took up residence in Rome when cultural and political divisions led to the dilemma of two reigning Popes. Eliminating this threat to the unity of Christendom was the focus of her attention to the end of her life.

Her health failed rapidly after she suffered a severe stroke at St. Peter's Basilica, and she died shortly after, surrounded by her devoted followers. A solemn funeral took place at the Church of the Minerva, the central church of the Dominican Order in Rome, where her body will rest under the main altar.

Imagine reading this obituary in a daily newspaper of the twenty-first century. Observant readers would pause to marvel at these accomplishments attributed to any individual, let alone a thirty-three year old woman. Accustomed to the succinct style of reviews of human lives, they would, nevertheless, surely question the religious, political, and social conditions that allowed this young laywoman to accomplish so much and exert such influence in so short a lifetime. They would want to know more, curious of the circumstances that made her achievements possible. What was the source of her personal power, her inspiration and intelligence? How did it all begin? Here are Dan Schutte's words, based on Isaiah 6:

> I, the Lord of sea and sky, I have heard my people cry.
> All who dwell in dark and sin, my hand will save.
> I, who made the stars of night, I will make their darkness bright.
> Who will bear my light to them? Whom shall I send?
> Here I am, Lord. Is it I, Lord? I have heard you calling in the night.
> I will go Lord, if you lead me.
> I will hold your people in my heart.[1]

Might this have been the intuitive call that Catherine received as a young girl and responded to with immediacy and eagerness? Without any concern regarding her age, her preparation, or her ability to address the difficult situations of a world about which she knew little, she would have answered God's call, "Here I am, Lord; I will go Lord." From her earliest beginnings, she had no fear, no recognition of inadequacy, only a total trust that God could accomplish in and through her all that He desired.

While many of Catherine's women disciples, often from af-

---

[1] Text and Music © 1981, OCP Publications 5536 NE Hassalo, Portland, OR 97213. All rights reserved. Used with permission.

fluent and sophisticated families, could read and write, Catherine was a true product of her middle class medieval world. She did not come from a home and family that made time and space for the education of their children. Neither would it be customary, or even possible, for neighborhood children to congregate each morning in schools and learning centers or even to gather round a revered figure who might convey to them the rudiments of literary learning. The work of the home, practical in nature, concerned with daily living, was the primary concern.

Both church and society educated medieval people through artistic representation, story, and legend. Their total environment invited visual images to explain their experiences, and they were adept in designing, understanding, and conveying meaning in this way. Gifted with extraordinary insight, Catherine perceived depth of meaning in images—verbal or artistic—and, in time, her own images would convey significance and discernment to challenge the keenest of intellects. The interplay of her inability to read and a religious and social environment that fostered an oral and visual culture would lead her to develop a deeply retentive mind. She would listen, she would ponder, and what would result over time would be wisdom beyond the ordinary.

As a third order Dominican Mantellate, Catherine and her companions were expected to pray aloud, and in unison, a variety of psalms and scripture texts. These words and phrases, heard daily, as well as the written script, would be indelibly engraved in her mind and later emerge in her letters, prayers, and conversations. In maturity, she would claim to have taught herself to read and write. At first hearing, this may sound odd, but our world is not without similar incidents related of exceptional people. Her reading ability would be limited, an extension of her oral knowledge; memories of prayer texts, for example, would lead to recognition of word forms. Writing would be at an elementary level; the one prayer that she wrote in her own hand may indeed be one that she had recited by heart from childhood. What she spoke orally, however, was profound in content. Her work, though dictated to and written by her disciples, brought her recognition as a prime representative of her time period in Italian literature. When assessing her writing, commentators consistently use the words, "she wrote" rather than "she dictated." They are concerned not with technique, but content, which may involve simple, everyday matters, individuals, groups, world shattering events, and heavenly conversation. She listened intently, pondered contemplatively, and what came forth was wisdom, both human and divine.

Her personal charisma seems to have been immediately recognized as, from her first days of public service, she attracted followers from the local neighborhood and from the nearby hospital of La Scala, where like-minded, spiritually motivated persons offered their service. Many local Dominican friars, Mantellate, and early converts formed an essential part of her devoted "family" for the rest of her life. The publicity that began to surface about her, both positive and negative, enlarged her reputation while both Dominican and papal formal recognition affirmed her validity as a servant of God, drawing her further into the public sphere, where she grew in the maturity necessary to address her new challenges.

Catherine's letters expressed a self-confident social and spiritual wisdom that affirmed her position in church and society. Her prayer of contemplation, in which the soul seeks after God, assumed a mystic intensity, in which mind and soul move into the depths of Godhead, becoming one, and natural wisdom is infused with divine wisdom. Her major work, *The Dialogue,* was set in this world of the Spirit, the realm of the Divine, in which was revealed to her God's deep love for all humanity, manifested in the gift of His Son, whose death and resurrection redeemed humankind and provided a new and secure path of entry into

Heaven. Her body of writing entitled this unlettered, thirty-three year old medieval laywoman to the unusual honor of being declared a Doctor of the Church by Pope Paul VI on October 4, 1970, placing her among the church's major theologians, in recognition of "the relevance of her teaching for the whole Church and for all time." This title acknowledges that Catherine "shares in a remarkable way in the teaching function of the church" making note of her "charism of exhortation," that is, her ability to communicate to others "the word of wisdom" and "the word of knowledge."[2]

Not unexpectedly, the source of Catherine's theology was not in learned texts, but in listening and learning from those whose own scholarship was systemic and advanced, coming to a profound and inspired understanding of what she heard and remembering it with thoroughness, exactitude, and clarity. In addition, her mystical knowledge, that is, "intuitive knowledge rooted in love," came from her deep "awareness of union with God experienced within" herself. Her declaration as a Doctor of the Church spoke of her charism of wisdom as a "mystic charism," indicating a special instinct and movement of the Spirit leading into the depths of God.

These official acknowledgments by the church, six centuries after her death, seem a fitting, if delayed, response to the profound love and dedication which this young woman bestowed upon her church at a time when, from a human level, one would say it was least deserving. Two popes claimed validity as leaders of the church, making war upon each other to achieve dominance, not necessarily of a spiritual nature. Urban VI, supported by Catherine (and by posterity) as the duly elected pontiff, became increasingly difficult to deal with. Ultimately, after

---

[2] Mary O'Driscoll, O.P., "Catherine the Theologian," 4-17, in *Spirituality Today,* Vol. 40, Spring, 1988. Interpretive material on this subject is dependent on O'Driscoll's scholarship.

Catherine's death, he succeeded in terrorizing his Curia, and was responsible for the physical torture of several of his cardinals, two of whom died in the process. In addition, it is believed that he, himself, died of poisoning from within the Curia.

The fourteenth century was a different time, one that saw the rise of national powers in conflict with papal dominance and with each other. Loyalties were continually changing; the political world was unstable, and the papal schism further complicated this shifting imbalance. The church had need of the support of kings and princes, of money and armies. Urban's papacy was bankrupt financially and becoming spiritually bankrupt as well. Despite the distressing condition of her church, Catherine's faith in God and dedication to the purification of the church continued to her last breath as she entrusted its future to a loving Father.

This presentation of Catherine's life will follow the metaphorical illumination of her journey to holiness described in her symbolic "Tree of Virtue" with its circle of soil, trunk, and crown exemplifying the essential stages of her human and spiritual development. Her tree symbol will expand to elaborate the stages of spiritual maturation in the "Tree of the Cross." Her ascent of the Cross from the "Feet" of Christ to the "Heart" and, finally, to the "Mouth" depict her mature journey of humility, peacemaking, preaching, and service to her neighbor and to God's Church.

Catherine's interpretation of this tree might also be extended to symbolize the church. In summer and fall, the Weeping Beech Tree, in full bloom, has a crown of rich green leaves that cascade downward from an overwhelming height, almost touching the ground. At first glance, it seems to portray the grief that Catherine experienced in the final days of her life, the sorrow she endured, a sorrow of failure to achieve her life goal, to purify her church, to restore it to its pristine virtue, and to eradicate its failures. Then, in winter, this Weeping Beech, stripped of leaves, reveals in its nakedness, not beauty, but an innate steadfastness and strength. There is wisdom to be found here as a poet revealed: "When one sees the tree in leaf, one thinks the beauty of the tree is in its leaves, and then one sees the bare tree."[3]

The leafless tree might symbolize the church as well, when the roots, the trunk, and the branches become clearly visible. These sources of life-giving nourishment, depicted by Catherine as the virtues of humility, charity, and patience, seasoned with discernment, continue to function as springs of continually renewed life to bring forth a rich and vibrant blossoming crown, a purified church. In dying, Catherine could leave her beloved church in the merciful hands of its Founder, trusting that, though trial and tribulation might assail the church down through the ages, seasons of change would renew the nourishment of the soil, the roots, the trunk, and branches of the church, enabling it, throughout all time, to be reborn in God's grace to that pure beauty, rich, vibrant, full of life, and source of grace for all believers.

---

[3] Samuel Menashe.

CATHERINE OF SIENA: TO PURIFY GOD'S CHURCH

PART ONE

The Circle of Family & Environment

1347-1359

Imagine a circle of soil traced on the ground,
and in its center a tree sprouting....
The circle in which this tree's root, the souls's love, must grow
is true knowledge of herself,
knowledge that is joined to me....
You can go round and round within this circle,
finding neither end nor beginning,
yet never leaving the circle.
This knowledge of yourself,
and of me within yourself,
is grounded in the soil of true humility,
which is as great as the expanse of the circle....
But if your knowledge of yourself were isolated from me
there would be no full circle at all.

THE DIALOGUE, 10:41-42

The Circle of Soil

Whoever goes from St. Catherine's house down towards the Piatta Valley, finds a low battlement construction on the right: Fonte Branda. If you want to draw water you have to descend from the street level to the lower part and look through the large pointed arches over the spring. And if, before entering, you pause and look up the hill, you can see standing out against the sky the massive church of St. Dominic, severe and mighty like a fortress.

Fonte Branda, St. Dominic's Church, the house of Jacopo Benincasa: the three vertices of a triangle in which one finds the first years of the life of St. Catherine of Siena. Fonte Branda, in the lower point, is the earthly aspect of life. It is the daily fatigue of attending to the material demands of a large family.... St. Dominic's Church, up at the top, is the life of the spirit. It is the house of Truth, the blessed place of eucharistic union. And the house, in the middle, is the convergent point of the forces of the other two vertices. It is the place where opposing elements are harmonized in Catherine's incomparable personality.

Giuliana Cavallini[1]

---

[1] *Things Visible and Invisible,* 1-2. I am happy to begin this work with a quotation from Giuliana Cavalini in tribute to her work in rescuing Catherine's *Dialogue* from centuries of erroneous interpretation. Even more, however, I wish to acknowledge the generosity, openness, and respectful encouragement she offers to those who attempt to continue her revelation of Catherine.

The buildings identified by Cavallini embrace three sources of Catherine's early development, and provide the ingredients of her circle of soil: family life, religious influence, and civic awareness. The Siena of Catherine's day was identified as the City of the Virgin and is known, even today, as the City of Art. The first appellation recognized its inherent religious stance while the second confirmed the importance of an artistic program that from medieval times not only aggrandized the city-state but provided potent religious images to mirror the sermons and values preached in the churches. For the unlettered, like Catherine, these artistic creations stimulated realistic images to dominate her thinking and appear in her "mind's eye" in what today are referred to as "visions."

Until she was approximately twelve years of age, Catherine's life was marked by a growing seclusion, perhaps loneliness, and by solitary excursions throughout her neighborhood. Except for her sister Bonaventura and her gentle father, Giacomo Benincasa, family life seemed an often noisy and querulous environment. Death and disease became an accepted and recurring circumstance accompanied by the terror, fear, dislocation and trauma that a global pestilence would cause. Influenced by fourteenth century medieval spirituality, she moved in a world informed by legends of the saints, by painted miraculous scenes, influenced by the Sienese civic identification with the Virgin Mary, and especially of an intimate personal relationship with the divine person of Christ. Siena offered Catherine a world of images that became her schooling. The churches were refuges, sources of religious story, peopled by monks and friars whose learning, voiced in the vernacular language of her understanding, made God and the saints, virtue and vice, good and evil, church and society the focus of her developing understanding.

Exploring her family background, parentage, siblings, and

family life during her earliest years necessitates an examination of the internal and external circumstances that directed their lives and provided the initial human developmental influences. Issues of war, social unrest, and natural disasters in many ways dictated the character of private lives and interacted with the spiritual and political atmosphere in the Sienese city-state where civic, religious, and familial ideals were so closely interwoven that they were often one and the same. Part One of this study will consider these nutrients of the circle of soil in which the seed of Catherine's life awakened, broke free from its protective covering, pushed out tentative roots, and extended a delicate shoot. How fragile yet ordinary is this beginning, reliant on its soil of environment, nourishment, and loving attendance. Yet, in Catherine's case, this is the beginning of a life that will achieve a trinity of greatness: of virtue, of accomplishment, and of sanctity.

CHAPTER ONE

The Inner Circle: Family Environment

- 1 -
Parentage

[T]he initial seed for development toward an identity for a newly evolving individual precedes and has its origins well before [birth]. The contributions of the parents whose genes fused to birth that person were not only genetic but have already been and will continue to be psychological and experiential as well. Each parent, and the pair as a unit, directs his/her mental attitudes toward the unborn from their first awareness of conception, even before that at its anticipation... the automatic surname that attaches to the infant carries with it a generational line of transmission of common traits in the identity of the lineage.

Leo Rangel[2]

So much of Catherine's early history remains obscure that a response to Rangel's observations can be made only in a general way. Her parents, Lapa and Giacomo Benincasa, had given birth to twenty-two children by the time they conceived Catherine and her twin, Giovanna. From what has been reconstructed of the

---

[2] "Identity and the Human Core" in Bosma et al, *Identity and Development*, 30-31.

family history, it is almost a certainty that many of their children had died either in childbirth or in early infancy since records exist to identify barely half of their progeny. Did the uncertainty of bringing a live child to birth affect them? Were they happy at the advent of yet another birth? Since Lapa has been characterized as one for whom childbearing was the purpose of her existence, who saw the world in the simple terms of creating numerous, prosperous and well-regulated families, there is a strong likelihood that the coming birth pleased her.[3]

The economic situation in Siena had been in decline since the mid 1330s. Living costs had risen; an epidemic had depleted resources; crops were poor; Florentine mercenaries had overrun the countryside; trade had diminished; industry was at a standstill; and the famished population rebelled. The ruling Nine seemed unable to reverse these conditions.[4] Yet, it appears that Giacomo Benincasa's occupation as dyer for the wool trade did not suffer from this decline. One biographer, commenting on the monetary position of the family, noted that Giacomo lived in a substantial house within the city walls and owned not only his house and workshops but also a farm and a vineyard outside of the city.[5] Levasti's account indicated that Giacomo came into possession of this house in October of 1346, less than a year before Catherine's birth and the same year that he took his eldest son, Benincasa, into partnership. It can be assumed then, despite the depressed local conditions, that the family fortunes were solvent as the parents awaited the birth of another child.

From her father, believed to have been a Franciscan tertiary, Catherine received a gentle and peaceful nature, a religious inclination, as well as the ability to bring reconciliation to op-

---

[3]   Arrigo Levasti, *My Servant Catherine*, 2.

[4]   Diana Norman, ed., *Siena, Florence and Padua: Art, Society and Religion, 1280-1400*, Vol. I, 16.

[5]   Alice Curtayne, *Saint Catherine of Siena*, 4.

posing opinions. He was a successful man of business, dedicated to his family, as well as socially responsible since it is believed that both Giacomo and Benincasa held representative positions during the Rule of the Nine.[6] He was remembered as having quietly paid an unjust debt without condemning or responding maliciously to the accuser. Industrious and hardworking, he was deeply committed to his family and capable of exercising limitless patience with his wife. Giacomo's sister Agnes, after the death of her husband Chele di Duccio, became a Mantellate (a lay third order Dominican), and a painting of her survives, inscribed Beata Agnese Benincasa.[7]

Catherine's maternal grandfather, Nuccio Piacenti, a quilt maker by trade, was a poet as well. That Catherine's later letters, so full of symbol, metaphor and flowing language, earned her a reputation as one of the few representatives of her time period in the history of vernacular Italian literature, may be due to this genetic legacy, a facility with word and tongue inherited from her grandfather.[8] A surviving document signed by the Master General of the Dominican Order grants to Nuccio Piacenti and his wife Cecca participation in all the prayers and good works of the preachers in return for their devotion to the Order.[9]

All accounts of Catherine's mother, Lapa, depict a voluble, excitable woman, one given to frequent mood swings. Levasti characterized her as an excessive talker, extravagant in feeling with "enthusiasms that were as facile as her rages." Raymond of Capua wrote that her outbursts were loud and frequent, often bringing the neighbors running to see what was wrong. She was also described as "aggressively busy," displaying "uncompromis-

[6] Levasti, 1.
[7] Augusta Theodosia Drane, *The History of St. Catherine of Siena and Her Companions*, Vol. I, 10.
[8] Francesco de Santis, *History of Italian Literature*, Vol. I, 124.
[9] Drane, Vol. I, 11.

ing precepts and tireless energy." Nevertheless, she ruled her large household effectively as a gentler woman might not have been able to do.[10] To her credit, Levasti stated that she loved her children to excess with a tenderness that was extravagant adding, however, that her moods could change quickly. Finally, we come to the name Catherine, *Caterina,* chosen for her at birth. Did her parents select this name to honor the great Saint Catherine of Alexandria, the early fourth century martyr who dazzled learned men with her brilliant discourse, the woman, undaunted by suffering, who gave her life for her faith? Images of this saint had begun to appear in Siena around the time of Catherine's birth and, since Catherine was not a common name given to Italian children at this time, if her parents chose this Catherine as a model for her, it would indeed have the nature of prediction.[11] Later, in her major literary work, *The Dialogue,* Catherine's references to this saint will indicate her interest in and admiration for her namesake.

- 2 -
The Black Death, 1348

The mortality in Siena began in May. It was a cruel and horrible thing: and I do not know where to begin to tell of the cruelty and pitiless ways. It seemed that almost everyone became stupefied by seeing the pain.

---

[10] Curtayne, 6.

[11] Waley lists the popular names chosen for Sienese girls in the 1280s: Gemma, Benvenuta, Fiore, Buonafemina, Divizia, Diamente and Riccha. Catherine does not even appear. It is among the popular masculine names that we recognize both male and female selections of the Benincasa: Giovanni, Buonaventura, Giacomo, Pietro, Benvenuto and Benincasa among others. Daniel Waley, *Siena and the Sienese in the Thirteenth Century,* 139-140.

And it is impossible for the human tongue to recount the awful truth. Indeed one who did not see such horribleness can be called blessed.

The Chronicle of Agnolo di Tura del Grasso[12]

Catherine Benincasa's infancy and childhood took place at a most inauspicious time in the history of her native Siena. Her birth, generally accepted as March 25, 1347, preceded by thirteen months the initial outbreak of the Black Death, a lethal visitation of death unparalleled in history.[13] What impact would this experience of unmitigated dread and devastation have on a precocious child, just entering into her second year of life? What effect would it have on her developing psyche, exposed for an intense period of four to five months to the unremitting grief, fear, horror, loss and suffering of her family, neighbors, and fellow citizens? The contemporary Sienese chronicler, Agnolo di Tura del Grasso, noted, "so many died that all believed that it was the end of the world" and "it was all so horrible that I, the writer, cannot think of it...."

An examination of the burial record of the Church of San Domenico, the center of Dominican life in the Fontebranda district where Catherine's family lived, brings the tragedy to life.[14] Not only does it afford insight into the impact of the plague in terms of loss of life, it also suggests the emotional toll exerted in the close knit neighborhood. An examination of the necrology of this small local cemetery, when seen as a microcosm of similar burial places throughout the city, supports to a great degree the information historians have gleaned from records of the pe-

---

[12] In William Bowsky, ed., *The Black Death: A Turning Point in History?*, 13-14.

[13] Judged by cumulative loss of life, physical damage and emotional stress the Black Death has been ranked as the second greatest disaster in world history. The Second World War, inclusive of the Holocaust, is the greatest, according to the geographer Harold Foster. Reported by Robert E. Lerner, "The Black Death and Western European Eschatological Mentalities," 77.

riod. The registrar of the *cimitario* confirms Agnolo's assertion that the plague began in May recording fifty-five burials in that month as opposed to the more normal numbers of seven in April and two in May of the previous year. Sixty-six burials followed in the first seventeen days of June 1348; then, suddenly, nothing. From June seventeenth through the end of July, no further recordings appear until the record resumes in August with four entries, then three in September and November as the record resumes normality. Between June seventeenth and the beginning of August, the lack of citations in the necrology gives evidence of Agnolo's lament: "And the victims died almost immediately. They would swell beneath their armpits and in their groins, and fall over dead while talking.... Members of a household brought their dead to a ditch as best they could, without priest, without divine offices. Nor did the death bell sound. And in many places in Siena great pits were dug and piled deep with the multitude of dead."

The necrology of the little cemetery in the Camporeggio demonstrates the day to day impact of the plague in this small local environ. The early entries in May have a regularity indicating that the plague had not yet been recognized as the horror that it would become. Men are identified by name, sometimes by occupation or title, and *sepultus est* followed by the date of interment. Women are identified by the title *domina* as well as their relationship to a male figure: wife, mother, daughter, sister then *sepulta est* and the date. No ages are supplied. As the month moves forward and the impact of the plague intensifies, the record indicates multiple deaths in the same family. The mother, sister and father of Friar Bartolomeo Mini succumb within a week.[15]

---

[14] *I Necrologi di San Domenico in Camporegio*, 5-101.
[15] Ibid., #751, #762, and #765, 74-75.

- 3 -
A Survivor's Grief

For years it lay in an iron box buried so deep inside
me that I was never sure just what it was. I knew I
carried slippery, combustible things more secret than
sex and more dangerous than any shadow or ghost.
Ghosts had shape and name. What lay inside my iron
box had none. Whatever lived inside me was so potent that words crumbled before they could describe.

Helen Epstein[25]

Considerations of the life of Catherine of Siena make scant
reference to the context of her early years. Her biographer,
Raymond of Capua, introduces her family, their social status, the
tenor of the household and moves quickly to reveal the outstand-
ing nature of a child he sees as pre-selected for greatness. Though
he alludes to many later private conversations with Catherine,
none of those he recorded refer to memories of her earliest experiences. Should we then conclude that there were none, or
should we consider that, like the children of the Holocaust, Catherine, too, had memories that would "never die"?

Historians concerned with the plague in Siena carefully sort
available data to draw conclusions regarding its effects on population, crime, taxation, wealth, land ownership, political stability, and similar public issues. Little first hand evidence exists,
however, beyond Agnolo's anguished attempt to put words on
paper to mark the profound nature of the experience of his fellow citizens. Indeed, in most medieval history, a veil of silence
is drawn over personal and private life so we are left to wonder

---

[25] *Children of the Holocaust*, 1.

how survivors regained control of their lives, how families reorganized to cope with loss, and how children dealt with the soul stirring scars of such an unprecedented upheaval.[26] Yet, it is in this early period that the first seeds of Catherine's early and determined choice of an independent and ascetical lifestyle were sown.[27]

Stories of the twentieth century Holocaust victims, and especially of their offspring, offer insight into the after effects of surviving an experience of horror, together with the endeavor to

---

[26] In the absence of personal testimonies contradictions surface. For example, when Agnolo states, "Father abandoned child, wife husband, one brother another" and "none could be found to bury the dead for money or friendship," we can look to the evidence in the San Domenico necrology. Forty-nine clerics succumbed, many in service to the victims; the faithful registrar of the cemetery put himself at daily risk to record each interment; the precise identification of victims indicates the cooperation of close relatives; and Agnolo himself records that he buried his five children with his own hands. Similarly, holocaust survivors are apt to report that in the camps it was everyone for himself, while at the same time telling stories of being helped by, or helping another, a contradiction which one writer reports as occurring so often "that it amounts to a double vision at the heart of their testimony," or two truths that co-exist in the memory. See Terrence Des Pres, *The Survivor: An Anatomy of Life in the Death Camps*, 30.

[27] Noting the aftermath of the Black Death, Agnolo wrote, "all who survived gave themselves over to pleasure: monks, priests, nuns, and lay men and women all enjoyed themselves, and none worried about spending and gambling. And everyone thought himself rich because he had escaped and regained the world." Historians usually consider three reactions to the devastation of the plague: hedonism, self punishment or projection of anger. We can assume, I think, that Catherine would not be influenced by the first group, those noted by Agnolo; possibly somewhat by the second, though not in the commonly discussed excessive reaction of groups of flagellants roaming the streets whipping themselves; nor even the third, the seeking of scapegoats. One indirect result of the plague was to exacerbate the position of those already on the margins of social acceptance, for example, strangers, beggars, lepers and Jews. In various locations, including northern Spain, Chinon and Chambéry in the French Alps, Strasbourg, Germany and Poland, rumors spread indicting the Jews for responsibility in spreading the plague by poisoning Christian wells. Despite the intervention of medical people and the pope, the rumors persisted since, in the trauma of the period, there was a need to place blame. See David Herlihy, *The Black Death and the Transformation of the West*, 65-66.

possible that Catherine was reminded frequently of these two facts. In later years, when Catherine wrote to her brother Benincasa in Florence to chide him for his lack of concern for their mother, she called him to responsibility by reminding him of "the milk she gave you from her breast."[44] Since this was not stated symbolically, but as an actual fact, it is apparent that Catherine may have been schooled to believe that this was a generous act and that some return was expected.

In the midst of Lapa's nursing and child bearing, we can imagine that the family home was a busy one, that washing, cleaning, cooking and serving meals was a demanding requirement. As the years passed, children of two generations would be underfoot. The workshop of the family dyeing trade was in the adjacent portion of the lower level of the house. Therefore, the men of the family and their helpers would be ever present, and the noises and odors emanating from the ground floor would rise to encompass every level of the household. An atmosphere of peace and harmony would be in short supply for both Lapa and the child Catherine.

Many components of child development in Catherine's earliest years can be traced to her sister Bonaventura's supportive relationship. We are told that infants begin to develop "specific attachments to particular people around the third quarter of their first year of life." When attachment figures are available in early years, a child develops a sense of security and inner confidence which will become the basis for a later adult capacity to form relationships.[45] Given the loving affiliation between Catherine and Bonaventura, it may be that it was her substitute care-giving that enabled Catherine to manifest the early sense of security and the inner confidence of an outgoing child loved by the neighbors

---

[44] *The Letters of St. Catherine of Siena,* Vol. I, T18, 33.

[45] Anthony Storr, *Solitude: A Return to the Self,* 9, 16, 148.

and later, the attractive personality that drew so many followers. In addition, this inner security would lay the foundation for Catherine's "capacity to be alone" and to thrive independently, characteristics which would become such an essential part of her later life.

Aside from what has already been mentioned in regard to Lapa's shared memories and the possibility that her grief may have distracted her, or even caused her to withhold affection from Catherine, several circumstances are significant. Levasti described Lapa, despite all her limitations, as one whose "tenderness for her children was extravagant." The substitute relationship of Bonaventura as a loving and reliable second mother was equally evident and surface indications reveal that Catherine developed as a happy, autonomous, and competent child.

- 6 -
Early Childhood

The big house in which [Catherine] lived was built against a sharp incline. It had two doors in front: one gave access to the workshops, full of the odors of dyes and crowded with apprentices; the other opened on a staircase leading to the dwelling rooms. There was a fantastic touch about this staircase, because there was a back door at the top of it giving on to the level road so that what seemed the ground floor viewed from the back was the first floor from the front. Through the back door, one entered Monna Lapa's kitchen on one side and a little terrace with a garden on the other side. The staircase was indeed the best coign of vantage to see all that was going on and Euphrosyne took pos-

session of it. On it, she could fly from the wonders of
one street to the magic of another; from the mysteries
of the workshop, to the kitchen, which was always
interesting. Tremendous meals were prepared at the
open hearth; it was also the room in which the
Benincasa dined, and the women sat there weaving
when evening came on. Catherine found other uses
for the stairs: checking her childish devotions by saying as many Hail Marys as there were steps. For this,
it was better than a rosary of beads.

Alice Curtayne[46]

All accounts of Catherine's early childhood comment on her
sweetness and happiness. Levasti's descriptive adjectives include
lively, pretty, attractive, talkative, and possessed of an understanding beyond her years. Raymond's account, repeated here by
Curtayne, has the neighbors calling her "Euphrosyne," translated
as joy, and constantly carrying her off to their own houses "to
hear her shrewd little sayings and to enjoy her charming childish
gaiety."[47] Her habit of repeating the Hail Mary as she went up
and down the stairs, was seen by Raymond as remarkable, a sign
of her early holiness.

Curtayne has given us an imaginative visual interpretation
of the staircase, the setting of this prayer practice, conveying comfortable domestic surroundings that indicate an environment of
trust and freedom, yet one that also included parameters.
Catherine's earliest explorations took place with supervision that
was liberal enough to allow for the kind of autonomy to which
Erik Erikson referred when he wrote of this stage, "From a sense
of self-control without loss of self-esteem comes a lasting sense

---

[46] *Saint Catherine of Siena*, 7.
[47] Raymond of Capua, 27, #27.

of autonomy and pride."[48] Catherine's playful use of the stairway also indicated the signs of development seen when female children begin to operate in a "larger scope of action" and experience wider opportunities to use their own mental and physical resources to articulate a larger sense of self.[49]

Catherine's freedom to wander outdoors must have been cautiously restrained until fear of contamination from the Black Death had eased. Thus, the stories of her playing in her mother's garden with other children of her age, teaching them prayers and even experimenting with a cord used as a discipline, would have come later. Similarly, visits to the Church of San Domenico a few minutes from her home—where the adjacent cemetery was the scene of frantic and numberless burials—could not have occurred until well after the danger of infection had passed.

This edifice, which reportedly fascinated Catherine, hovered over the Benincasa residence and must have seemed to a child to reach to heaven itself. Here, the incense, the music, the singing, and the sermons would have delighted her. Above all, perhaps, the intense silence of the vast empty interior, its stillness, broken only by the whispered voices and the sandaled footsteps of the white robed friars, might have invoked in her what was deeply buried, the immeasurable loneliness for the one who was lost to her, her twin. At this vulnerable age when the young child is most open to the experience of attachment, the memory of the one to whom she was most intimately connected in her mother's womb was a further connection to this sacred place which became both heaven and haven. She must have thought that, in contrast to the noisy busyness of home, the church of San Domenico offered a sanctuary where she felt an at-home-ness, a connectedness and a deep longing to remain there.

---

[48] Erik Erikson, *Psychological Issues: Identity and the Life Cycle*, 68.
[49] Jean Baker Miller, "The Development of Women's Sense of Self," 16-18.

Early in her experience, then, at a time when a child begins to develop a capacity to function separately, the religious atmosphere provoked in her a strong attraction, which would become central to her developing self. In the period when a child is becoming aware of herself as loving the people who cared for her and to be sad to be separated from them, she had the experience of being separated forever from a loving relationship with her dead twin.[50] Consequently, relationship may have assumed for her both an earthly and a heavenly character.

- 7 -
Youth

Since adolescence denoted the transition from childhood to adulthood, what constitutes 'development' in adolescence hinges on how one views the childhood that preceded it.... Recent research on infancy and early childhood reveals the young child to be far more social than psychologists previously imagined.... [Recent researches] document the interpersonal capabilities and the social nature of young children: their responsiveness to others and their appreciation of standards.... the young child is now observed to initiate and sustain connection with others, to engage in patterns of social interaction with others, and, thus, to create relationships with them.

Carol Gilligan[51]

---

[50] Carol Gilligan and Grant Wiggins, "The Origins of Morality in Early Childhood Relationships," 114-115.

[51] "Adolescent Development Reconsidered." viii.

Studies of childhood development from the ages of five to twelve define this period as one preoccupied with learning. The title "school age" emphasizes the contemporary notion that at this point all children, in one way or another, are given over to the care of schools and teachers whose impact on their development is a fundamental one. The question of education is not directly addressed in stories of Catherine's childhood, but it is apparent that she had no formal schooling. According to custom, it was the mother who would provide her child with basic instruction; but since Lapa herself could not read or write, she would be unable to teach her children. Still it was a "learning" time for Catherine who would educate herself by listening attentively to the spoken word and observing intently every image around her. Her intelligent curiosity, her creative imagination, as well as a meditative propensity, intensified the learning potential of one who, all evidence indicates, was gifted with a precocious understanding and a keen perceptive aptitude.

Reconstructing Catherine's interactions with her large family is difficult; however, a family tree, contrived by Grottanelli for a 1966 edition of Catherine's letters, identifies five of her brothers and seven of her sisters.[52] Niccoluccia, who may have been the eldest daughter, had married Palmiero dalla Fonte before the 1348 plague since we know that the Benincasa family adopted her husband's younger brother, Tommaso dalla Fonte, orphaned during the plague. Maddalena also was married early to Bartolo di Vannini and probably lived outside the family home at this time. Bonaventura, Catherine's closest family member and surrogate mother, newly married to Niccoló Tegliacci when Catherine was four or five, may have been an adolescent at Catherine's birth (though some accounts list her as the eldest daughter). Other members include unmarried sisters, Lisa and Nera; Catherine's

52 Grottanelli, 296-297.

twin, Giovanna; and the last born child, Nanna. Her brothers Benincasa, Bartolo, and Stephano became dyers like their father and worked in the family business. Their wives and children were part of the extended family. Also mentioned in the family tree were brothers Niccoló and Sandro who appear neither in the letters nor Raymond's *Legenda*. Her biographer Levasti comments: "In Catherine's life her brothers and sisters play a very minor part and, except for Bonaventura, they move in the background as colorless figures who seem to have no influence over her, and do not help us understand her."[53] Perhaps this only appears true because we know so little about them.

Urbanization in medieval life restricted what had been a broader role for the female in rural areas where every member of the family—husband, wife and children—had been expected to make significant contributions to the labor required for the survival and well being of the family unit. In city life, as in the Siena of Catherine's time, a few husband and wife teams operated a family shop or business as a complementary endeavor though women, for the most part, had ceased to be equal helpmates in manual labor and trades. Instead, women concentrated on the home and homemaking endeavors. Specialized trades, such as dyeing, appeared to be a male domain. In the Benincasa household, there was a discrete separation of roles in which the women prepared and served meals, cared for the children, and saw to the general well being of the family. None of the women participated in the operation of the workshop, certainly a loss for a trade in which the natural creative flair of women might have revolutionized the world of texture and color. At her young age Catherine would have absorbed these "cues" which indicated the different values that society placed on the female and male.[54]

---

[53] Levasti, 2.

[54] Barbara Newman and Philip Newman, *Development through Life: A Psychological Approach*, 107.

The family composition offers some explanation as to why Catherine appeared uninvolved in the household chores, with her contribution apparently limited to running errands. The women responsible for the family quarters included Lapa, daughters Nera and Lisa, Benincasa's wife, at least one servant girl, and Bartolo's wife Lisa who joined the household when Catherine was a young girl. Either Catherine lacked domestic instincts or Lapa's natural impatience, combined with her age, may have made her less willing or able to instruct Catherine in the household arts. A child comes to an understanding both of her gender and her role in society at an early age.[55] Thus, Catherine's freedom to wander the city, to spend time in churches, and to feed her imagination must have been an important factor in her choice of a lifestyle different from the other women in her family.

Frequent errands to the market and to Bonaventura's home on the other side of the city gave her the opportunity to explore and to study her city and the people she met along the way. Her errands may have brought her to the public market, then located in the Campo, where her curiosity would have taken her inside the Palazzo Pubblico. Here she would be introduced to the political realities demonstrated in the Lorenzetti cycle of paintings depicting aspects of Good and Bad Government. Young children find potential for learning in every new encounter, especially learning that is directed outward to the environment, and demonstrate ability to acquire complex artistic skills. Therefore, it is quite possible that through her informal learning in her city, Catherine imbibed its political realities and developed the artistic sensibility that would later emerge in her prolific use of symbol and metaphor as she described in her adult writings what she saw in her "mind's eye."[56]

---

[55] Ibid., 104-105.
[56] Storr, 153-163.

One wonders at the family's lack of supervision as the child often seemed to be absent from home for extended periods. One story describes Lapa as upset and irritable when Catherine, sent on an errand, was overly late in returning. Lapa's remonstration, loud and excessive, evoked a temperate but firm response. Catherine told her mother that, in the future, she could punish her in whatever way she wished, but she was not to lose control of her tongue to "curse anyone, good or bad," because "that is a thing unbecoming your venerable age," and "wounds me to the heart."[57] Raymond tells us that her family members were "astounded" at this show of moral strength.

---

[57] Raymond of Capua, 39, #40.

CHAPTER TWO

The Outer Circle:
Civic and Religious Awareness

- 1 -
Siena

It is not the rational order of many Baroque towns that
we find in Siena; its little universe is many-sided, for
it represents the very body, soul, and spirit of Man.
The town is built along the curves of three ranges of
hills spread out like the veins in a leaf. One can look
across from each height to another part of the town,
separated by a valley yet still remaining one and the
same city, with its earthen-red towers and houses....
The beauty of Siena is not merely the result of an unconscious or 'natural' growth; it has been consciously
built up by its citizens, as a work of art, with a keen
sense of unity but also with that deep respect for the
inherited rights of the castes, the professions, and the
clans, which is the special mark of the Middle Ages.

Margaret McDonough Brown[1]

The glory of the medieval city was its conception as *civi-*
tas, the residence of citizens who dwelt in safety behind walls

---

[1] *"Sena Vetus Civitas Virginis"* in Jacob Burckhardt, *Siena*, 1.

erected to keep danger out and to preserve security within. These cities were constructed for and developed to nurture human beings in a time when the material and spiritual worlds comprised two parts of one communal whole, when religious and temporal power interacted for the common good. Throughout the history of the Sienese commune, there was a coordinated partnership between two governments: one supreme in matters temporal and the other in matters spiritual. Sienese citizens paid allegiance to both and rejoiced in the success and greatness of the church no less than in the success and greatness of the state.[2]

From 1287 to 1355, the Nine Governors and Defenders of the Commune of the People of Siena, popularly referred to as "The Nine," governed the Commune of Siena. During this period, when members of the noble families were excluded from governing, the Nine were members of the mercantile-banking oligarchy. They were elected to pursue twin goals: creating an environment that inspired civic pride and building on established religious principles to espouse the virtues of justice, concord, and peace to provide for the common good of all citizens. As leaders of the Commune, they oversaw the pursuit of a city planning effort that encompassed all societal, political, and religious aspects, as well as an artistic program that created what Sienese still claim as a "city of art." This process of building up the fabric of her environment continued into Catherine's day, but after 1355 a radical series of changes in government introduced her to the realities of political discord and violence.

Reconstruction of the Duomo, the cathedral consecrated to the Virgin from at least 913, began around 1226; revisions and alterations continued well beyond Catherine's lifetime. The center of city government, the Palazzo Pubblico, was initiated in 1297 and completed in 1326, while a bell tower was added between

---

2   Ferdinand Schevill, *Siena, The History of a Medieval Commune*, 76.

1325-1344. This elongated structure, the Torre della Mangia, of which it was said that to be Sienese was to be born in its shadow, matched the height of the bell tower of the Duomo perched on the adjacent hill top, thus equating civic and religious power and authority. Fronting the Palazzo Pubblico, the large open public space of the Campo had the effect of an amphitheater. Within its boundaries, the construction of a fountain bringing water to the heart of the Campo by 1334-1336 was a marvel of medieval engineering, celebrated by its joyful name, the Fonte Gaia.

Inside the Palazzo Pubblico, the walls were lavishly decorated by the great Sienese artists of the time. In 1315 Simone Martini painted a Maestà, an enthroned Virgin surrounded by saints and angels, for the Great Council Hall; an inscription below it reminded the councilors to be concerned with justice as they ruled the land. Between 1337 and 1340, Ambrogio Lorenzetti created frescoes in the adjoining chamber of the Nine, the Sal de Nove. Covering three massive walls, these frescoes depicted allegories of good and bad government with expansive scenes portraying the effects of good and evil in the city and in the countryside. These frescoes visually educated the citizens of Siena in the Aristotelian, Augustinian, and Thomistic principles of governance. Elaborating medieval ideals of virtue, of peace and justice, of wisdom and concord, these frescoes promoted not only the common good of the citizenry but also the expectation of virtuous behavior within the commune. Every citizen of Siena was familiar with this message, and children like Catherine grew up imbued with these inspiring and persuasive values. Her later political views reflected this idealistic understanding and influenced her exhortations to civic and religious leaders.

Exposed as they were to sensitive and dramatic portrayals of civic themes and religious experience in visual imagery, the religious temperament of the Sienese embraced a strong mystical bent, leading them to have faith in visions and to rely on the direct intervention of the Almighty. Their perception of the intimate relationship between the Virgin and their City, of Siena being held lovingly to the Virgin's breast like a child being nursed, demonstrated this medieval facility in joining the material and spiritual worlds. In the *Divine Comedy*, Dante has a Sienese noblewoman, identified as Pia dei Tolomei, say, *"Siena mi fè,"* Siena made me.[3] This expression of the close identification that a medieval woman felt toward the city of her birth, upbringing, and life long residence could easily be repeated by Catherine who, like Pia, was a creature of her city. Though a canonized saint and Doctor of the Church, Catherine Benincasa to this day, has remained known only as Catherine of Siena.

- 2 -
Visual Learning

But the fourteenth century did not think of... works of art in the same way that we do. They were not meant to be objects hung on the walls of museums and admired only for their beauty. Rather, the paintings and statues were, first and foremost, holy things intimately connected with the liturgies that were performed before them in the churches. These holy images were thought to contain the power of the beings they represented; they were viewed with awe. There are numerous records of carved Christs and painted saints miraculously intervening in the lives of those who worshiped them.

Bruce Cole[4]

---

[3] *Purgatorio,* Canto V, line 133-134; tr. by Charles Singleton, Bollingen Series, Princeton, 1973.

[4] *Sienese Painting,* xii.

Everywhere, in churches and in public buildings of Siena, art and artists flourished. Catherine's early wanderings in the streets and her penchant for visiting churches introduced her to a visual knowledge of Christ and his mother, of saints and holy people, of holy stories depicted in panoramic scenes that invited participation. Listening to sermons from the pulpits and studying these lifelike images, she grew in spiritual knowledge and human understanding. Above all, the painted metaphors of saints and saintly stories fed her mind as she grew more deeply into relationship with Christ. As her solitary wanderings led her to question and identify her deepest needs, feelings, and impulses, we can see how important to her maturing imagination and creative mind was her capacity to be alone, to evolve the inner security and strength that would make her capable of aesthetic achievement.[5]

In the quiet beauty of the streets, churches, and meeting places of her city, she allowed the inner world of her imagination, "the most reverent mirror of the inner world," to play freely in the world of symbols, "the only means of expressing divinity."[6] Describing personality types identified as self-actualizing creative, Maslow found in them the "creativeness of all happy children" who are "relatively unfrightened by the unknown, the mysterious, the puzzling, and are often positively attracted by it."[7] In her wanderings throughout the churches of her city, Catherine had ample opportunity to interact with mystery, to be drawn into contemplation of it, and to generate new images to portray the depth of the relationship growing in her soul.

Throughout Siena, the image of the Virgin was the domi-

---

[5] Storr, *Solitude,* 15, 21, 69, 70.

[6] John O'Donohue, *Anam Cara: A Book of Celtic Wisdom,* 95.

[7] Abraham A. Maslow, *Toward a Psychology of Being,* 138. Maslow elaborated that these self-actualizing persons do not neglect the unknown, deny it, or run from it, or try to believe it is really known.

nant one since, from 1260, it was known as the City of the Virgin, *Civitas Virginis*. In September of that year, threatened with invasion by the Florentine armies, the citizenry marched to the Cathedral, led by Buonaguida Lucari. Here, they joined the Bishop and clerics in procession to the high altar of the Virgin and cried out in unison, "Misericordia, Misericordia" ("Mercy, Mercy"). Buonaguida prayed, "Glorious Virgin, Queen of Heaven, I, a miserable sinner, give and dedicate to you this city of Siena and the lands around... that you may defend and deliver her from the hands of those arrant curs of Florence, who would subdue her." The following morning, the citizen army engaged and defeated the Florentine host at Montaperti.[8] This "miracle" wrought by the Virgin's intercession was commemorated every year on August fifteenth as the Virgin's image was carried in procession around the city. No Sienese child could be unaware of the significance of the Virgin to the city.

As she went to and from her sister's home, Catherine often may have taken the route which led between the Duomo and the hospital opposite it, Santa Maria della Scala. Earlier frescoes, lost since the eighteenth century, adorned the façade of the hospital from 1335, testifying to the obvious religious nature of the original institution.[9] These representations from the life of Joachim and Anna, parents of the Virgin, echoed the exterior decoration of the Cathedral opposite it, depicting scenes from the life of the Virgin Mary. The faces of the two buildings, with their connecting themes, demonstrated the medieval relationship between the Cathedral, as the place of the "word," and the hospital, the place of the "deed," a message of faith disseminated in sermons from church pulpits. The artistic decoration of the two buildings, fac-

---

8   Henk Van Os, *Sienese Altarpieces, 1214-1460*, Vol. I, 11-12.

9   Hayden J. Maginnis, "The Lost Façade Frescoes from Siena's Ospedale di S. Maria della Scala," 180-194.

ing each other across the Piazza of the Duomo, created the ambiance of an outdoor church which often served as a gathering place for processions that would circle the city on special occasions. Examples include the August fifteenth commemoration of the Virgin saving the city at the battle of Montaperti, the Palm Sunday procession around the walls of the city to the Porta Salaria to welcome Christ to the city, and the many processions of the various confraternities on their feast days.[10] On numerous occasions, Catherine must have paused and gazed upward in awe at the enormous scenes seemingly hanging from the sky above her.

On almost every altar of every church and in every public building, the Virgin and her Child reigned. Customarily, panels of two or three saints appeared on each side of the central Madonna and Child; interestingly, female saints were frequently represented. The presence of Mary Magdalen, Catherine of Alexandria, Agnes, Lucy, Dorothy, and others in these grand polyptychs, panel paintings and altarpieces, must have given Catherine inspiration and encouragement in her desire to respond to God's call. The great Sienese painters of the day—Duccio, Simone Martini, Pietro and Ambrogio Lorenzetti—participated in creating these images in the half century preceding Catherine's birth, when the artists of Siena were recognized for their superior innovative and naturalistic creative talents. With their brushes, they created human and motherly images of Mary unlike earlier iconic representations of the Byzantine tradition. The Child, too, became playful and smiling in his interaction with the loving mother and with the viewer.

---

[10] Daniela Gallavotti Cavallero, *Lo Spedale di Santa Maria della Scala in Siena: Vicenda di una Committenza Artistica*, fig. 3, 15.

Madonna del Latte (1340)

The development of humanistic qualities in painting is apparent in the image of the Virgin nursing her child and a delighted Christ child playfully partaking. One of the most famous, and the earliest among these, is that of Ambrogio Lorenzetti.[11] Here, an active squirming baby, still grasping his mother's breast, pauses to look out at the spectator with a mixture of surprise and curiosity, creating "one of the most lifelike and human infants of the fourteenth century." Touching deeply into the consciousness of all Sienese, for whom a mother's sustaining milk was of daily reality, this image became part of local lore as citizens proclaimed the Virgin's special affection for their city claiming, "in order to give your milk to Siena [you] deprived the heavenly Child of his share."[12] Catherine's later visionary experience of being invited to feed at the breast of Christ would be a natural extension of this predominant medieval symbol of an intimate and mutual relationship. It has been said that Catherine did not have to create images to express her later visions because they were so prevalent in the world about her.

- 3 -

Augustine, Gregory the Great, Dominic

For those who cannot read, art serves as the text, teaching the illiterate what should be worshipped, even inspiring them with the "ardor of compunction," that burning fire of repentance essential to reform.... Yet all these communications from God would go unno-

---

[11] Cole, *Origins*, 146-148, fig. 76.
[12] Judith Hook, *Siena: A City and Its History*, 130.

ticed and misunderstood were it not for the preacher
whose role is central to Gregory's program of reform....
The tie of unselfish love between teacher and disciple
is a microcosm of the disinterested charity binding the
whole Church as a new family. If the teacher cherishes
his spiritual children, they in turn help stabilize their
father.... Through them new members of the Church
come to life: "the Church's children [are] born through
the mouth of the preacher."

Carole Straw[13]

The reforms initiated by Pope Gregory the Great in the sixth
century had a lasting impact on the Christian world. To reach all
classes, both learned and unlearned, medievals were deliberately
taught a religious metaphorical language conveyed in visual representations. Gregory the Great had directed, "For to adore a picture is one thing, but to learn through the story of a picture what
is to be adored is another. For what writing presents to readers,
this a picture presents to the unlearned who behold it, since in it
even the ignorant see what they ought to follow; in it the illiterate read."[14] Consequently, engaging and expressive artistic images were widely accessible and understood by all classes of the
laity by Catherine's fourteenth century. In addition, prayer practices prescribed for the illiterate encouraged entrance into painted
scenes in a devotional, imaginative, and experiential way, creating a climate of opinion that accepted the intimate relationship
of the human and the spirit world.

---

[13] *Gregory the Great: Perfection in Imperfection*, 200-201. The sense of this quotation
is based on Gregory's *Moralia*: 30. Straw characterizes Gregory the Great as "the
first exponent of a truly medieval spirituality." Ibid., 264.

[14] Gregory the Great (590-604) in *Selected Epistles, Library of Nicene and Post Nicene
Fathers* XIII, 2nd series, trans. and ed. James Barmby (Grand Rapids: William B.
Eerdmans, rpt. 1952), p. 53. Quoted in *The Medieval World View* by William R.
Cook and Ronald B. Herzman, 112.

For example, artistic iconic language always represented Charity as a female figure whose outstretched hand offered her heart to God. Catherine will describe giving her heart to Christ as a sign of her total love and receiving Christ's heart in return. Medievals knew and understood these images that translated mysteries of faith. They also created new images to convey their understanding of the spiritual life. For example, recognizing marriage as the most intimate of human relationships, artistic representations of a human's union with the divine were demonstrated by a betrothal ceremony.[15] For Catherine, the seal of her intimate union with Christ will take place in a visionary betrothal. Contemporary writers who analyze the medieval image underscore its "importance as the center of the affective life of the whole community" and emphasize the engagement of the whole being, both intellect and senses.[16] They describe the mystic's need of such a language to communicate a personal relationship of such great significance as their direct apprehension of God.[17] Noffke confirms "the total subservience of image to theology in Catherine's mysticism."[18]

Two centuries before Gregory, Saint Augustine had elaborated on the various means God used to communicate to human beings: through an instrument, like the divine scriptures; through some element of the world, as to the wise men through a star; through lots in choosing Matthias to take the place of Judas;

---

[15] According to Levasti, the concept of spiritual marriage can be found in pagan mysteries, in neo-Platonism, in the Fathers of the Church, in St. Bernard, with psychological exactitude in Teresa of Avila and theological exactitude in John of the Cross. The marriage marks the highest grade of spirituality that the mystic can achieve. 42.

[16] Margaret R. Mills, *Image As Insight: Visual Understanding in Western Christianity and Secular Culture*, 29, 33.

[17] Elizabeth Alvilda Petroff, *Body and Soul: Essays on Medieval Women and Mysticism*, 4.

[18] Suzanne Noffke, O.P., "The Physical in the Mystical Writings of Catherine of Siena," 124.

through a human, as through a prophet; through an angel, as to some of the patriarchs, prophets, and apostles; through some created sound effect, as voices coming from heaven, though no one could be seen with the eyes. "Finally," he wrote, "God speaks directly to a man, not outwardly through his ears or eyes but inwardly in the mind... when someone understands God's majesty or will, like Peter himself as a result of that vision, when by thinking it over to himself he recognized what it was the Lord wished him to do."[19]

Catherine's emphasis on seeing "in her mind's eye" revealed her understanding of Augustine's teachings, which had a pervasive influence on medieval spiritual comprehension. His impact is further evidenced in one of Catherine's most recurrent images, the trinity of memory, understanding, and will. In *De Trinitate*, Augustine wrote: "Now this trinity of the mind is the image of God, not because the mind remembers, understands, and loves itself, but because it also has the power to remember, understand, and love its Maker. And in doing this, it attains wisdom.... Therefore, let the mind remember its God, to whose image it was made, let it understand and love him."[20] Noffke, commenting on the patristic, and especially Augustinian echoes in Catherine's works, verifies the influence of Catherine's Augustinian and Dominican mentors.[21]

Most significant to Catherine's spiritual development in her own lifetime was the presence, in close proximity to her home, of the monastery of Dominicans whose avowed purpose of existence was to preach and teach. The Dominican Order came into being in the early thirteenth century, when the preaching and

---

[19] Saint Augustine, *Sermon Twelve*, in John E. Rotelle, O.S.A., ed., *The Works of Saint Augustine*, Part III, Vol. 1. See Sermon #12, sec. 4, 299 (394 CE).

[20] Harvey Egan, S.J., *An Anthology of Christian Mysticism*, 69.

[21] Noffke, "The Physical and Mystical," 109.

teaching mission of the church was in critical need of revision. The rise of heretical groups, prevalent in those years, was in some sense a response to disillusionment with the official church, but more to the general worldliness of the secular clergy who often abdicated their responsibility to educate and inspire the laity. Monastic groups in the church, which upheld a high standard of learning and practice, lived in monasteries pursuing spiritual lives while the needs of the faithful were left to uneducated and, sometimes, disinterested local clergy. In this intellectual climate, several lay groups arose, among them the Waldensians, impelled by a desire for a more evangelical and penitential expression of faith, modeled on the lifestyle of Jesus, the apostolic preacher who "had no place to lay his head" and "fasted forty days in the desert." At the same time Catharism, imported from North Africa to Albi in southern France, was making great headway, due as much to ignorance of the inherent Christian meaning of the faith as to the appeal of the tenets of the heresy. The Albigensian heresy, as it became known, proclaimed the duality of two separate created substances: one good, governing all that was spiritual, and the other evil, responsible for the material world including the human body. This heresy, therefore, embodied a denial of central Christian doctrines of the Incarnation, the Virgin Birth, and the dual divine and human nature of Jesus Christ.

Saint Dominic, born in Castile, an area newly liberated from the Moors and, therefore, in what might be considered the frontiers of Christendom, traveled with his bishop, Diego of Osma, through southern Europe, the territory most affected by heresy and lack of religious instruction. They began to realize the need for a combination of well-argued Catholic doctrine and preachers living an apostolic lifestyle, modeled on Christ's own sending forth of disciples as described in the Gospel of Luke, "He sent them out to preach the Kingdom of God and to heal the sick." Imbued with piety, zeal and an intense desire to devote himself to the salvation of souls, Dominic, an Augustinian Canon, conceived the idea of founding an order of men who would respond to this great need of the church. Dominican preachers would live an itinerant lifestyle, one completely based on personal poverty and dedicated specifically to the education and stimulation of the piety of the faithful.[22]

After some years of personal dedication to this mission, Dominic was invited by Bishop Fulk of Toulouse to establish a house in his diocese. Dominic gathered a religious community of preachers to assist the bishop in fulfilling what was, in this time period, a bishop's unique prerogative and obligation as the responsible teacher and preacher within his diocese. Though the conversion of heretics remained an important goal, Dominic considered the instruction of the faithful equally important. From the beginning, he conceived the mission of his incipient Order of Preachers as addressing the whole doctrinal mission of the church. Venturing to Rome in 1215 for the meeting of the Fourth Lateran Council, also concerned with the need for education of the laity, Dominic sought official approval for the foundation of his Order. With the adoption of a recognized Rule, that of St. Augustine, dedicated to salvation of souls through emphasis on poverty and fraternal charity, and having completed arrangements for a proper education for his men, the Order of Preachers received papal approval. Thus, Saint Dominic became "not just a preacher, not just the father of preachers, but the instigator of a preaching mission reaching out to the whole world."[23]

The significance of Dominic's emphasis on preaching and teaching, and on service to the church in the Dominican tradition, was evident to Catherine from her childhood. She had received catechetical instruction and was prepared for Holy Com-

---

[22] Simon Tugwell, O.P., ed., *Early Dominicans: Selected Writings*, 11-15.
[23] Ibid.

munion at the Dominican Church. There, the sermons at daily liturgy were of a high caliber, a worthy instruction for such an eager mind. As she grew older, once her penchant for religious commitment became evident, she was taken more exclusively under the wing of the Dominicans.[24] Levasti suggests that a Dominican Friar, Angelo Adimari, who was in Siena in 1352, could have been her confessor, offering her advice in formulating a pattern for her holy lifestyle. If this is so, then her early ascetic practices must have been seen as childish and harmless imitations of the activities of the saints, as perhaps they were at this early stage, for no one seems to have objected or tried to interfere.

It is interesting, however, that for all her desire for a religious commitment, Catherine never showed interest in any local religious community of women. Though there were no female Dominicans at the San Domenico location, the historian Daniel Waley indicated that in 1307 as many as 363 nuns were housed in at least ten monasteries in Siena. There were eighty-nine hermits—male and female—within one mile of the city limits. Two blood sisters, Lucia and Palmerina, were anchorites "imprisoned in cells" outside the nearby Camollia gate.[25] Though these numbers may have diminished due to losses in the 1348 occurrence of the Black Death, Catherine seems never to have considered any such option in the pursuit of her religious longing. She was, from earliest childhood, uniquely Dominican and aspired to serve God under their direction and live out their mandate of preaching and teaching.

One concise delineation of the historic tradition of sanctity identifies asceticism as the prevailing ideal of antiquity, mysticism as the form representative of the middle ages, and an ac-

---

[24] Giacinto D'Urso, O.P., *"Il Pensiero di S. Caterina e le sue Fonti,"* 377-380.
[25] Waley, *Siena and the Sienese,* 135-136.

tive life of charity as the prototype of the modern age.[26] In its earliest years, the Dominican Order integrated all these elements in its spirituality. Dominic and his followers customarily used the discipline, fasted rigorously and regularly, and lived as mendicants dependent on the good will of the laity even for their daily bread. Mysticism, though not a mandated way of prayer, appeared among its members with steady regularity, especially among women. Finally, the active life of service to the neighbor, primarily through preaching and teaching, was the bedrock of its foundation. We will find the ascetic, the mystic, and the life of active service manifested in Catherine's ministry as well.

- 4 -
Imagination

The people who later devote their lives to pursuits in which imagination plays a major role have often started to do so in childhood to a greater extent than the average because circumstances of separation, loss, or enforced isolation have impelled them in that direction.... [T]he development of an imaginary world can sometimes serve as a retreat from unhappiness, a compensation for loss, and a basis for later creative achievement.

Anthony Storr[27]

---

[26] John Coakley, "The Representation of Sanctity in Late Medieval Hagiography: Evidence from the Lives of Saints of the Dominican Order," 3.

[27] *Solitude,* 106-107.

Looking at Catherine as a young child, growing into a youth of twelve, we seek clues to a flesh and blood person reacting to the stimuli of her surroundings. From stories of these years, selective in their content and colored by her later sanctity, we can imagine a small, bright-eyed, inquisitive youngster, wandering independently and somewhat randomly through the narrow streets of her city. She may have entered into the open space of the Campo just to feel the excitement of the bustle and noise in order to observe everyone, to drink in the atmosphere, and to discover the life that existed outside the confined space of her home. In this period when church paintings were a major instrument for the education of the illiterate, and given her propensity to wander into churches, we can imagine Catherine studying the colorful painted images lining the walls and adorning the altars. Which paintings impressed her precocious mind, provoking images to enliven her prayer? Did they speak of sin and penance, of solitary lives, intense holiness and self-abnegation? Did she discover components of a life that was attractive to her and begin to envision means to fulfill her desires?

Between the ages of three and five, as the developing child moves around more freely, she asks questions, is consumed with curiosity, expands her imagination and, Erikson states, "hears God's voice," and develops a conscience.[28] When she was five or six, Catherine literally had an experience of God in a vision seen in the sky across the Fontebranda valley above the heights of her own church of San Domenico. Christ, his hand raised in blessing, appeared in papal garb surrounded by Peter and Paul, giants of the early Church, and John the disciple whom Christ loved so tenderly. The effects of this vision would change her life indelibly and direct her future. In Eriksonian terms, a sense of total purpose was evoked.

---

[28] Erikson, *Psychological Issues,* 74-82.

Altarpiece for the Church of San Domenico (c. 1305)

A possible artistic source for this vision existed in a location where Catherine would have encountered it almost daily. It is believed that this altarpiece by the painter Duccio, commissioned by the Dominicans, hung over the main altar of the Church of San Domenico during Catherine's lifetime. The figures surrounding the central Virgin and Child provided an array of men significant to Dominican history: on the left, Augustine and Peter, on the right Paul and Dominic.[29] In pinnacles above these figures were four angels and, in the center, Christ as a grown man. Peter and Paul represented the Roman Church, confirming the tradition that they inspired the founding of the Dominican Order. Saint Augustine's presence represented the heritage and Rule that Dominic had adapted for the Order. In keeping with the mandate of the Dominicans as teachers, all the saints carried books representing *Logos*, the Word, which Dominicans were called to preach. Even the mature Christ figure, above the Virgin and Child, held a book. Ordinarily, in medieval iconographic language, the image of a book represented a Doctor of the Church, in this case, making the image a Dominican extension of the artistic tradition.

Because of Catherine's interest in the Dominicans from her earliest years and her frequent presence in the Church of San Domenico, it is reasonable to suspect that the persons appearing in this painting influenced the vision that she saw suspended in the sky over this very church. Did she incorporate the presence of Peter and Paul and interpret the mature Christ figure to be John? Was her smiling Christ in papal attire, with his hand raised in blessing, the Saint Augustine of this work, dressed as

---

[29] Hans Belting, *Likeness and Presence: A History of the Image before the Era of Art*, 401-404, fig. 243; Van Os, *Altarpieces*, Vol. I, 34, 63-64, fig. 38; Norman, ed., *Siena, Florence and Padua*, Vol. 1, 68, pl. 65.

he was in a bishop's cope and miter, a book in one hand and his right hand raised in blessing? The happy carefree child became transfixed by this experience, becoming withdrawn and meditative. Though at the time she confided in no one, her every activity became dominated by the memory of her vision. How she must have longed to experience it once again, to examine it more carefully and to seek closer definition of what remained in her memory. Interrupted by her brother Stephano in the midst of the vision, she did not have time to savor the details, to look closely at each face. She must have wondered: Was it really Peter, Paul and John that she had seen; had they spoken to her? Did the memory of the divine countenance so dominate her thoughts that the others had receded in clarity? No answer came; the vision did not reappear. Soon she conceived the notion of becoming a solitary, a hermit hidden away in a cave like the desert fathers of old. One day she ventured beyond the gates of the city, found a cave, entered it, centered her self, and prayed for the vision to return. The day passed and before dusk, she returned home, apparently without need for explanation. No one had missed her.

Altarpiece for the Carmelite Church in Siena (1329)

Again, we find an artistic clue to this experience in Pietro Lorenzetti's monumental painting for the Carmelite Church in Siena. The lengthy panorama depicted in the predella below the central Madonna and Child represented incidents from the history of the Carmelite Order. From the left, emerging from a pink walled city was a procession composed of citizens, wealthy riders and soldiers led by religious figures. A blue-grey church, a pink fountain, and a group of kneeling Carmelites occupied the right side. In the distance, behind this grouping, unfolded a scene depicting the countryside "unlike anything seen in Sienese painting before." Amid a peaceful landscape of gentle hills, dotted with flowers and bushy trees, were white robed hermits reading, praying or silently contemplating in front of their cave-like structures.[30] Was this the inspiration for Catherine's one-day experiment as a hermit?

Raymond recorded that Catherine had "come to know by pure revelation the lives and deeds of the holy Fathers of Egypt" and had "felt a strong inclination to imitate them." We may wonder, however, if this superbly life-like painting, with its profuse use of color and naturalistic detail, had not reminded her of the stories of hermits and suggested a way of life that would provide the solitude and freedom to worship that she so desired. This possibility merits additional consideration since Raymond records that Catherine left the city for her eremetical experiment by way of the San Ansano gate, in the vicinity of her sister Bonaventura's home where Catherine was a frequent visitor. Since the Carmelite Church was located adjacent to the Ansano gate, and given Catherine's penchant for visiting churches, it is more than probable that she dropped in here more than once to study the huge and awe-inspiring painting.

This painting also provides a superb example of the Sienese artistic capability of portraying stories that emanated from historical legends in a realistic and engaging manner. For example, one of the smaller sections of the lengthy predella portrayed another important medieval concept significant to Catherine's developing sense of religious imagery. An angel, hovering over the sleeping form of the father of Elijah the prophet, informs him that Elijah will have many followers, a prophecy of the future Carmelite Order. The message, inscribed on a long white cloth held by the angel, invoked that commonly held medieval assump-

---

[30] Cole, *Origins*, 10-115, fig. 58; Van Os, *Altarpieces*, 91-99; Joanna Cannon, "Pietro Lorenzetti and the History of the Carmelite Order," 18-28.

tion that God speaks to the mind, the highest capacity in a human being, and the mind, even in sleep, is capable of entering into and experiencing the realm of the divine.

- 5 -
Called to Holiness

[W]hat the holy girls and boys took to be signs of divine election their families received with considerable doubt and much anguish. Even in the so-called age of faith and miracle, parents who discovered their seven-year-old children whipping themselves until the blood ran or praying all night on their knees took alarm.... On their part, ascetic children knew they would encounter parental distress and opposition, and invariably they practiced their austerities in private.

Donald Weinstein and Rudolph Bell[31]

Catherine's vision changed her life. The carefree jaunts through the city, the playful mingling with children her age became less important. A pre-adolescent child becomes absorbed in self-evaluation, with a desire to achieve a meaningful purpose to match some internalized goal that is surfacing from within. Perhaps, Catherine began to equate her self worth with her ability to actualize the divine call of her vision in imitation of the saints' lives as preached in the churches. At about the age of six

---

[31] *Saints and Society*, 37. This study concludes that for female children, seven was the common year for the manifestation of religious impulses; that celibacy was central to a decision since arranged marriages occurred so early; that the family was the first context in which the child's independence and determination was tested; and that most parents reacted with alarm to the ascetic practices of their holy children; 18, 45.

or seven, she made a promise of virginity to dedicate herself completely to God. This vow set her apart from other young girls of her age whose ambitions would normally tend toward an enthusiastic acceptance of duplicating their mothers' social roles as caregivers and child-bearers.

The vision demanded an absolute choice to serve God, so Catherine began to secretly adopt the methods of holiness that were known to her. Monks and friars scourged themselves. The Disciplinati groups in the city alternated prayer with flagellation, often in public processions. The desert fathers rejected the solace of company to pray alone. Visual images of gaunt figures of John the Baptist and Mary Magdalen demonstrated their rejection of food. Sleep was a luxury; therefore, Catherine stayed awake keeping vigil during the night hours when the local Dominican monks slept. Her attraction to these friars in the monastery a few yards from her home deepened. Raymond tells us that she would rush out into the street to kiss their footprints after they had passed by. Fascinated by their work of preaching, teaching and saving souls for Jesus, she even toyed with the idea of disguising herself as a man to become a Dominican as the legendary Euphrosyne reputedly had done. Yet, it appears that her family took little notice of her unusual behavior until she turned twelve, an age when Sienese parents, like the Benincasa, began to seriously consider a marriage arrangement for their young girls.

When a child approaches adolescence, she becomes more sensitive to the expectations of others, though she also remains keenly aware of her own designs. When Catherine found herself for the first time in a direct confrontation both with her family's plans for her future and with the social norms that society would impose upon her, this produced painful conflict. At first, Monna Lapa's efforts to engage Catherine in preparations for marriage addressed very fundamental changes appropriate to every medieval young girl of marriageable age. Primary among these was to stay at home; it would be unseemly for her to wander the streets alone as she had done as a child. Some arrangements seem ludicrous to us today, for example washing her face and neck to accommodate more mature clothing. Others are more basic to every culture: dressing becomingly, fixing her hair more stylishly, learning to be somewhat of a coquette, and dying her hair. The natural dark locks were to be changed to gold, a style indicating maturity in a young female, to increase her attractiveness.

In Ambrogio Lorenzetti's famous painting, *The Effects of Good Government,* demonstrating the demeanor of the well-governed city of Siena, there is a clear depiction of the surface changes that Monna Lapa was seeking for her child. In the forefront of an open space, formed by the juncture of several narrow streets, a group of young women dance hand in hand in a serpentine line. As they circle and bend under the arms of two that form a kind of bridge, one sings and makes music with a tambourine-like instrument. Their colorful flowing dresses are cut modestly low revealing a broad circle of the neck and shoulders, hence the need for careful washing. Their golden hair is caught up and rolled at the nape of the neck or braided to encircle the face, then decorated with a corona of colored cloth. The young women seem to be unabashedly advertising themselves while around them life goes on in the business of the city shops and pathways. How Lapa must have longed to see her beautiful young daughter participate in these courting activities. Despite all her attempts at persuasion, Levasti tells us: "Catherine listened tranquilly and continued to live as before."

- 6 -
A Resilient Child: Vulnerable but Invincible

We have learned that such resilient children have four
central characteristics in common: an active, evocative
approach toward solving life's problems, enabling them
to negotiate successfully an abundance of emotionally
hazardous experiences; a tendency to perceive their
experiences constructively, even if they caused pain
or suffering; the ability from infancy on, to gain other
people's positive attention; a strong ability to use faith
in order to maintain a positive vision of a meaningful
life.

Emmy Werner[32]

In a taped interview with a family of Holocaust survivors,
the parents were asked what they had left, what their ordeal had
done to them? The mother confessed: "We are left with loneliness. As long as we live, we are lonely." The father, barely able
to speak, whispered: "Nothing to say. Sad." In contrast, the daughter responded to the same question: "I think I'm left with a lot of
strength, because you can't have parents like this.... You can't
grow up in a household like that without having many, many
strengths...."[33] As Catherine grew from childhood to the age of
twelve, a similar contradiction manifested itself within her: loneliness and strength. As a survivor, she mirrored the loneliness of

---

[32] "Resilient Children," 69.

[33] Lawrence L. Langer, *Holocaust Testimonies, The Ruins of Memory*, x-xi. In a recent
interview, Hadassah Lieberman commented on the effects of being raised the daughter of Holocaust survivors. "There's a certain strength to the way you're raised,"
she stated, "a certain, almost, I don't want to use the word guilt—that's not the
right word—but you do feel a pressure that you have to make it, you have to
move forward for all the people that didn't make it." *The Boston Globe*, August 11,
2000, B6.

this mother and father who experienced the Holocaust and, with the strength of their daughter, chose to become part of the future, connected to the world in which she lived. Studies of resilient children teach us that surviving adversity can have a steeling effect rather than a scarring one. Resilient children are oriented toward the future, living ahead, with hope.[34]

In her early years, Catherine's loneliness was forged with strength. The courage to be alone demonstrated her budding maturity and strength of purpose. She could mingle in a living vibrant world where neighbors acknowledged her and strangers accepted her. At the same time, she created an inner world of her own where she could have a relationship with God and the saints and make plans for her own future. She began to learn how to deal with those who would attempt to limit her independence and judgment, as we saw in her measured and respectful response to her mother when her discipline was accompanied by an unreasonable outburst. Children entering their early teens must learn to navigate between compliance and autonomy.[35] Lapa had not been angry with Catherine for correcting her; instead, she was impressed. When she told her husband of the incident, Giacomo "gave thanks to God in his heart" and pondered on the wisdom of his daughter.

By the age of twelve, Catherine had overcome her early vulnerabilities. The establishment of a close bond with Bonaventura had provided her with ample affection and attention. She was fortunate to encounter people who gave meaning to her life and encouraged her to believe that things would work out. This emotional support, from outside of the immediate family, came from the close knit Fontebranda neighbors as her biographers indi-

---

[34] Lois Murphy, "Further Reflections on Resilience," 101.

[35] Brian Bigelow, Geoffrey Tesson & John Lewko, *Learning the Rules: The Anatomy of Children's Relationships*, 79-87.

cated from Lapa's stories. The fountain at the foot of the hill was a place of work, but surely also of play and interaction with numerous townspeople. Despite the many stressful events in her early life, Catherine had come to experience an acceptable balance of protective factors that enhanced resiliency; in addition, she had her indomitable faith, the comfort of her vision, and the sense of being called to perform great work for God's church.

Her childhood vision remained a pervasive influence that dominated every other consideration, set in motion her life plans—however indistinct they remained at this time—and made her impatient for the freedom and independence to pursue her Dominican calling. The vow of virginity was taken with serious intent and nothing between the ages of seven and twelve seemed to deny it until, unexpectedly, she was faced with a family discussion of her marriage arrangements. This impending conflict between her dream of the future and that of her family evoked consternation, resolution and impasse on both sides.

PART TWO

Spreading Roots:

BEGINNING A PUBLIC LIFE

1360-1374

Charity, it is true, has many offshoots,
like a tree with many branches.
But what gives life to both the tree and its branches is its root,
so long as that root is planted in the soil of humility....
The tree finds its nourishment in the soil
within the expanse of the circle,
but uprooted from the soil it would die fruitless.
So think of the soul as a tree made for love and living only by love.
Indeed, without this divine love, which is true and perfect charity,
death would be her fruit instead of life.

THE DIALOGUE, 9:40, 10:41

Rooting and Nurturing the Tree of Virtue

The circle and the tree are defined with an innate simplicity that theologians might take volumes to explain. The root of Catherine's tree, "the soul's love," demonstrates her continuous, lifelong process of growing in ever expanding circles of self-knowledge. This self-knowledge, tempered by a parallel growth in the knowledge of a loving and merciful God, produces humility to water the tree's roots and, in turn, give birth to the charity that will foster patience. These three, humility, charity, and patience, nourish a flourishing tree structure in which every other virtue can thrive. However, throughout her life, the tree will be only as fruitful as the soil of humility that sustains it and the roots that anchor it.

The events of Catherine's childhood promoted profound learning experiences. Years later when writing her spiritual testament, *The Dialogue,* she will depict the distractions and temptations of this time as sharp thorns blocking her entrance into the circle of soil. Though many might have run away, Catherine demonstrated her commitment to her divine call by braving the thorns, entering into the circle, and giving root to the tree of her future life. Now she is prepared to move deeper into that dual knowledge of self and God, into the pain and suffering that accompany the birth of ever deepening spiritual awareness.

In adolescence and the early years of adulthood, Catherine withdrew from family and society into solitude. During this retreat and isolation, in the midst of long intervals of acute suffering from lurid sensual temptations accompanied by self-doubt, she entered a period of deep affinity with the divine, developing her foundational theory of self-knowledge in the continuing process of relational encounter with God. Segregated in her room, freed of family pressure, she devoted herself completely to responding to her visionary call to holiness. Finally permitted to exercise her free choice, she sought admission into the Dominican Third Order. Freed from the disadvantages and limitations that her youth and inexperience had placed upon her at the time of her vision, she was now mature enough to profit from the guidance of spiritual counselors and eventually by divine wisdom itself. This solitary period will mark a new beginning and Catherine will never look back from what she will learn.

With her symbolic mystical marriage, a medieval concept of the culmination of a deep spiritual union of the human and the divine, Catherine was inspired to leave solitude, to re-enter society to demonstrate her new understanding of the duality of love of God and love of neighbor. Ministering to her neighbors in the streets of her city, she had many opportunities to test the maturity of her spirituality and courage. Some fellow citizens would admire her while others would question her validity as she responded to the needs of God's church and God's people.

In seeming contradiction then, it was in solitude that Catherine became empowered so that on her return to society, she began, almost immediately, to manifest mature human relational skills. She attracted followers. Some would become life long and intimate friends as well as advisors and disciples. What a profound gift was this human affirmation to Catherine as she embarked on her calling to a public role, as yet undefined, and certainly uncharted for a woman of her time and position. Equally important in this equation was Catherine's unique ability to freely bestow the gift of love and friendship, of support and validation to so many throughout her public life as her tree of virtue began to flower and produce a crown of fragrant blossoms and blessings for her neighbor.

CHAPTER THREE

Expanding and Deepening Roots

- 1 -
A Second Cycle of Death

[T]he early adolescent becomes aware of death, and the late adolescent attempts to impart a meaning to death (as well as to life) that transcends everyday events and infuses the future with hope. Failure to endow the future with optimism results in death of the spirit or suicide.

Audrey Gordon[1]

When Monna Lapa despaired of her own ability to convince Catherine to prepare herself for marriage, she turned to Bonaventura for assistance. The already strong bond between the two had grown even more meaningful. Bonaventura was able to encourage Catherine to participate in some of the traditional preparations. Catherine's dark hair soon exhibited a tinge of gold coloring; she began to use powder and rouge and to dress with some concern for fashion. Levasti suggests that Catherine's "religious fervor declined," and Bonaventura rejoiced that soon she would be able to convince Catherine to marry. Then, on August 10, 1362, when Catherine was fifteen, Bonaventura died in childbirth.[2]

---

[1] "The Tattered Cloak of Immortality," 28.

[2] *Necrologi,* #1065, 88.

Catherine's grief was intense as was her sense of loss. The one person to whom she could relate in total confidence was suddenly gone. Nine months later in April of 1363, barely recovered from the loss of Bonaventura, the Benincasa family had to face a second visitation of the dreaded plague in Siena. On April eighteenth in the first month of the plague, the last cherished child, Nanna, was taken. Then, Bonaventura's husband, Niccolò Tegliacci, died on June fifteenth; and, in the next generation, the daughter of Bartolo and Lisa succumbed to the plague on July second.[3] What took place in the Benincasa family was but a footnote to the larger tragedy in the neighborhood. Until its waning at the end of August, three hundred and seven deaths were recorded in the San Domenico necrology.[4] We know little about the impact of these events, but any family would grieve deeply, either alone or collectively, as memories of previous losses awakened emotions barely buried below the surface of normal living.

And what of Catherine? Her reaction to Bonaventura's death was one of deep personal loss compounded when her grief turned to remorse and then to guilt. She reproached herself for her lack of faithfulness, for wavering in her commitment to the beloved Christ of her vision. She had allowed her passionate resolve to live only for God to ebb away; she had been distracted from her prayer and earnest ascetic practices. She believed she had per-

---

[3] *Necrologi*, #1106, #1263, #1269, 90, 95, 96.

[4] The plague was no respecter of rank or wealth as fifteen members of the powerful Malavolti family succumbed, of whom nine were children. More than forty per cent of the total deaths recorded at San Domenico were minor children supporting the belief that in this outbreak children were highly susceptible. Unlike the local burial record of 1348, that of 1362 is exact and complete with only one unknown recorded; yet, it is again unrelenting in its repetitive character. The list states name, date and *sepultus* or *sepulta est,* sometimes more than a dozen in one day. Then, as suddenly as it began, the plague was over. From September to December, only four deaths were registered and the citizens were left to pick up their lives once again and continue on with their daily routines.

mitted the sister whom she loved so dearly to become more important to her than Christ, to whom she had pledged herself. Then, as she grappled with this self-torment, Nanna, her mother's replacement for her dead twin, died; and to intensify the family's grief, her young niece also perished. Who can know the residue of culpability and self-doubt that surfaced from the wounds of childhood loss? How many, she must have asked, must pay for her sin? For how many lost lives must she accept responsibility? How could she endow her future with optimism?

Early adolescence is probably the first period of life in which a sense of the future becomes a reality. The young person begins to feel conflicting demands from the various relationships in which she is involved: daughter, sister, neighbor, child of God. She feels the first pressures of multiple expectations, and she must learn to weigh the different values in each choice. Perhaps, for the first time, an adolescent realizes that her own expectations for the future are at odds, not only with her family's, but also with those of her peers, her friends, and the neighbors who have known her from birth. The second cycle of death occurred when Catherine was in the midst of this period of choice, a perplexing and confusing time of life for most young girls, bridging the worlds of childhood and the beginning stages of adulthood.

By nature, adolescence is also a time of intense preoccupation with the body which undergoes remarkable changes. In young females, hormones initiate the rounding of the pelvis, the growth of breasts, and the beginning of the menstrual cycle. Adolescents lose their self-confidence and turn to others for models of behavior.[5] To whom had Catherine turned for guidance but to Bonaventura who had been her trusted ally from earliest childhood? And how else would Bonaventura have counseled Catherine except to behave in the expected fashion of a

---

[5] John J. Mitchell, *The Nature of Adolescence*, 93-104.

twelve year old girl whose society recognized no interim stage between childhood and adulthood, no time set aside for a gradual process of maturation in preparation for meeting life's adult demands?

Bonaventura would not have subverted Catherine's holy desires deliberately. She would have counseled her, as she had been counseled, to move into the next phase of life: marriage. Bonaventura would not have considered that Catherine was abandoning her spiritual life. She would have seen her entering a life that would include, not only spiritual commitment, but also family and children, just as she had done. That Bonaventura died in the midst of these preparations is the tragedy. Catherine turned for advice to her adopted brother, Tommaso dalla Fonte, by then a Dominican friar in his middle twenties. He allowed her to believe that Bonaventura's behavior had been displeasing to God, consequently Catherine chastised herself for what she had considered her sin in adopting what was in reality a very normal style of life and behavior for her age. Later, in his account, Raymond revealed that he, too, told Catherine that Bonaventura's behavior had been displeasing to God.[6]

Contemporary psychologists suggest that the loss of an affiliative relationship in a female can be perceived not just as a loss of relationship, but as something akin to a loss of self.[7] It is no wonder that Catherine was thrown into turmoil by Bonaventura's death. At the same time, Catherine's earlier associates, those childhood friends who accepted her leadership in games of prayer and discipline, had lost interest in such practices, drawn instead to the very courting practices which Catherine's mother proposed to her and which she resisted even more strongly after Bonaventura's death. Who, then, would share her dreams of a

---

6   Raymond of Capua, 117, #122.
7   Jean Baker Miller, *Toward a New Psychology of Women,* 83-85.

future life dedicated to Christ alone? Catherine's response was to make a firm and independent decision about her future life direction. The memory of the childhood vision, so deeply implanted in her mind and heart, surged through her whole being. She determined to return to that earlier happier time of the divine call and her immediate and loving response. She would seek the companionship of God who loved her with an intensity that would go well beyond her childhood ideas of prayer and penance.

- 2 -
Family Conflict

Between the world of the spirit and the world of the flesh chastity was the great divide. No other virtue— not humility or poverty or charity—was so essential to either the performance or the perception of a holy life. Children who aspired to the religious life took a vow of chastity long before the onset of puberty made it a practical issue, and for both boys and girls the decision to remain virgin marked a turning point. In stories of adolescents who aspired to holiness the battle over chastity was a central drama—an internal struggle against temptations of the flesh and a social conflict with parents who wanted them to marry.

Donald Weinstein & Rudolph Bell[8]

Once again, Catherine's family seemed oblivious to her state of mind. Father, mother, and brothers proceeded with arrangements for a marriage and soon decided upon a suitable husband.

---

[8] *Saints and Society,* 73.

Catherine's response to their announcement was to confer once again with Tommaso who suggested that, to prove the seriousness of her commitment to her vow of virginity, she should cut off her hair. Lapa's emotional reaction and the family's anger with Catherine for this behavior prompted a harsh course of action: she would become servant to the family, be allowed no time for the leisure of prayer, and be deprived of the privacy of her own room.

As time passed, her quiet acceptance of her punishment and her continued dedication to her chosen lifestyle began to impress her father, a gentle holy man. Catherine, moved to pray to Saint Dominic for guidance, was rewarded with a dream in which Dominic offered her the protection of the "white habit" of his Order. Encouraged, Catherine faced her family decisively and confirmed her seriousness of purpose. Rewarded with her father's protection, Catherine's life became her own again. She was free to pray in privacy, as she willed, and free to concentrate solely on her spiritual life without interruption.

As she grappled with repentance for her unfaithfulness, Catherine began to develop a special devotion to Mary Magdalen. Like others of her time, Catherine would be influenced in her understanding of Magdalen's life by the work of the Dominican Friar Jacobus de Voragine. His *Golden Legends*, stories that collated the oral traditions of the lives of the saints with a wealth of detail, often apocryphal, were attractive to the medieval imagination.[9] According to the *Legends*, Mary Magdalen led a solitary and rigorous ascetical life after the Resurrection of the Lord. She was fed only by angels who came to her in her solitude. This dramatic telling of Mary Magdalen's life of prayer and total abstinence may have influenced Catherine's own choices as she re-

---

[9] Jacobus de Voragine, *The Golden Legends*, 355-364.

turned with increased fervor to a rigid ascetic spiritual regimen.[10] She used the scourge three times a day, trained herself to eat almost nothing and to sleep very little at night on a hard board. Still, her mother persevered in her attempts to divert her child from her purpose. She forced her to sleep with her in a soft bed and took her to the local health spa in order to provide a diversion and to contribute to her health and well being.

Meanwhile, Catherine continually begged her mother to intercede for her acceptance into the local Dominican Third Order, the Sisters of Penance, or the Mantellate as they were popularly called because of their distinguishing black flowing mantle.[11] Finally accepted, her dream of donning the "white habit" of Saint Dominic seemed within reach. Permission to adopt this way of life set Catherine apart, clearly indicating her complete dedication to prayer and the service of God, and resolved her adolescent conflict. Her choice of the Dominican Third Order, the Mantellate, as the group that would meet her needs and provide her with a sense of belonging, coincided with her passage into early adulthood. This demonstration of personal choice indicated the beginnings of that power over self and others that would characterize Catherine's future way of life.

---

[10] For a development of the influence of Mary Magdalen on Catherine, see Caroline Walker Bynum, *Holy Feast and Holy Fast: the Religious Significance of Food to Medieval Women,* 166-167.

[11] The Mantellate were originally reluctant to accept Catherine because of her youth and single status; most members were widows.

- 3 -
A Dominican Tertiary

After her clothing she went joyfully back home into her cell, which she never intended to leave except to go to church. She was to complete a year's novitiate, under the guidance and supervision of the Friars and Sisters. She wished to observe the Rule scrupulously— indeed to surpass it in severity. No one would now weary her with worldly conversation; she would henceforth pray, meditate, implore all day and all night; she was free to stay as long as she liked in the company of God. She must have felt an overwhelming joy at being mistress of her own time, after overcoming such great difficulties, and at being able to dedicate herself to the life of the spirit and the progressive realization of ever loftier ideals.

Arrigo Levasti[12]

The Dominican Third Order had its origin in 1285 in response to the desire of lay persons to participate more fully in the spiritual life practiced by the friars. Originally, third orders had usually consisted of married couples; however, in Catherine's day, members of the Mantellate were usually widows who lived in their own homes. Entrance to and profession in the Third Order followed a pattern similar to that of the friars. During a probationary period, the candidate was vested with a habit to the accompaniment of prayers, blessings, and hymns in the presence of the Dominican community. At the end of this period, a permanent profession was made which obliged the member to live according to the rule of the Third Order until death.

---

[12] *My Servant Catherine*, 30.

This rule called for the daily communal recitation of the canonical hours of the Church, and confession and communion on the four main feasts of the liturgical year: Christmas, Easter, Pentecost, and either the feast of the Assumption or the commemoration of Mary's Nativity. More frequent communion was allowed only with special permission. Though no formal canonical vows were taken, the evangelical counsels of poverty, chastity, and obedience, modeled on the values taught by Christ in the Gospels and exercised by the friars, stimulated many to a deeply religious way of life. Most women, in addition to prayer, performed works of mercy. Sometimes these acts of charity were directed exclusively to their own members, but many visited the hospitals, consoled the afflicted, mourned with the dying, and interceded for sinners. They were humble, devout, and not usually involved in intellectual pursuits. The protection of the Dominican Order safeguarded these women within the norms of church structure in times when other groups of women, for example the Beguines in northern Europe, often encountered difficulties and opposition in their efforts to establish independent communal groups.[13]

Becoming a member of the Dominican Third Order of Penance in late 1364 or early 1365 when she was between seventeen and eighteen years of age, marked the official confirmation of Catherine's special religious role in the community. The religious habit that she wore, white gown and veil with a flowing black mantle, readily identified her position in the church. Membership in the Mantellate placed Catherine directly under Dominican authority. Theoretically, the sisters were responsible to the Master General of the Order. In practice, the provincial superior appointed a local friar as immediate director. He was responsible

---

[13] These women lived in dedicated groups primarily in northern Europe. They were not officially sanctioned by the Church but engaged in prayer and good works.

for calling monthly meetings, presiding at the election of a prioress, celebrating Mass for the group, preaching for them, and interpreting their rule.[14] He had complete authority to correct penitents who transgressed or neglected the rule as well as a fair amount of control over their freedom of action; for example, no Mantellate could travel outside her city without his express permission.[15] Members promised obedience both to him and to the prioress.

A routine of communal prayer, participation with other members in the morning liturgy at San Domenico, frequenting the sacrament of Penance and receiving the Eucharist when permitted established a routine that gave order to Catherine's previously isolated program. She added to the tertiary requirements private vows of poverty, chastity, and obedience, total silence except with her confessor and total seclusion except for attendance at prayer and liturgy in the Cappella delle Volte, the private chapel reserved for the Mantellate in the rear of San Domenico. The Dominican spiritual director assigned to the sisters gave instruction in the tertiary rule on the first Friday of each month; in addition, Catherine profited from individual counsel and conversation with many of the friars.[16] This direction gratified her longing for spiritual knowledge, giving her the comfort of guidance in her developing contemplative life. Most importantly, her membership in the Mantellate signified acknowledgment by her family that she was free to pursue a dedicated life, secure from talk and planning for marriage. At last, she would be allowed the privacy and uninterrupted time to dedicate herself to ever increasing knowledge, love, and intimacy in her relationship with God.

---

[14] Thomas J. Johnston, O.P., "Franciscan and Dominican Influences on the Medieval Order of Penance: Origins of the Dominican Laity," 115-117.

[15] Later this will become a problematic issue in Catherine's life that will need to be rectified before she can be of service to the world outside Siena and to the church at large.

[16] D'Urso, *"Il Pensiero,"* 377.

In this new lifestyle, with its long sought resolution of the struggle to respond to her childhood vision, Catherine manifested a degree of adult independence, of having initiated an authentic self expression and, in her own estimation at least, a certain kind of power. In this newfound opportunity to "be her real self" Catherine's behavior displayed many of the characteristics that Maslow described as accompanying a "peak experience." There is, he says, the "appearance of calm sureness and rightness, as if they knew exactly what they were doing, and were doing it wholeheartedly, without doubts, equivocations, hesitations." Sensing oneself to be "the responsible, active, creating center of her activities," Catherine became "more decisive, looking more strong, more single-minded" and, as her family discovered, "more apt to give the impression that it would be useless to try to stop her."[17]

- 4 -

Conquest of Self

I believe myself that often in these early stages, and again later, it is the Lord's will to give us these tortures, and many other temptations which present themselves, in order to test His lovers and discover if they can drink the chalice and help Him to bear the Cross before he trusts them with great treasures. I believe it is for our good that His Majesty is pleased to lead us in this way so that we may have a clear understanding of our worthlessness; for the favors which come later are of such dignity that before He grants them

---

[17] Maslow, 106-108. Maslow writes that the person in a peak experience feels more like a prime mover, more self-determined, more fully responsible, and with more "free will" than at other times.

He wishes us to know by experience how miserable
we are, lest what happened to Lucifer happen to us
also.

Saint Teresa of Avila[18]

When Catherine entered into the solitude of the small room
that would be her home for the next three years, she must have
experienced great joy and relief. Now, at last, she could begin
her spiritual life in earnest. All that had gone before was merely
preparation for this serious undertaking. She was eighteen years
of age, on the threshold of adulthood, and with her newfound
freedom, she could approach God in a mature manner. The next
three years would lay a foundation for a future that would take
her far from this small room and engage her in many public endeavors that would test the spiritual resources, the strength of
character, and the depth of virtue that she would begin to achieve.

What we most long for, however, when it is finally achieved,
does not always have the anticipated satisfaction. In silence and
solitude, the mind mechanically recalls words, gestures and
thoughts that would barely penetrate the consciousness of a person living in the noise and bustle of daily life. In silence, thoughts
resonate loudly and stimulate the imagination. Soul stirring and
seductive temptations often intruded upon Catherine's anticipation of uninterrupted loving companionship with Christ. Spiritual visions alternated with the appearance of tormenting devils
bent upon breaking her will and distracting her from the intimate life with Christ that she sought. Instead of the sweet presence of the Lord, Catherine found herself often in the midst of
temptations, unsought and enduring. At one time, when she asked
Christ where he was when these embarrassing visions flooded
her mind, the comforting reply was, "I was in your heart."

---

[18] *The Autobiography of St. Teresa of Avila*, 130.

Over time, such gentle assurances in the midst of her anguish and distress helped her to realize that the purpose of this suffering was to ground her in the virtue of humility. She came to realize the limitations of her own spiritual strength so that she would become more dependent on the goodness and strength of God. Her struggle would lead her to recognize the powerful allure of human passion and its potential to mislead even the most resolute souls. Small victories in these encounters with temptation not only made her strong but also initiated a growth in wisdom that would stand by her throughout her life.

She learned, directly from the Lord, Raymond tells us, how to distinguish between visions that came from God and visitations of evil spirits who strove to mislead her.[19] The devil's visitation began in a sweetness soon replaced by terror, while a sacred visitation might come in the midst of suffering, bringing in the end peace, greater truth, or humility. She learned that when she remained calm in the midst of these frequently frightening encounters and when she waited patiently for them to pass, the Lord would comfort her and strengthen her in the struggle in which she was engaged. She learned that ascetic practices alone would not result in deeper intimacy with God, that abstinence from food, the use of the discipline, and harsh treatment of her body were only means to an end, a way to develop control of her passions and lead her to grow in virtue. She learned the importance of self-knowledge that came, not by concentrating on herself but by concentrating on God, who taught her to understand who she was and in contrast, who Christ was: "I am He who is; you are she who is not."

Gradually, the course of Catherine's life settled into a calmer routine, and her spirituality matured. Christ appeared to her in

---

[19] See Chapter 4, "Gifts of Friendship," for an explication of the pivotal role of William Flete in this period of Catherine's spiritual development.

his crucified form to show her that her suffering was not in vain but was, in truth, a source of power when endured in union with his redemptive agony of death and dying. She learned to read the psalms aloud with her sisters in the Mantellate chapel in San Domenico; this communal prayer brought her great joy. Her interior world became less exclusive, less focused on her own soul; possibly the instructions of the Dominican director of the tertiaries was a persuasive force in this attitude. Her prayers began to embrace the welfare of the church and the spiritual condition of society.

Catherine's thoughts began to focus on the traditional imagery of mystical marriage, the union of the soul with a divine bridegroom.[20] As her visions included more intimate conversation with her Lord, she increasingly longed to become the bride of Christ, but she had learned by now that she was the receiver of grace, not the instigator, and she waited in patience. Finally, her prayers were answered in 1368 while in the streets of her city, Sienese celebrated boisterously and voluptuously the eve of the somber fasting days of the season of Lent, the Feast of Carnival. Seen in her "mind's eye," the Virgin Mary took Catherine's hand and presented her to her Son, who placed a ring on her finger and espoused her to him in faith in the pres-

---

[20] The medieval interpretation of mystical marriage was based on the human understanding of the intimacy and close relationship of the marriage union. This was a frequent subject of medieval painting. One which may have been of particular influence to Catherine, since it was available to her both in time and in place, was that of Catherine of Alexandria by Barna of Siena, believed to have appeared as early as 1350. In this painting two life size figures dominate the upper portion of the canvas and extend hands across the center of the painting; Christ puts a ring on the finger of Catherine of Alexandria whose name is inscribed in her halo, *Katurina*. Of further significance for Catherine of Siena's future life is what appears in the bottom portion. Two adult males, having dropped their weapons, embrace each other in a gesture of reconciliation. What makes this painting so pertinent to the life of Catherine of Siena is that her mystical marriage, sealing her union with God and her willingness to enter into a public ministry, will initiate her active participation in reconciling warring families, especially in the Sienese context of the vendetta.

ence of Saint John the Evangelist, Saint Paul, Saint Dominic, and King David who provided music on his harp. The vision ended, leaving Catherine in great joy. The ring on her finger, visible only to herself, comforted her throughout her life.

- 5 -
Contemplation in Action

Discernment is the essence of mysticism in action. The medievals were greatly interested in it, and they kept asking a number of simple but intriguing questions about it: How am I to know when to eat and when to fast, when to sleep and when to watch, when to go into solitude and when to go into action. How am I to discern the voice of the Spirit so as to follow his gentle guidance?

William Johnston, S.J.[21]

Catherine had hardly settled into the sweet communion of intimate spousal relationship when she understood that she was being urged to leave her room and rejoin her family. Her discomfiture was understandable since, at almost twenty-one years of age, she at last felt that she was within reach of the goal she has been seeking from childhood. That she heard the divine voice, deep in her soul, urging her to forsake this spiritual intimacy caused her great pain. However, she began to realize that, despite the physical loss of solitude, her communion with God would not be altered. Intuitively, Christ led her to comprehend that her love for him must be manifested through service to oth-

---

[21] *The Inner Eye of Love*, 155.

ers, that the spiritual life did not provide a refuge from the world, but generated energy to live in and to serve in the world.

The Rule of Saint Augustine, the inspiration of the Dominican Rule and communal life, interpreted charity as directed to the dual love of God and neighbor, while Dominican spirituality translated this dual love directly into service to others in the ministry of preaching and teaching. How deeply Catherine had imbibed this understanding of mission at this point in her life is unclear; however, as she began to realize and to assent to Christ's call to leave solitude, she did raise the question of her gender and the appropriateness of her entering into a public role. Though aware of her innate dignity as one created in the image and likeness of God, she nevertheless indicated her keen awareness of the limitations that her society placed upon women. She noted that men had no esteem for women who circulated freely in the city and that they would think it unseemly for her to preach and teach. In Raymond's account, the Lord replied that he would send "women who of themselves will be ignorant and frail, but whom I will fill with the power of God and the wisdom of God."[22] She reached a consoling understanding that her spiritual intimacy with the Lord would continue. Thus comforted, Catherine accepted God's will for her, despite her misgivings and, as instructed, she began to join the family at mealtime.

We can only wonder at the reaction of the family when Catherine suddenly reappeared at the dinner table after an absence of three years. Their confusion would equal Catherine's own chagrin at returning to a routine that had become strange and intolerable to her. Yet, she seems to have thrown herself into the domestic affairs of the household with characteristic vigor and intensity. Soon, her charity extended into the neighborhood with visits to the ill and hospitalized and, with her father's permission,

---

[22] Raymond of Capua, 41-42.

she began to distribute the family goods to the poor. Finally, she comprehended that love and service to her neighbor demonstrated her love of God. All true mystics discern this reality and, in classical terms, they "return to the marketplace."

- 6 -
The Streets of Siena

The same people walked the streets daily. There was mutual instant recognition.... Every neighbor had his or her particular identity associated with a trade, a name, a reputation, a clan or a family. Strangers were immediately picked out in the streets and doubtless stared at. Births, marriages, and deaths were neighborhood events—for the common knowledge and feeling of all. Wedding parties were shared with neighbors. Funerals were the affair of the neighborhood, and a ritual mourning was provided not only by the women of the bereaved family but also by a host of women from the parish, while kinsmen and other neighbors gathered in front of the house.

Lauro Martines[23]

If there is cause to wonder about the family's response to Catherine's arrival at the dinner table, imagine the reaction of her neighbors as the twenty-one year old reappeared in the streets of her local parish community. The Benincasa home faced on a main thoroughfare, the Strada della Oca (Street of the Goose), now known as Via Santa Caterina, which rose steeply upward

---

[23] *Power and Imagination*, 76.

from the Fontebranda gate in the city walls to the heart of the commune. The fountain at the foot of the hill was the main source of water for the area; hence, it was a gathering place for women and children as well as the dyers, the wool and leather workers of the valley. Here, local gossip would begin and circulate freely. Catherine would be well known from her childhood. Every event of her life would have been discussed, analyzed, digested and become part of the lore of the district. Yet, as one of their own, she would be sympathetically judged and taken into the hearts of her neighbors.

Catherine was as much a part of her district as were all children growing to maturity under the supervision of this watchful, loving, solicitous, yet gossipy extended medieval family. Neighbors would be predisposed to marvel at her re-entry into the life of the community, having carefully observed her over the previous three years. They were familiar with her daily passage from her home to the Church of San Domenico, as well as her prayer in the company of her tertiary companions in the Cappella delle Volte, and her frequent lapses into ecstasy following her reception of Holy Communion. Every facial and bodily expression would be of interest and subject to conversation. Neighbors would be anxious to call to her attention the needy, the hungry, the ill, and the dying, and thus to participate in the holy adventure in which she was involved.

Catherine, together with her neighbors would be electrified in June of 1368 by the arrival at San Domenico of important guests of the friars: Pietro I, King of Cyprus, accompanied by three hundred knights, sumptuously dressed and riding magnificent horses. Renowned throughout Europe as a great Crusader, Pietro was known as the Defender of Christianity in the East. His arrival must have stirred the populace to discussion of the Holy Places and the need for further crusades to redeem them. The Dominicans, supporters of the crusades, would imbue their sermons and conversations with the exploits of their guests, and thus raise communal consciousness of the wars waged in the far reaches of the Holy Land. Introduced to this significant issue of her time, Catherine would adopt the attitude of her Dominican brethren and zealously support the interests of the church in furthering the crusades.

A few months later, Catherine's neighbors would grieve with the Benincasa family at the loss of their beloved husband and father, Giacomo. Catherine would be deeply moved by the support of the neighbors. She would be touched by the loving stories that people customarily recount at the death of a person generally known for holiness, generosity, and kindness in the neighborhood. Mourning would affect the whole community when, by tradition, the women gathered to weep and pray together in the family dwelling while the men gathered outside in front of the house. The cemetery register of San Domenico noted that the revered neighborhood dyer, *Iacobus Benecase, tinctor,* was buried there on August 22, 1368.[24]

- 7 -
Political Realities

The government of the *Riformatori...* was... a government of artisans; though patriotic and energetic, their rule was extremely oppressive, and burghers and nobles alike murmured. There were continual plots, followed by banishments, torturings, executions. The Salimbeni were expelled in 1374, their houses and possessions wasted; but they gathered together in the

---

[24] *Necrologi,* #1458, 103.

contado, captured many castles, and carried on a formidable war against the State.

Edmund G. Gardner[25]

Barely recovered from the loss of their husband and father, in early September, the Benincasa family was caught up in, and dramatically affected by, the violence accompanying one of the many reversals of political power that disrupted the commune. Siena had experienced a lengthy period of stable government from 1287 to 1355 under the rule of the Nine. Their power, rooted in the mercantile elite, began to wane about the time of the Black Death when newly rich and upwardly mobile citizens grew restive and angry at their continued exclusion from government. With the end of the rule of the Nine, a thirteen-year period of tumult and continued political change disrupted the city. At first, leading representatives of the guilds, calling themselves the Dodici, or the Twelve, governed. Then, on September 2, 1368, when dissatisfaction over representation forced them from power, an interim, short-lived aristocratic government of the Noble Consuls assumed control. They were quickly and violently overthrown on September 23rd and replaced by the council of the reformers, the Riformatori, as "humble guilds men, mostly artisans, craftsmen and petty shopkeepers" rose to prominence.[26]

The historian Lauro Martines provides an interesting insight into the physical conditions that made a medieval city like Siena ripe for violence. City walls enclosed crowded populations in narrow streets lined with massive family dwellings; specific trades concentrated in certain streets and quarters; noble clans or clusters of socially prominent families resided in the upper levels of

---

[25] *The Story of Siena and San Gimignano*, 40.

[26] Valerie Wainwright, "The Testing of a Popular Regime: The *Riformatori* and the Insurrections of 1371," 121.

the city. When violence broke out in the streets, groups could quickly assemble with like-minded classes or guilds.[27] Violence was an intrinsic element of politics, the only vehicle for getting redress of just and urgent grievances; hence, Martines concludes that, in this period, its perpetrators could interpret violence as a constructive force in politics.[28]

Catherine's brothers were intimately involved in this evolutionary power struggle. Supporters of the Twelve—Bartolo's name had been listed as a potential representative of his guild from the parish of San Antonio in the administrative district of Camollia[29]—the three Benincasa brothers were in danger of their lives as revolutionaries roamed the city on September 2nd. When friends came to warn them to seek shelter in the parish church, Catherine intervened. Showing worldly wisdom, she led her brothers through the streets of the city, through angry mobs who stepped back in respect as she passed, and brought them safely to the hospital of the Misericordia, leaving them in the charge of her disciple, the rector, Matteo di Fazio dei Cenni.[30] She told them to remain in hiding for three days and then to come home. At the end of that period, peace had been restored and her brothers were safe, while all those who had taken refuge in the parish church were killed or taken prisoner.

With the fall of the provisional government of Noble Consuls on September 23rd, the Benincasa brothers were once again allied with the government in power as two of them, Benincasa and Stephano, appeared as nominees for the list of potential representatives for the guild of dyers under the Riformatori.[31]

---

[27] Lauro Martines, "Political Violence in the Thirteenth Century," 345.

[28] Ibid., 349.

[29] Wainwright, 124, n. 38.

[30] Levasti, 73. In some accounts the hospital is identified as La Scala.

[31] Wainwright, 124, n. 41.

Throughout the rule of this new government, continual changes, some violent and some orderly, occurred within the structure of leadership. Civic and family feuds became part of the daily life of Siena, and Catherine's skills as mediator gained her a reputation for being a counselor and promoter of peace and justice. Unable to maintain commercial prosperity, Sienese fortunes diminished over the years. Eventually many craftsmen and tradesmen were forced to leave the city and seek prosperity elsewhere. Among these were the three Benincasa brothers who, in October of 1370, took up residence in Florence.

Catherine was truly a product of her city, educated in, and acutely aware of its volatile political situation, the economic distresses among the guilds, and the famines that afflicted the city whenever crops failed in the rural agricultural area outside the city walls, the *contada*. All these realities affected her family, eventually affecting her in her attempts to reconcile conflicting groups. More importantly, at this time, they affected the well being of her neighbors whom she had been directed to love and serve as a demonstration of her deep love of Christ to whom she was betrothed. One of the more famous incidents recorded of her occurred under this regime in 1375. A young Perugian, Niccolò di Toldo, was accused of defaming a senator, arrested, and condemned to death. Catherine befriended him and accompanied him to his death.[32] This incident may have set the tone for Catherine's relationship with the Riformatori, of whom the Sienese Chronicler Donato wrote, "Everyone was afraid of them."[33] Needless to say, Catherine was not.

As she moved among the needy and afflicted, the neighborhood stories grew, and her reputation soared daily, forcing

---

[32] Noffke, *Letters*, I, 82-89.

[33] Wainwright, 170.

Catherine to deal with the notoriety arising from the love and respect, and sometimes jealousy, that came back to her from the outpouring of her heart to her fellow citizens. For the rest of her life, she would at times withdraw totally to the solitude of mystic contemplation only to leave it with renewed strength to respond to others and to address the ills of her church and society.

Women survive, we are told, as long as they strive to achieve the fulfillment of the ideals they have chosen and with which they identify. Having done this, they attain a position that enables them not only to transform themselves but also the society in which they live.[34] In this period of her life, Catherine made a major step toward the fulfillment of her life goals. She emerged from solitude and took up the cross of daily living, to practice the second great commandment: loving her neighbor with the same love that she lavished on her Maker.

---

[34] C. Margaret Hall, *Women and Identity: Value Choices in a Changing World*, 4.

CHAPTER FOUR

Deepening Self Knowledge

- 1 -
Gifts of Friendship

Friends are particularly helpful to women who are committed to heightening their awareness of self. Self-revelation occurs through the many conversations and nonverbal interactions over long periods of time. These exchanges touch deep levels of self that might not otherwise be experienced. Our innermost beliefs, thoughts and feelings are articulated when friends make time to listen to us. Identity is clarified for each woman when experiences are shared; especially when there are parallels in their lives. Differences between friends also contribute towards clarifying identity and defining how our lives and values contrast with theirs.

C. Margaret Hall[1]

Even while secluded in her home, Catherine came into contact with men and women who would have a powerful influence on the person she would become. As she began to circulate in her neighborhood, several Sienese Mantellate became her earliest companions and remained lifelong friends and supporters.

---

[1] *Women and Identity,* 118.

The gift of friendship has a profound effect on any young person, especially friends who discern and value your interior gifts and encourage you to pursue your calling. In Catherine's case, these friends guided and supported her in discovering and living out the relationship of mystic bride, attentive to whatever tasks the Lord would ask of her. Two early friends and counselors were the Augustinian hermit, Friar William of Flete, and the young Dominican, Bartolomeo Dominici. Another young Dominican, Tommaso da Siena, though not an intimate, would later become a forceful influence for her future canonization.

William of Flete, O.S.A.[2]

William of Flete, also known as William of England, lived in the wood of the lake, Selva del Lago, four miles outside the city of Siena. The wood was known to Sienese as Lecceto because of the abundance of *lecci* or ilex trees, and Flete was known as the hermit of Lecceto as well as *il baccelliere,* because of his Bachelor's degree in theology. A member of the English Austin Friars of Saint Augustine, Flete left Cambridge University in 1359 when he was well on his way to a Master's in theology. The academic life, for which he was preparing, became unacceptable to him, and he left his native England to take up residence outside of Siena in a hermitage of his Order. His lifestyle and theological training in Augustinian spirituality identified him as a holy man gifted in spiritual counsel, and he was well known to many Sienese who sought his direction in their spiritual quests.

An earlier published work, *A Treatise on the Remedy against Temptation,* examined the role of temptation in the spiritual life. Because of his reputation in this matter, it is believed that

---

[2]   Unless indicated otherwise, information for this section is found in Benedict Hackett, O.S.A., *William Flete, O.S.A. and Catherine of Siena,* 79-100.

Catherine's adopted brother and earliest counselor, the Dominican Tommaso dalla Fonte, uncertain of his ability to guide Catherine himself, had brought her to Flete when she was experiencing terrifying temptations during her time in solitude. Contact may have occurred as early as the summer of 1367 but definitely by January of 1368, when Catherine was twenty years of age. Flete has not always been fully recognized for his influence on Catherine's thought and spiritual development.[3] However, the fact is now accepted that he, along with the Dominican Bartolomeo Dominici, provided theological guidance in the interim period between 1368 and 1374 and that both were well versed in the Augustinian theology that influenced and gave direction to her early spirituality.

The influence of William of Flete was sound and supportive during the foundational period of Catherine's spiritual development and the years when she initiated her public ministry, a time when she grew in self-confidence, in maturity and in reputation. Very likely, this maturing was due in large part, not only to Flete's wise and beneficial counsel, but also to his generous acknowledgment of her spiritual giftedness. Her understanding of the Augustinian concept of the interdependence of the knowledge of self and the knowledge of God, together with the explicit meaning of inspired symbols, like the circle and the tree with its graft of discernment, more than likely were clarified in discussions with Flete. In one of her earlier letters sent to the Sisters at the Monastery of Santa Marta in Siena, she described the effect of abiding in that circle where love of self and of God become one. "I don't think it is possible to have virtue or fullness of grace without dwelling within the cell of our heart and soul... that is holy knowledge of ourselves and of God," she

---

[3] Levasti, 153; Levasti's prediction that further study of Flete's writings would reveal more about his influence on and relationship with Catherine has been addressed in Hackett's work, cited above.

wrote. Sharing her own knowledge of the acceptance of God's will that she had so recently gained, she added, "I want you to want things to go not your own way but the way of the one who is. You will then be stripped of your own will and clothed in his."[4]

For his part, Flete was one of Catherine's staunchest supporters, encouraging his own Sienese followers to believe in her, stating "the Holy Spirit is truly in her." Several years later, when the church was disrupted by the crisis of a dual papal leadership, the Great Schism, Catherine called upon as many notable holy persons as possible to come together in Rome in support of the papacy of Urban VI. Flete declined her invitation, choosing to continue his life of solitude and contemplation in Lecceto. Here was a dividing point between the Augustinian hermit, committed to solitary contemplation and the Dominican tertiary, called to an apostolate that, overflowing from the depths of contemplation, led her to an active ministry for the church and for her neighbor. These differing views of vocation severely tested their friendship; however, at the close of her life Catherine acknowledged the value of Flete's unique contribution to her own spiritual development when, on her death bed, she appointed him spiritual director of her fellowship of faithful followers.

Bartolomeo Dominici, O.P.[5]

Bartolomeo arrived at San Domenico about 1368 and, at his request, was introduced to Catherine by Tommaso dalla Fonte, his former classmate. A friar of intellectual distinction, he recognized intuitively the spiritual stature of Catherine and encouraged Tommaso to believe in her validity as well. At Bartolomeo's urg-

---

4   Noffke, *Letters*, I, T30, 49, 51.
5   Levasti, 63-65; Kenelm Foster, O.P. and Mary John Ronayne, O.P., eds. & trs., *I, Catherine: Selected Letters of Saint Catherine of Siena*, 19-20.

ing, Tommaso began to keep notes about her, recording incidents of her early life that otherwise would have been lost. One of the first to join Catherine's circle of friends, Bartolomeo lived to bear witness to her sanctity at the official inquiry into her canonization in Venice in 1411 when he recounted how youthful she was when he first knew her, and the sweetness and gaiety of her countenance. Acknowledging his own youth—he was about four years older than Catherine—he reported that he never felt the embarrassment in her company that he might have felt with any other young woman; indeed, he stated that the more time he spent with her, the less troubled he was by human passions.

Soon after his arrival in Siena, Bartolomeo became one of Catherine's confessors and for the rest of her life remained one of her closest friends, accompanying her on her journeys to Pisa, Avignon, and Rome. Catherine's influence was such that she attracted men of more than average culture and ability, and Bartolomeo's intelligence and learning were readily acknowledged. A discerning student of literature and fine speech, his report that Catherine was wonderfully eloquent when she spoke of the honor of God and the salvation of souls, can be readily accepted. He encouraged her contact with Flete. Catherine's salutations in letters written to him in the early years convey her devotion and respect. She referred to him as "very loved and dearest son in Christ" and "very loved and dearest brother and son in Christ Jesus."[6]

Tommaso da Siena, O.P.[7]

Though not among her intimate followers, Tommaso da Siena, more popularly known as Caffarini, became acquainted

---

[6] Noffke, *Letters,* I, T105, T200.
[7] Levasti, 67-68.

with Catherine about this same time. As a young Dominican aspirant, sixteen or seventeen years of age, he, too, was brought to visit her cell by Tommaso dalla Fonte. Fascinated by her, he began to observe her constantly, whenever he could: in church, conversation, prayer, and charitable activity. He was absorbed with the more miraculous and ascetic aspects of her life. Miracles impressed him enormously, and he made a collection of them, accepting even the most fantastic versions. His concentration on the extraordinary seemed to blind him to Catherine's wisdom and the depth of her inner life. Perhaps, because of this lack of understanding of the profundity of her spiritual life, there was never a close and enlightened friendship with him such as she had with Bartolomeo and later with Raymond. Relations were friendly, and his work in translating Augustine might have pleased and helped her. Levasti says, however, that a letter he wrote to her, instructing her in a particular translation was cold and scholastic, imparting little interest in the spiritual meaning of the psalm in question. Yet, Caffarini would become a potent force in pressing for Catherine's canonization after her death.

Three Mantellate [8]

Monna Alessa dei Saracini was a widow of noble birth who had given her possessions to the poor and joined the Order of Penance. She maintained a home in Catherine's neighborhood that became a refuge when the overcrowded Benincasa household threatened to overwhelm her. Alessa was perhaps Catherine's closest female confidant; she traveled with Catherine frequently, and was her choice to lead her spiritual family of Mantellate after her death.

Francesca di Clemente, familiarly known as Cecca, was also

---

a widow of noble birth and the mother of three Dominican sons who died in the plague of 1374 and a daughter, Giustina, who later became a religious at Montepulciano. She had great affection for and loyalty to Catherine with whom she became acquainted during their service to the sick in the Hospital of *La Scala.*

Lisa Bartoli Benincasa, Catherine's sister-in-law, the wife of Bartolo, had observed at close range Catherine's struggles within the family. Gentle and pious, supportive and sympathetic, she loved to converse with Catherine about spiritual matters and had complete trust in her miraculous powers. She became a Mantellate after her husband's death in 1374 and the two remained lifelong friends.

Both Alessa and Cecca served as scribes for Catherine's earliest letters. Their lighthearted comments appended to Catherine's very serious missives suggest that the friends provided laughter and happiness to lighten Catherine's serious nature, as good friends often do. Who can calculate the power of their affirmation of one whose life had been so circumscribed and solitary?

- 2 -
The Sienese Religious Temperament

Numerous Sienese from the town's twenty odd parishes joined a variety of religious confraternities.... Some confraternities concentrated on personal worship and the singing of lauds, others focused on almsgiving, still others dedicated themselves to such worthy deeds as support of poor prisoners. These institutions varied in important details; certain of them, for example, demanded the exclusive allegiance of their members,

or were open only to those practicing a particular occupation. But all were similar in origin and impulse,
and none have been shown to have had any political
involvement with communal political life.... [The] traditional, structured, comfortable Sienese church would
not suffice for the spiritual needs of many who were
imbued with a strong religious bent.

William Bowsky[9]

The Sienese civic ideal embraced the highly religious nature of the majority of its population, not only in its building and
aesthetic programs, but also in charitable considerations. Estimates
suggest that a high proportion of adult Sienese, especially among
the middle class, were members of at least one of the confraternities, or guilds of pious laymen and women and that some confraternity, religious group, or social organization addressed almost every human need.[10] Twelve of these were flagellant confraternities, that is, requiring a weekly group ceremony of using
the discipline.[11] The idea of serving one's neighbor, then, was
not unusual among the laity; rather, it was a calling experienced
by a multitude of the Sienese citizenry. This was the atmosphere
to which Catherine emerged from seclusion. Moving around her
city, meeting so many service-oriented, charitable and devout
people, Catherine not only learned from them, but later she would
draw them to herself, continually adding followers to her spiritual family.

A major center of charitable activities was the hospital, Santa

---

[9] *A Medieval Italian Commune*, 265-266.

[10] A member had to be at least twenty years of age, a working artisan, be interviewed
by a priest, attend daily Mass, go to confession twice monthly, receive communion four times a year and pledge oneself to charity toward one's neighbor. Francis
Oakley, *The Western Church in the Later Middle Ages*, 122-123.

[11] Waley, *Siena and the Sienese*, 150.

Maria della Scala, one of the great Sienese institutions of the middle ages. Erected directly opposite the cathedral steps, hence the name La Scala,[12] the hospital was a work of charity initiated by the cathedral canons possibly as early as the late ninth century but definitely by the year 1090.[13] Siena was a stopping place on pilgrimage routes for those journeying to and from Jerusalem or Rome and to the most significant site of the period, Saint James of Compostella in Spain. Christians along the routes would offer hospitality by erecting hostels, providing food and nursing care for ailments such as blisters and swollen feet. Santa Maria della Scala began in response to these needs of pilgrims. Over the years, its charitable program expanded to include a variety of social needs, for example, a foundling home, orphan asylum, poor house and finally a full-scale hospital.[14]

In 1192, as a result of a petition to Pope Celestine III, the hospital was removed from the control of the cathedral canons, and La Scala became a civic institution. Operated by confraternity members, it enjoyed the financial support of the commune

---

[12] Another interpretation of the name *La Scala* appears in a painting by Vecchietta, *The Allegory of the Origins of the Spedale della Scala*, dated 1441 and depicting a legendary founder, a cobbler, whose mother's dream led to the founding of the hospital. In her dream, the legend asserted, Beato Sorore's mother saw children ascending a ladder (*scala*), which became the logo of the hospital, into the arms of the Virgin Mary. This legend, invented as late as the fifteenth century, has been interpreted either as an attempt to trace the foundation of this most ancient of European hospitals to a humble lay artisan rather than to clerics, or as part of a fifteenth century effort to cement lay control. In some versions of the myth, Sorore's body was later "discovered" and relics became available. Keith Christiansen, Laurence Kanter, Carl Strehlke, *Painting in Renaissance Siena: 1420-1500*, fig.15, 50; Cole, *Sienese Painting, Vision of the Virgin*, fig. 19, 32; in Gualtiero Belluci and Piero Torriti, *Il Santa Maria della Scala in Siena: l'Ospedale dai Mille Anni*, this painting is entitled *Sogno della Madre del Beato Sorore*, 77-79; in Henk W. van Os, *Vecchietta and the Sacristy of the Siena Hospital Church: A Study in Renaissance Religious Symbolism*, it bears the title, *The Blessed Sorore and the Education of the Foundlings*, fig. 11, 106, 21; Schevill, *Siena*, 93.

[13] Belluci and Torrito, *Il Santa Maria della Scala*, 11.

[14] Ibid., 27; Christiansen, et al, figs. 10-18, 46-50, Schevill, *Siena*, 90-93.

as well as generous benefices and endowments from wealthy Sienese. Papal approval of the transfer of power was commemorated in a fresco of 1442 attributed to Domenico di Bartoli, one of an elaborate schedule of paintings commissioned in the fifteenth century to adorn the vast interior spaces of the hospital.[15] Others engaged to decorate the building included Lorenzo di Pietro, known as Vecchietta, and Priamo della Quercia. Their prominence and the quality of their art, confirms the continuing reputation of the hospital and the prosperity that it enjoyed.

The extent of the charitable work of the hospital can be gleaned from these fifteenth century paintings. Four concentrate specifically on the lay confraternity members as they carry out their works of mercy: the care of the sick, the reception of pilgrims, the distribution of bread, the nursing and education of orphans, providing marriage dowries for orphan girls, and the feeding of the poor.[16] The inclusion of the image of the cathedral in the background of one painting, depicting the distribution of alms, recalls the medieval concept of "the word" received from the pulpit begetting "the deed" in the hospital.

The sponsoring disciplinant confraternity that served and supported the institution consisted of lay volunteers, men and women who lived according to stringent rules they had framed and voted themselves, governed by a rector elected in a general session of the members. The nature of membership in the confraternity as a lay-religious calling—they were third order Augustinians—became apparent in the rules regarding the spiritual life of its members which stipulated times of confession, reception of the Eucharist, and attendance at Mass. Each Friday, the obliga-

---

[15] Bellucio and Torrito, *Il Santa Maria della Scala,* 99-107; van Os, *Vecchietta,* 1; Christiansen, et al, figs. 17, 51. The La Scala Hospital has only recently ceased to function as a hospital; it is now designated a museum.

[16] Belluci and Torrito, *Il Santa Maria della Scala,* 112-142; van Os, *Vecchietta,* 21; Christiansen, et al, figs. 10-14; 46-50.

tory *disciplina,* or self-flagellation, took place in the guild chapel under the supervision of the prior who led the singing of hymns and the recitation of prayers that accompanied the penitential rite. Good conduct was required of members; swearing, gambling and drinking in taverns were forbidden. On some occasions, members processed with their banners, publicly performing the discipline.[17]

According to medieval custom, the city streets were off limits during the night hours. The communal bell tolled the evening curfew which required all citizens to remain indoors until the morning bell signaled the opening of the city gates to day time normalcy. This custom frequently resulted in many members of the various confraternities being forced to spend the night in the crypt, the lower floor of the hospital building. Many groups had rooms there; one, which took its name from its nightly use, the Cappella delle Notte, was the chapel where Catherine, herself a frequent volunteer at the hospital, stayed when the evening curfew prevented her return home.[18] These night hours were often spent in conversation and prayer with other spiritually minded persons. Catherine's group included Dominican friars, lay women and men whose discussions concerned the church and its problems, as well as personal spirituality. The participation of many educated and deeply spiritual persons made these discussions a rich experience. Not only did Catherine's political and religious insights deepen but also her family of followers grew.

Catherine's experience, however, was not a completely positive one. Though many were drawn to her and became her ardent followers and supporters, others were apt to view her with

17 Waley, *Siena and the Sienese,* 151-152.
18 Many of Catherine's followers later formed a Confraternity of *Santa Caterina delle Notte* which still meets in this place where she would often fall into an exhausted sleep; Henk van Os, *Sienese Altarpieces, 1215-1460: Form, Content, Function,* Vol. II, 125.

skepticism, slandering her in denial of her remarkable spiritual character. These detractors unwittingly contributed to Catherine's human and spiritual development by creating the climate of hostility and animosity in which one is forced to choose between despair and greater self-autonomy. For Catherine it was the latter. Opposition drew her inward to conquer self-doubt, to grow stronger in virtue, compassion, and tolerance. Her biographers tell of the leprous prostitute Cecca, the acerbic tertiary Andrea, and the cancer victim Palmerina, to whom she continued to offer comfort and care despite their harsh vitriol and ingratitude.

Some among her own tertiary community refuted her charity, accusing her of posturing, pretending, seeking attention, and even of having lost her virginity. Some friars, as well, denied her validity, at times ejecting her from the church building during her ecstasies. Catherine bore all of this in union with Christ, affirming her more mature comprehension that suffering, not self-imposed but unbidden, was the key to holiness. Consequences followed, however. In 1371, Catherine was called before the Prioress of the Mantellate and forced to defend herself against the malicious gossip that was circulating; her forthright innocence caused the Prioress to immediately dismiss charges. Later, towards 1374, the gossip and jealousy resulted in Catherine's exclusion from Mantellate meetings.

- 3 -
To Be Filled with Power and Wisdom

Thou shalt love is a command that calls for three steps:
first, saying *yes* to belonging; next, to look and see what
our *yes* implies; finally, to act upon that *yes*. One step
leads to the next. If we have said the first *yes* with full
conviction, we will surely care enough about those to
whom we belong to inform ourselves about them....
Thou shalt love implies all the effort it takes to find
out what I personally can do to act upon my *yes* to
belonging in a given case. And little as it may be, there
is always something I can do. Most importantly, therefore, *Thou shalt love* implies that I go ahead and do
what I can, because I belong and have said, *Yes I will*.

David Steindl-Rast[19]

As Mary had questioned in response to the angel at the An-
nunciation, Catherine, too, pondered in her heart how God's will
was to be accomplished in her. As she recalled Christ's promise
to send women, filled with power and wisdom to do his work in
the world, she prayed to know what it was that God was asking
of her. How could she actually demonstrate her great love for
God through her neighbor? She felt called to do more than feed
the hungry, nurse the sick, and console the dying, as did all tertiary members. She longed to understand the true nature of her
vocation.

One piece of her answer came one autumn day in 1370
when, deeply engrossed in her prayer, she became unconscious
as in a coma, not an unusual occurrence. Her companions, however, noticing the unusual length of her rapture and the fact that
her body was growing cold and lifeless, became alarmed and

---

[19] *Gratefulness, the Heart of Prayer*, 175.

called others to join them. Touching her seemingly lifeless body, they were certain that she had died, and they wept together, mourning her loss. Soon, word of Catherine's death spread through the neighborhood, and people gathered in the street outside her home, as was the custom. After four hours, Catherine began to return to life. As she grew stronger her friends rejoiced, but Catherine wept bitter tears for what had been lost. She had been in the presence of God, who charged her to return to earth and to enlarge her sphere of apostolic work.

A second piece of her answer came through unexpected conversions because of her prayers; for example, two criminals being led to public execution for their actions, recanted publicly before their deaths. A growing number of local followers who came or were sent to her seeking her wisdom and guidance made public and dramatic conversions; for example, Andrea di Naddino del Bellanti, a prominent member of the ruling Nine and Giacomo Tolomei, scion of a prominent family. Her support among the Dominicans increased as Friars Matteo Tolomei and Simone da Cortona became her followers. More women joined her: Francesca and Ghinoccia Tolomei, Caterina di Ghetto, Caterina della Ospedaluccio, Giovanna di Capo, Agnola di Vannino, among others. Neri di Landoccio dei Pagliarisi and Stephano Maconi, well educated young men of noble families, became her devoted disciples, scribes, and companions until the end of her life. Two interesting conversions occurred as Fra Gabriele da Volterra, Franciscan minister of the Sienese province, and Fra Giovanni Tantucci, friar of the local Augustinian hermits, came to challenge her authenticity and expose her as an ignorant fraud. Immediately on meeting her, they experienced a change of heart, transformed their own lifestyles, and became dedicated followers.[20] Disciples began to seek her influence in bringing harmony and

---

[20] Gardner, *Saint Catherine*, 92-94.

resolution to local disturbances, and she was increasingly called upon to end family vendettas. Her name began to be heard outside of Siena, likely by way of her Dominican friends. We know from her own letter to her disciples in 1374 that Pope Gregory XI sent an emissary to Siena to speak to her and to ask for her special prayers.[21]

New uncertainties presented themselves: how to measure the impact of the increasing numbers of disciples and followers; how to comprehend what it meant to receive the recognition of men and women educated in the ways of the world, seeking her counsel in the ways of the Spirit. As these disciples continued to gather round her, a human manifestation of the divine workings in her life, how could Catherine any longer doubt that God intended her to become a public figure and that, if she waited in patience, she would know the time, the place and the circumstances?

Soon the direction and purpose of Catherine's life changed dramatically when she was drawn into the broader designs of the church and of the Dominican Order. In May of 1374, her twenty-seventh year, she was invited by the Master General of the Dominican Order, Elias of Toulouse, to present herself at a General Chapter meeting. About five hundred Dominicans gathered in the Spanish Chapel of the Priory of Santa Maria Novella in Florence. No official record of this encounter remains, and for years, it was considered by many to be a trial. The equanimity with which her supporters recorded the summons and made reference to the event suggests that it was designed to permit the leadership of the Dominican Order to become informed about Catherine's spiritual life and the extraordinary events that were beginning to be reported about her.

From their founding, Pope Gregory IX had encouraged the

---

[21] Noffke, *Letters,* I, T127, 40.

Dominicans to assume roles as directors, confessors, and protectors of religious women dedicated to living out intense spiritual lives either singly or in small groups. These roles placed them in the position not only of teaching and preaching, but also of guarding these women from error and protecting them from those who would place them in danger by accusations of heresy or witchcraft. In Catherine's case, since she had been under Dominican tutelage from her childhood, she was well known to the Sienese friars, and many of them were already among her ardent followers. In addition, Arrigo Levasti reports the presence at the Florence chapter of Fra Angelo degli Adimari, who had been stationed in Siena during Catherine's childhood; he had served as her confessor, knew her well, and could attest to her fidelity to the church, her deep spirituality, honesty, and openness.

Whether Catherine was interviewed by a select group of the leadership or by all the members of the chapter is not clear. In any case, it appears that she was less to be tested than to be affirmed. The meeting demonstrated the interest rather than the opposition of the order since, if there were serious questions, she would have been silenced without any recourse. As a result of this meeting, Raymond of Capua was appointed the official confessor of Catherine and her followers. His standing in the order as an esteemed scholar, one who had a grasp of and experience with mysticism as well as a reputation as a cultured man, wise in political matters, attested to the esteem in which the Dominicans held Catherine. She, in turn, received protection from slander and the annoying behavior of those who questioned her authenticity, and at the same time gained access to sound spiritual and theological direction and support.

To refer to the pairing of Raymond of Capua and Catherine as director and directee as a match made in heaven could sound trivial; however, for Catherine, this was an absolute fact. In her writings, she referred to Raymond as "father and son," and "son given to me by that gentle mother Mary," referring to a promise made by the Virgin during her time in solitude that she would give her a spiritual director.[22] Long after Catherine's death, Raymond would refer to Catherine as "my own Mother and Teacher."[23] Similarly, in referring to him in letters, Catherine often used the term "John," indicating the similarity between their relationship and that of Jesus and John the beloved disciple.[24] Before the official connection was established at the Florence chapter, it is believed that Raymond had been aware of Catherine, that details regarding her reputation and her unique holiness had been conveyed to him by Bartolomeo during conversations in nearby Montepulciano and in Florence.

When they met, Raymond was forty-four years of age and Catherine twenty-seven. He came from a family of judges, counselors, and administrators in the area of Capua, Naples, and Sicily. His father, Pietro, was judge and counselor under Robert of Anjou, King of Naples, while his brother Luizi served in the army of Queen Giovanna of Naples.[25] Following in the family pattern, Raymond had begun to study law at the University of Bologna when he felt called to become a Dominican. He took the habit at the convent in Bologna, eventually being ordained for the province of Rome. His years of initial training, 1347-1355, cover the span of Catherine's early life. His theological training completed, he is believed to have been a lector in theology at Rome and at Bologna from 1355-1363 when the second wave of the Black Death swept through Siena. For the next four years, he was Rector at the Monastery of Montepulciano where he wrote his first

---

[22] Noffke, *Letters,* II, T226, 5.

[23] Raymond of Capua, xlviii.

[24] Conversation with Giuliana Cavallini who was the first scholar to acknowledge this connection.

[25] Biographical data on Raymond, unless otherwise noted, is from Kearns' introduction to his translation of the *Legenda.*

Legenda, the life story of the popularly proclaimed local saint, Agnes of Montepulciano. From there he went to Rome, where he served as prior of the Minerva, the station church of the Dominicans in that city. By August 30, 1373, he was listed as a resident of the monastery of Santa Maria Novella in Florence, in time for the chapter gathering.

At the conclusion of the Dominican chapter, Catherine remained in Florence for a few weeks, during which her reputation spread throughout the city. People flocked to see her, to touch her, and to speak to her. Several devout believers, members of the ruling Guelf party, typically allied with the papacy, greeted her. These men would soon draw her into the dilemma of the Papal/Florentine relationship. To all, Catherine spoke, not of politics, but of the love of God, the reform of one's life, loyalty to the church, the importance of a crusade, and the need to bathe oneself in Christ's redeeming love.

On June 29th, Catherine departed Florence to return to Siena where another devastating visitation of the Black Death was ravaging the city. Once again the necrology of burials in the cemetery of the Church of San Domenico provides a measure of the impact of this third visitation of the plague on the entire city. From January through May, a total of only five interments were entered in the cemetery record[26] while the accelerating numbers in June alerted the citizens to impending danger.[27] From June to October, two hundred and fifteen citizens in Catherine's district suc-

---

[26] *Necrologi,* #1563, #1564, 111.

[27] In June the seventeen deaths included six men, five women, two boys and four girls, #1565-#1581, 11-112; in July the forty-nine consisted of eight men, nine women, twelve boys and twenty girls, more than double the number of the previous month, #1582-#1631, 112-113; the high point of the plague occurred in August when the burial record indicated seventeen men, fourteen women, thirty-two young men and twenty-six young girls, eighty-nine in all, #1632-#1719, 113-116; by September there was a waning: thirteen men, four women, twenty-one young males and four young females for a total of forty-two, #1720-#1761, 116-118.

cumbed to the plague. At least eight members of Catherine's family fell victim in this outbreak: her brother Bartolo, husband of Lisa, and four of their children; the daughter of her brother Benincasa and her two sisters, Lisa and Nera.[28]

Now twenty-seven years of age, Catherine exhibited her maturity, inner power, and authority as she took to the streets to care for the numberless victims neglected by those who either fled or refused to become involved in the crisis facing their neighbors. She demonstrated her leadership abilities when she gathered her band of followers to attend to the dead and dying, encouraging the weak and fearful with the example of her own indefatigable energy, courage, and dedication. Raymond of Capua was a case in point. Arriving in Siena on August 1, 1374 at the beginning of the most virulent period of the plague, he responded to Catherine's leadership and direction by going into the streets to console and bless the sick and dying. He wrote: "I knew I was bound in charity to love my neighbor's soul more than my own body, so with Catherine urging me on I resolutely made up my mind to visit and comfort and instruct as many victims as I could...."[29] As would happen often in their relationship, the director himself received direction; Raymond's decision was made firm by Catherine's resolve. We are told that, among the friars of San Domenico, it was only Catherine's followers who braved the danger of infection.

---

[28] Ibid., #1633, 113; #1643, #1646,#1647, #1649, 114; #1706, 116; #1762, 118.
[29] Raymond of Capua, 239, #254.

- 4 -
Pope Gregory XI

On 29 December 1370, as soon as the nine days de-
creed by custom for the obsequies of Urban V were
over, the cardinals went into conclave; the next morning they unanimously elected as pope, Roger de Beaufort, son of Guillaume de Beaufort and Marie du
Chambon. Cardinal Roger took the name of Gregory
XI and was crowned by Guy de Boulogne on 5 January, 1371. Born in 1329 he was then forty-two years
old. The new pope had had a rapid career from one
ecclesiastical honour to another. At eleven he was already canon of Rodez and of Paris, at nineteen his
uncle, Clement VI, had made him cardinal-deacon of
Santa Maria Nuova (28-29 May 1348). Instead of giving way to the charms of the ostentatious way of life
at Avignon, the young man had gone to Perugia, there
to attend the lectures of the famous jurist Pietro Baldo
degli Ubaldi. Through this association with the master, he had acquired a profound knowledge of law and
an unusually balanced judgment. His biographers tell
us that Baldo was so proud of his disciple that he took
pleasure in quoting his judicial opinions.

Guillaume Mollat[30]

When Gregory XI was elected to succeed Urban V (1362-
1370) he was forty-two years old. Under his uncle, Clement VI
(1342-1352), the new pope had risen rapidly from one church
position to another while remaining a deacon; hence, to allow
his selection as pope, he was ordained to the priesthood one

---

[30] *The Popes at Avignon, 1305-1378*, 59.

day before his election. Historic opinion regarding Gregory's character varies. Guillaume Mollat, the major revisionist historian of the Avignon Papacy, noted his high moral qualities and cultivated mind, his prudence and discretion, his modest demeanor, his piety, goodness and affability, the uprightness of his character, and his steadfastness of purpose in word and deed.[31] Another historian, Thomas Okey, described him as a cultured aristocrat, gentle when obeyed but hard and passionate when opposed, sickly in body and pale of complexion, and poorly endowed with the qualities of mind and body necessary to guide the church in the stormy days of the Italian wars.[32] A third historian, Gene A. Brucker, called Gregory "perhaps the most competent and dedicated occupant of the Holy See in the fourteenth century," noting that he was "scrupulous in his regard for the rights of his subjects."[33] A fourth, Paul R. Thibault, stated that the blame for the growing discontent in the Papal States rested solely with Gregory who left control of his lands to subordinates and indicated that his priorities were elsewhere.[34]

Catherine's biographer, Arrigo Levasti, indicated that Gregory was a man whose sense of justice and long-suffering patience may have been taken for weakness, his constancy and firmness for obduracy. Instead, he notes, Gregory was very frank, disliked sudden decisions, reflected at great length about questions concerning the state, and tried to avoid violent clashes. However, when moved to act, he did so wisely and struck boldly and authoritatively at the church's enemies. Levasti stated that Gregory appreciated being told the truth, since most people tried to hide it from him and he believed in the revelations of the saints

---

[31] Ibid.

[32] Thomas Okey, *The Story of Avignon,* 171.

[33] Gene A. Brucker, *Florentine Politics and Society, 1343-1378,* 270, 279, note 108.

[34] Paul R. Thibault, *Pope Gregory XI: The Failure of Tradition,* 137-138.

and the admitted superiority of mystics.[35] No source accuses Gregory of vices or personal failings that would bring disrespect to the papacy. It is a fact, however, that the political situation during his reign was so complex and complicated, that it would not have admitted an easy resolution by the most skillful negotiator.

Catherine's and Gregory's interests intersected soon after the beginning of Gregory's reign. From his election to the papal throne, evidence shows that Gregory intended to return the Papal Court to Rome. A marginal drawing in a fourteenth century manuscript in the Avignon archives, dated 1348, depicts the voyage to Rome of his predecessor Urban V. Two cardinals accompany the Pontiff; one is the future Gregory XI.[36] This experience undoubtedly influenced Gregory's determination to make a speedy and permanent return of the papal seat of government to Rome. Crowned on January 5, 1371, Gregory informed the Cardinals in Consistory on May 9, 1372 that he intended to return to Rome "very shortly." Early in the following year, 1373, Gregory informed the kings of England, Aragon, Castile, Navarre, Portugal, and France of his intent. In July of 1373, Birgitta of Sweden, the visionary who had long been a supporter of the papacy and a vocal advocate of its return to Rome, died. The next month Gregory became involved in reform measures for the Dominican Order with the cooperation of the Master General, Elias of Toulouse, as part of an overall effort to unify the order, which had been somewhat decentralized since the plague of 1348. One of the reforms included the legislation of a general chapter of the Dominican Order of Europe to be held once in every two-year period.[37]

---

[35] Levasti, 197, 223. Thibault comments that Gregory "admitted on a number of occasions that his deputies in effect had the power to conceal things from him," Ibid., 136.

[36] Philip E. Burnham, Jr., "Cultural Life at Papal Avignon, 1309-1376," 94-95.

[37] Mollat, 60, 162, 166-167.

In March of 1374, Gregory sent a special messenger, identified as the former confessor to the deceased Birgitta of Sweden, to seek Catherine's prayers "for him and for holy church" and granted her "the holy indulgence."[38] Two months later, in May of 1374, Catherine was summoned to Florence where the Dominican biennial chapter was in progress. Here, she was removed from the authority of the local Sienese Dominicans and made subject to the Master of the Dominican Order under the direct charge of Raymond of Capua. By September 6, 1374, Avignon was busily engaged in preparations for the departure to Rome[39] at about the same time that Catherine received an invitation to visit Pisa. This sequence of events suggests that Gregory and his advisors desired Catherine's overt endorsement of the papacy's return to Rome, a risky public affairs undertaking. Thus, they prompted her public validation through the Dominican Order, ensuring her protection from error and scandal.

---

[38] Noffke, *Letters,* I, T127, 40.
[39] Mollat, 162.

PART THREE

The Blossoming Crown:

PISA, FLORENCE, AVIGNON
1374-1378

This tree, so delightfully planted,
bears many-fragranced blossoms of virtue.
Its fruit is grace for the soul herself
and blessing for her neighbors....
The marrow of the tree (that is, loving charity in the soul)
is patience, a sure sign that I am in her and she is united with me....
To me this tree yields the fragrance of glory and praise to my name,
and so it does what I created it for and comes at last
to its goal, to me, everlasting Life....
And every fruit produced by this tree
is seasoned with discernment, and this unites them all.

THE DIALOGUE, 10:42

Seasoning the Fruit with Discernment

In her wonderfully graphic image of the tree of virtue, Catherine depicted with abundant detail the interactive process by which one becomes proficient in the life of virtue. Constant growth in self-knowledge within the knowledge of God produces the humility that nourishes the circle of soil. This nutrient is essential to further the growth, first of charity then of patience, the life giving marrow that will permeate the whole tree structure. These crucial three—humility, charity and patience—develop as needed, according to the circumstances of each one's life, to nourish first the soil, then the roots and, finally, a flourishing tree structure in which every other virtue can thrive. Thus, Catherine demonstrates that the life of virtue requires harmonious and interactive development imitative of the mutually supportive processes of nature.

However, when Catherine adds to the natural structure of her tree a "graft" of discernment, she indicates an alteration of its nature. Tree grafts have the purpose of strengthening the tree's nature, enriching its innate quality, sweetening its fruit, thereby, enhancing its growth. Similarly, Catherine sees discernment as a gift that alters, enhances, and changes forever the nature of one who seeks perfection. Discernment is like a transfusion which, entering into the very marrow of the tree, courses throughout the entire structure in company with the essential triad of humility, charity, and patience. As charity and patience receive life from humility, so, too, discernment is virtuous only if it is rooted in humility.

In *The Dialogue* there is a further explication, "Discernment is that light which dissolves all darkness, dissipates ignorance, and seasons every virtue and virtuous deed. It has a prudence that cannot be deceived, a strength that is invincible, a constancy right up to the end, reaching as it does from heaven to earth, that is, from the knowledge of me to the knowledge of oneself, from love of me to love of one's neighbor."[1] As Catherine entered adulthood, opportunities to exercise this discernment multiplied and assumed added complexity as, leaving the confines of her city of Siena to enter into the world beyond, she encountered political dilemmas that threatened to weaken or even destroy the purity and moral fiber of God's church. In her meetings with church and political officials, Catherine dedicated every ounce of her human and spiritual energies to the purification of the church, the return of the papal court to its rightful place in Rome, and the achievement of peaceful and harmonious relationships. Letters of exhortation multiplied: to the pope; to religious and political leaders; to warring families; and to ordinary people seeking her guidance and/or the mediation of political and family disputes. Catherine was a woman called to a life that had few parallels in her time or even in ours. She has much to teach us about the dynamic process of self-discovery and her actualization as a woman of spiritual power, authority, and independence in a world poised to thwart, admonish, and deny it.

---

[1]   Catherine of Siena, *The Dialogue*, #11, 44-45.

CHAPTER FIVE

The World of Action

- 1 -
Mature Wisdom

If the term "adult" means anything, its meaning must
be social. One does not declare oneself adult; one is
perceived to be. Unavoidably, the qualities we call
adult are on the side of "sanity," "normality," rational-
ity, continuity, sobriety, responsibility, wisdom, conduct as opposed to mere behavior, the good of the
family or group or species as distinct from the desires
of the individual.... In its purest form, adulthood is expressed in the characters of saints, sages, and culture
heroes.

Wallace Stegner[2]

Catherine of Siena's progress to adulthood must be looked
at in an accelerated manner since her entire life span consisted
of only thirty-three years. During the years when she aged from
twenty-eight to thirty, Catherine's life experience expanded rapidly as she began to influence and be influenced by events in
the world around her. Unlike other women of her time, or of
almost any time, her impact extended to the centers of power in

---

[2] "The Writer and the Concept of Adulthood," 227.

her world. Her journeys from Siena to Pisa, Lucca, Florence, and Avignon introduced her to leading personages in the growing conflicts that embroiled church and state. Her correspondence widened, giving her access to persons of significance whose power—religious, political or military—could impact the position of the church and determine the outcome of world events. After the Florence Chapter, Catherine's position within the Dominican Order assumed greater stability. Her growing circles of followers and supporters from every rank and station, her experience of the political realities of her native Siena, together with her mediation of long standing enmities in local family vendettas, testify to the expansion of her mission. Catherine began to experience, as did Dag Hammarskjöld in his own era, that "the road to holiness necessarily passes through the world of action."[3]

Erikson reminds us that goals and values important in childhood have continuity in new settings and that experiences of earlier life stages have significance in the resolution of later ones in what he calls the engagement of the self and the world.[4] In the public arena, Catherine's letters were her voice, the intelligent, informed, and determined expositions of her position on spiritual and political matters. At times, the childhood learning she achieved in the churches and paintings emerges. Her conception of governance echoes the commitment to peace, justice, and the common good etched in the inscription below the *Allegory of Good Government* in the Palazzo Pubblico, "Wherever this holy virtue—Justice—rules, she leads many souls to unity, and these, so united make up the Common Good." This message impelled her three desires for the church: the return of the Papal Court to Rome, the internal reform of the church through the appointment of worthy administrators and cardinals, and the calling of a crusade.

---

[3] *Markings*, 122.
[4] Erik Erikson, *The Life Cycle Completed*, 59-60.

- 2 -
The Avignon Papacy, 1309-1378

The popes of the tenth, eleventh and twelfth centuries had been deeply involved in the local politics of Rome. In the thirteenth and fourteenth centuries the internationalising of papal power and papal claims made that involvement seem claustrophobic, limiting and, in the face of popular hostility and aristocratic intrigue, dangerous as well. In any case the popes were increasingly involved in the growing complexities of international politics. From Charlemagne to Frederick II it was the emperors with whom popes had to reckon. In the late thirteenth and fourteenth centuries other rulers, especially the kings of France, loomed on the papal horizon and posed a threat to papal independence.

For most of the fourteenth century, the bishops of Rome lived far away from Rome, in the fortified city of Avignon. The seventy-year exile of the popes at Avignon was a disaster for the Church, and came to be known as the Babylonian Captivity of the papacy. Yet it came about by accident.... In 1309 Clement V settled at Avignon. It was a sensible choice, for it was not strictly speaking French territory. The surrounding region was part of the Papal States, and the city itself was subject to the Kings of Sicily, until bought by the popes in the mid-century. It was near the sea and far more centrally placed for most of Europe than Rome had been. The move was not at first intended to be permanent, the Pope camping in the Bishop's palace, his curia billeted around the town, and only a minimum working archive being kept in the city.

Eamon Duffy[5]

---

[5] *Saints and Sinners: A History of the Popes*, 122.

In 1303, toward the close of the pontificate of Boniface VIII (1294-1303), a confrontation occurred with King Phillip the Fair of France over papal taxation of the clergy. The defiant monarch loosed his soldiers on the pope, in residence in Italy in the town of Anagni; this move was a blatant signal that clerical supremacy over lay leadership had come to an end throughout Europe. The rising civic, financial, and military power of kings and princes, at first geared toward independence, soon became, especially on the part of France, a thirst for dominance. In this climate of change, Clement V (1305-1314), after residing in several Italian cities, found his way to Avignon, which became the official papal residence for the next seventy years.

Those who survey the history of the Avignon popes record both positive and negative factors in this seventy-year period of papal governance. On the positive side, many were learned men of good character; several provided sound administration and financial insight previously lacking. The code of Canon Law and the office of the Curia received needed reorganization, existing universities were upgraded, additional ones established, and preaching missions to the East were encouraged.[6] Residence outside of Italy distanced the popes from the nepotism and vendettas of ancient Roman families that had influenced earlier papal leadership.

Many of these conditions, however, had negative side effects. Frequently, efficient administration became an end in itself while needed reforms were ignored. In contrast, a pope who concentrated on the larger issues often ignored administrative concerns, thereby producing chaos within the machinery of governance.[7] The new centralization strained good will as papal control extended into areas previously the realm of local governance.

---

6   Ibid., 122.
7   Geoffrey Barraclough, *The Medieval Papacy*, 152.

For example, all episcopal appointments down to the lowest local level, including monasteries and priories, became the responsibility of the pope, reducing the rights and power of local authorities. Inadvertently, this not only increased secular authority over local church leaders, but what was originally intended as reform led to added papal opportunities for financial gain in the sale and/or taxation of these benefices.[8]

Both the Hundred Years War between France and England and turbulent internal conditions throughout the Italian peninsula contributed to an unsettled political climate. John XXII (1316-1334) is reported to have spent sixty-three percent of his income on warfare while two thirds of all the revenues raised by the Avignon papacy was expended on hired mercenaries and payments to cooperative allies.[9] Financial necessity led to increases in taxation as the expenses of the curia became exorbitant. Exclusive of broader church interests, the ordinary internal expenses of the Avignon court soared, requiring such a volume of exchange that Avignon emerged as an important banking center of Europe.[10]

Though the idea of returning to Rome had never been fully abandoned, it was John XXII's successor, Benedict XII (1334-1342), who initiated the building of the papal palace at Avignon, and in 1348, his successor, Clement VI (1342-1352), purchased the county of Avignon from Naples.[11] Clement VI had close ties with the King of France, and as pope, he followed his lead on international lines; thus, during his reign, the papacy came to be seen more and more as an instrument of France. Similarly, the nationality of the cardinals contributed to this mindset. Not only

---

[8] R.W. Southern, *Western Society and the Church in the Middle Ages,* 158-159.

[9] Duffy, *Saints and Sinners,* 125.

[10] Walter Ullmann, *A Short History of the Papacy in the Middle Ages,* 287, 289.

[11] Ibid., 287-288.

were all Avignon popes of French origin, but of the 134 cardinals they created, no fewer than 112 were French as were at least seventy percent of all curial officials.[12] It was during the papacy of Clement VI that the lifestyle of Avignon acquired its reputation as profligate, luxurious, wasteful; additionally, nepotism became a regular practice. All these conditions detracted from the historic universality of the papal role as the Father of all Christians.

The Black Death ravaged Avignon during Clement's pontificate, provoking devastation similar to what has been documented of Catherine's childhood in Siena. Sixty-two thousand inhabitants perished, and it is recorded to his credit that Clement remained in the city tending to the victims in a courageous manner.[13] Clement's three successors, Innocent VI (1352-1362), Urban V (1362-1370) and Gregory XI (1370-1378) were all men of good character who lived simply and were reformers in spirit. It became their responsibility to repair previous damage that had seriously alienated the public.[14] They administered the existing system without abuse and tried to tame excesses, to check the greed and materialism of the officials of the curia, and reduce expenses. However, by this time, more than good personal qualities were needed.

So low was the prestige of the papacy that, during the reign of Urban V, the idea of resettling in Rome became a reality. Urban entered the holy city in 1367 remaining until September of 1370 when the resumption of the Hundred Years War called him back to France. Three months later he died. It would be Gregory XI, the last Avignon pope, who would make the final journey to a city which had been reduced to little more than an overgrown

---

[12] Duffy, 123-124.
[13] Duffy, 125.
[14] Barraclough, 153.

village where, on the steps of Saint Peter's, grass grew and goats grazed.[15]

The devastation of the Black Death, the continuous warfare in Italy, France, and England, as well as the failure of the papacy to maintain credible spiritual leadership, finally led to a broad based concerted reaction among the laity. Throughout Europe, "a new wave of genuine religion, coming from below, from the people, sprang into life: a real opportunity for the papacy if it had known how to use it."[16] Popular religious fervor found its impetus in basic historical Christianity, the life of Jesus, devotion to the Eucharist, and primarily the sufferings of the Passion of Christ, rather than in the abstract intellectual and theological systems built up in the previous centuries. In Siena, a group founded by Giovanni Colombini reflected this development and provided a milieu acceptive of Catherine's later associates and their public ministry. Made up of wealthy, prominent citizens, they were devoted to poverty and made public processions through the streets and public spaces of the city calling out the name of Jesus.[17] Spiritual expressions, similar to these and the lay Disciplant Confraternities seen in Siena, became widespread; trepidation and dismay regarding the church surfaced among writers and chroniclers everywhere, and often came forth in mysticism.[18]

---

[15] Ullmann, 292.

[16] Barraclough, 154.

[17] Karen Scott, "Urban Spaces, Women's Networks, and the Lay Apostolate in the Siena of Catherine Benincasa," 113-114.

[18] Barraclough, 157.

- 3 -
Pisa

I've received a letter from you, and the sight of it warmed my heart. From this I've come to realize that it is not my virtue or goodness... but only your love and goodness and that of those holy women that has moved you to write to me so humbly, inviting me there. I would gladly fulfill your wishes and theirs, but for now I'm excusing myself, for my physical condition makes it impossible. Besides, I see that right now I would be a source of scandal. But I trust in God's goodness that, if he sees it is for his honor and the salvation of souls, he will see that I come free of constraint, in peace, without any further gossip.

Catherine of Siena to Piero Gambacorta
in Pisa, late 1374 [19]

Shortly after sending this letter, Catherine accepted this invitation from the leader of the Pisan Republic. Catherine's allusion to her physical condition has been interpreted as exhaustion following her labors among the Sienese plague victims in July through October of 1374. Her reference to being a cause of scandal was due, not to her personal reputation, but to tensions in political relationship between Siena and Pisa, following the seizure of rural Sienese fortresses by the Pisan Knights of Saint John with the encouragement of Gambacorta.[20] With her companions Alessa and Cecca, who would serve as scribes for many of the Pisan letters, Catherine stayed at the home of a Pisan disciple, Gherardo Buonconti. She indicated in a letter to a Sienese

---

[19] Noffke, *Letters,* I, T149, 62-63.
[20] Ibid., see notes 9, 10.

follower that, after two months, "We've never left Gherardo's house; we'll go out when God decides we should."[21] Catherine's restraint is interesting in that the political situation regarding the papacy and Tuscany was peaking at this time, and Pisa was more central to events than Siena.

The Pisa to which Catherine journeyed in early 1375 had a quite different aspect from her native Siena. An urban center on a flat plain, it was surrounded by a broad, fertile countryside which provided exportable agricultural products to foster the prosperous commercial trade for which Pisa had become famous in the tenth and eleventh centuries. Bounded on the northeast by the mountainous Alpine hills, the Arno River flowed majestically west from Florence through the heart of the city and continued on to the Tyrrhenian Sea. Here, a seaport gave Pisa access to trading and political endeavors as far reaching as the eastern Mediterranean. In addition, Pisa was situated on the coastal land route, the *Via Aemilia*, which connected cities of the north with Rome and brought overland trade to the heart of the city and beyond.[22]

At the time of Catherine's visit, her host, Piero Gambacorta, governed Pisa. A member of a powerful and wealthy Pisan family, he had come to leadership in 1370. His daughter Tora, drawn to Catherine, later became a Dominican acknowledged by the church as Blessed Clara Gambacorta. Piero was a "peaceable and beneficent man"[23] who would soon find himself embroiled in the political problems that would lead the Tuscan communities to organize in opposition to the papacy. Since Pisa was the port city through which church dignitaries traveled between Avignon and Tuscan Italy, and since Raymond who was with her had a semi-official role in papal planning for the crusade, Catherine was

---

[21] Ibid., I, T69, 67.

[22] David Herlihy, *Pisa in the Early Renaissance: A Study of Urban Growth*, passim.

[23] Noffke, *Letters*, I, T149, introductory notes, 60.

in a position to meet many churchmen and public officials to discuss papal concerns in person. At the same time, she became increasingly aware of the human limitations, if not corruption, of many highly placed churchmen.

Catherine's correspondence expanded during her stay in Pisa. The early letters have a personal nature, written either to followers who had sought her advice and encouragement or to bring the needs of others to the attention of those who could provide assistance. Soon, however, politics began to invade her messages when news circulated that Gregory would officially announce a crusade, as happened on July 1, 1375. In a letter to Giovanna, Queen of Naples, immediately following this declaration, Catherine joyfully informed her that Gregory had requested several leaders of religious orders to spread the word of the impending crusade and to find leaders who would be willing to participate. She asked Giovanna to "fire up your desire and get ready" so that when the moment arrived she could send military aid.[24]

At the same time, Catherine contacted Niccolò Soderini, a Florentine loyal to the papacy; Monna Pavola, Abbess of a monastery in Fiesole outside Florence; her friend, William of Flete at his hermitage in Lecceto; Don Giovanni de' Sabbatini, a Carthusian monastic of Bologna; and Queen Mother Elizabeth of Hungary to influence them to support the crusade.[25] From some of her comments in these letters, it appeared that Catherine, perhaps remembering Francis of Assisi's peacemaking journey to the East, had a simplistic idea that an entourage of religious persons would join the military force in a kind of holy pilgrimage. She was obviously ill informed of the negative aspects of former crusading ventures which engaged in looting and murder as they passed

---

[24] Ibid., I, T133, 125.
[25] Ibid., I, T13, 129-130; I, T144, 114; I, T66, 157-158; I, T141, 145; I, T145, 170.

through Europe, in some cases assaulting and molesting enclaves where Jewish residents dwelt. For Catherine the emphasis was on the glorious venture of fighting, even dying for the church, and for the return of holy places in Jerusalem where Christ had once lived, suffered, and died.

Catherine's ensuing letters continued to promote the crusade, but soon a second issue emerged: the difficulties between the church and Florentines who had begun to foster the notion of a union of Tuscan cities in an anti-papal league. In her letter to Giovanna of Naples, Catherine not only sought her support in the crusade "so that we may all go as one splendid company," but she also asked assistance for the church adding, "Surely it is a foolish and mindless child who does not help such a mother when a rotten member opposes her and rebels against her."[26] In a letter to her follower, Matteo di Fazzio d'Cenni, the rector of the Misericordia Hospital in Siena, Catherine rejoiced in the progress being made regarding the crusade but declared, "Christ's bride is being persecuted by Christians, by false and rotten members."[27]

Several letters from this period depict her growing concern about persons whose activities threatened to disrupt peace in Italy and consequently weaken the papacy. In a lengthy and rather severe letter to Bernabò Visconti of Milan, who was waging war with the papacy, Catherine warned him that he "would be cut off from the body of holy Church like a gangrenous limb." She urged him to make amends and to "go to the aid of your father as he lifts high the standard of the most holy cross."[28] In another letter directed to his wife, Regina della Scala, Catherine urged her to restrain her husband.[29] In her letter to the notorious mer-

---

[26] Ibid., I, T138, 102.
[27] Ibid., I, T137, 182-183.
[28] Ibid., I, T28, 136-137.
[29] Ibid., I, T29, 210.

cenary, John Hawkwood, the English leader of militant bands of soldiers who roamed Italy willing to fight for the highest bidder, she insisted "change your course and enlist instead in the service of the cross of Christ crucified, you and all your followers and companies."[30] Hawkwood had attacked one city after another, first at the bidding of the Visconti from 1369-1372, then of the pope in May of 1375 until bought off by the Florentines in June. He then began to extort money from other Tuscan cities to prevent his ravaging their territories

As her letters continued, a third point emerged: Catherine's direct connection with papal affairs. She informed Tommaso dalla Fonte, who had written from Siena urging her to come home because of gossip, "I want you to know that I'm afraid to have to put off doing as you told me, because the Archbishop has asked the Master General [of the Dominicans] whether I might stay several more days as a favor."[31] Again, in a letter to her followers in Siena, she sought prayers for the church "for she is much persecuted," reporting, "I have delayed my coming a bit for the sake of a certain service to the church and because the holy father wanted it."[32] Eventually, she not only wrote to the Elders of Lucca, she visited that city—believed to be at the request of Gregory—in an unsuccessful endeavor to retain their loyalty to the papacy.[33]

Though Catherine entered the realm of political affairs from this time forward, her letters were not distinctly political, in the sense of offering sage political advice and direction or entering into the intrigue of strategy. Rather, they contained encourage-

---

[30] Ibid., I, T140, 79.

[31] Ibid., I, T139, 196. Note that the permission was sought from Elias of Toulouse, not from the local Sienese superior; Catherine also noted that the master (theologian, Giovanni Tantucci) had written a response to her calumniators in Siena which she said "will surely quiet them down."

[32] Ibid., I, T132, 202.

[33] Ibid., I, T168, 243.

ment to the recipients to remain closely bound to Christ, to forsake evil, to defend the church, and to be loyal to the pope. The letters indicated a growing understanding of the wide-ranging efforts of Gregory XI to maintain the stability of papal power and the role of the church in the affairs of Italy. Papal diplomatic efforts seemed to be headed toward the accomplishment of at least two of Catherine's three desires for the church: the return of the papal court to Rome and the calling of a crusade. Her third desire, the internal reform of the church and the appointment of worthy administrators and cardinals, was a continued concern addressed in her letters.

Perhaps the most significant letter of this period is one addressed to Berengario, Abbot of Lézat and Apostolic Nuncio to Tuscany, in which Catherine responded directly to questions he raised regarding Pope Gregory XI. She listed the pope's personal failings and the public consequences that resulted. First, she noted his excessive attachment and concern for his relatives; second, his excessive softness and leniency in the correction of his subordinates allowing three particularly evil vices: "impurity, greed, and bloated pride" to hold sway in prelates who cared for nothing but "pleasure, positions of power, and wealth." Lastly, she addressed an issue that was paramount in her view of a restored and reformed church, the need to get rid of those shepherds who care about "nothing but food and beautiful palaces and splendid horses." She implored Berengario to work with the pope to appoint pastors and cardinals, not for "flattery, money, or simony" but because of their virtue and good reputation.[34]

Catherine's candid assessment of Gregory's role demonstrated not only her immersion in discussions with the church personnel she had met in Pisa, but also the self-confidence she

---

[34] Ibid., I, T109, 267-268.

exerted in her new role in church affairs. The tenor of her letters conveys a sense of comfort with her public role, with articulating her point of view, and impacting public events. Clearly, her support was being sought and her opinion solicited. Neither hesitating nor wavering in her interactions with the leaders of the church, her responses were lucid and forthright. A telling example of this occurs in an early letter to Gregory, whom she had not yet met personally. She wrote to express her disappointment at the creation of nine new cardinals—all French—who did not represent a reform mentality: "I've heard you have appointed some cardinals. I believe it would be to God's honor and better for you to be careful always to choose virtuous men. Otherwise it will be a great insult to God and disastrous to holy church. And then, let's not be surprised if God sends us his chastening scourges, and justly."[35]

Catherine remained in Pisa until at least January of 1376, to lend her prestige to the papal effort to maintain peace in the Italian territories, to raise support for a crusade, and to avert the formation and later, the expansion, of the anti-papal league in Tuscany. Eventually, however, the lines would be drawn, and almost all the Italian cities, including Perugia, Pisa, Lucca, Siena, Bologna, and Milan joined in the anti-papal rebellion under the leadership of Florence.

---

[35] Ibid., I, T185, 250.

- 4 -
The Anti-Papal League

Florence showed rather more skill in exploiting the discontent caused by the administration of Church lands by papal officers. Whether these were Frenchmen or not, they had incurred the dislike of the Italians.... It is only too true that many of these Frenchmen regarded Italy merely as a place where they could rapidly amass a fortune. Gregory XI did all he could to put right such abuses. The Vatican registers show many signs of his efforts; but they also prove how well-founded were the complaints of the populations of the Italian cities.

Guillaume Mollat[36]

The events that propelled the papacy and the Tuscan communes into open confrontation resulted from a mix of political unrest, mutual suspicion, distrust, and deception. The bumbling efforts of papal negotiators provided a major contribution as well as the newly aroused political ambitions among the artisan classes in Florence, similar to the activities of the Riformatori in Siena. Florentine relations with the papacy had been deteriorating since 1372. One source of discontent was the activity of the nephew of Gregory XI, Gerard du Puy, Abbot of Marmoutiers, Vicar-General of Perugia and leader of a powerful military force. Florentines suspected that du Puy was fomenting unrest in southern Tuscany in order to promote the territorial ambitions of the church. Suspicion increased after the 1374 outbreak of the plague when poor harvests throughout the region caused extreme shortages of food. The papal territories had supplies in abundance; yet, Gerard du

---

[36] *The Popes at Avignon, 1305-1378*, 165.

Puy was believed to have ordered an embargo that prevented grain sales to the Tuscan territories. Brucker suggests that "the antipapal forces in Florence utilized and manipulated events" such as these since, in a letter to the Florentines, Gregory later denied the charges.[37] In addition, the traditional leadership of the patrician nobility comprised of Guelfs, historically tied to the church, gave way to the newly empowered working class artisans of the guilds, the *gente nuova*, whose attitude to the papacy was hostile. In their efforts to extend control over all of Tuscany and weaken the papacy, the newly elected leaders, the Signoria, began a campaign to spread false propaganda about papal intentions.

A Conference of Tuscan cities, including Siena, Pisa, Lucca, and Arezzo, was held in Florence in early June of 1375. A major point of discussion was the fear that the cessation of hostilities between the church and Bernabò Visconti of Milan would loose mercenary troops, like that of Hawkwood, into the area. Papal legates, Berengario and Jacopo da Itri, assured the Tuscans that the papacy would hold out against Visconti and that Hawkwood would defend Tuscany. Members of the conference discovered on June sixth, however, that the peace treaty between the papacy and Visconti had been signed two days earlier even as these assurances were being stated. Suspicion and distrust deepened while the mood of opposition expanded.[38]

In late June of 1375, a new group of Signoria took office in Florence, headed by Luigi Aldobrandini, "an inveterate foe of the Guelf oligarchy and the papacy." Florence prepared to engage in war with the church by passing stringent anti-clerical provisions, forming an alliance with Bernabò Visconti of Milan and appointing a commission of "Eight" to direct the war effort. Four

---

[37] Brucker, 276, 283-284, 295.
[38] Ibid., 286-287.

citizens, authorized to initiate a federation of Tuscan communes, spread rumors regarding the papacy. For example, on July twenty-second, they contacted Piero Gambacorta of Pisa to report that a "trustworthy and reliable source" had revealed that "a certain abbot," hinting at Gerard du Puy, "is attempting to subvert the city of Pisa in the name of the church." Thus Pisa was induced to join the league on July twenty-fourth. On the thirteenth of August, Florence entered into alliance with Visconti, announcing in a letter that clarified their intent, "...we declare that this league... is to be extended to the pope and the emperor, and against them."[39]

Though the Florentines were guilty of exacerbating antagonisms that already existed and of creating a sentiment receptive to war, papal administrators, usually Frenchmen, were equally responsible for the impasse. Their ineptness, bad judgment, and constant interference in Tuscan disputes invited suspicion and recrimination. Their failure to coordinate the truce negotiations with the Visconti and those of Gregory's ambassadors to the Conference of Tuscan cities exemplified not avarice or lust for power but a chronic failure to comprehend the intricacies and involutions of Italian politics.[40] Surprisingly, however, once the League had been established, neither side to the dispute engaged immediately in overt warfare. Both pursued diplomatic channels to accomplish their ends. The Florentines sent letters to kings, princes, communes, and clerics to present their side of the issues, requesting either assistance or neutrality. Gregory also endeavored to encourage neutrality among the uncommitted states while continuing his two pronged effort to organize a crusade and to return the papal court to Rome.

---

[39] Ibid., 293-294.

[40] Ibid., 295-296. Brucker reports that one papal legate, Jacopo da Itri, Archbishop of Otranto, reported of his colleague, Abbot Lézat, Berengario, that he was "a man who knows nothing or very little." Both of these men corresponded with Catherine.

When the Florentines refused Gregory's peace offer in March of 1376, the pope responded by imposing a papal interdict on the city. Though the religious impact of this decision was painful to some—depriving all citizens of religious services including Mass and the sacraments—it was the political and economic consequences that intensified its effect. The interdict was extended to include a ban on trade with Florentine merchants throughout Europe and the East.[41] With this hardening of relationships between Avignon and Florence, Catherine's "political" activities entered a new phase.

Catherine's overarching concern was not only to prevent the formation of a league formidable enough to injure the papacy, but also to bring all the constituencies together in virtue and love of the church and of each other. From her first letter to him, she urged Gregory to take the initiative for peace. "I beg you," she wrote, "to communicate with Lucca and Pisa as a father, as God will teach you. Help them in any way you can, and urge them to keep holding their ground." Relying on her own experience, she reported, "I have been in Pisa and Lucca until just now, and have pleaded with them as strongly as I could not to join in league with the rotten members who are rebelling against you. But they are very anxious, since they aren't getting any encouragement from you, and are being constantly goaded and threatened by the other side."[42]

She begged Gregory to use "kindness to conquer their malice," and "with the bait of love and of your own kindness give peace to us poor children who have sinned."[43] When Gregory threatened military action, she wrote, "As for the soldiers you have hired to come here, hold them back and don't let them come, for they would ruin everything instead of setting things right." In

[41] Ibid., 309-312.
[42] Noffke, *Letters*, I, T185, 249.
[43] Ibid., II, T196, 20.

the same letter, she responded to his request for counsel, "My dear father, you ask me about your coming [to Rome]. I answer you in the name of Christ crucified: come as soon as you can. If you can, come before September, and if you cannot come earlier, don't delay beyond the end of September. Pay no attention to any opposition, but like a courageous and fearless man, come!"[44] In the summer of 1375, however, peace negotiations between France and England to end the Hundred Years War caused Gregory to delay once again. Then, the formation of the antipapal league caused another delay.

The contents of Catherine's letters to Gregory demonstrate not only her spiritual awareness but also an adult and mature articulation of her new knowledge of political realities. From her broader connections in Pisa as well as her interactions with church dignitaries, she grasped the human strengths and weaknesses that impacted the health and well being of the church through its leadership. Her letters to Gregory reveal the accumulation of knowledge and understanding dating from her childhood exposure to the Sienese paintings of Justice, Peace, and Concord. They had provided an introduction to issues reflecting a world beyond her narrow horizons and prepared her now to communicate forcefully both spiritual and political wisdom.

Catherine's letters to Gregory were written between January of 1374[45] and Gregory's arrival in Rome in early 1377 and continued sporadically until his death in 1378. As was her custom, she concentrated on the reformation of the individual as the surest means to effect radical change in society as a whole. The cause of peace demanded Gregory's personal reform. Like the image of the ruler in the *Allegory of Good Government*, he must acquire the requisite virtues, depicted in the fresco as Prudence, Justice, Fortitude, Temperance, and Magnanimity. He must

---

[44] Ibid., II, T229, 190-191.
[45] See Noffke, I, 244, Intro., T185.

root out vice in himself and make an urgent demand for more ethical standards in those who ruled under him. Invested with authority, he had the responsibility to use his power to eradicate the evils that were the cause of the social injustices that led citizens to rebel against the church. Catherine's language matched the strength of her conviction as she called Gregory to his duty. Using the spiritual prestige that flowed from her inner power, she modeled for Gregory the proper use of his authority to correct evil where it existed. She warned him that if he failed to do this, he would be severely rebuked by God, adding, "If I were in your place I would be afraid of incurring divine judgment."[46]

What Catherine identified as the greatest weakness in Gregory's exercise of authority was his failure to correct those who had failed in their duties and his lack of discernment in appointing virtuous and able administrators. She urged him to uproot these weeds in the garden of holy church.[47] According to Catherine, appointments to high office of men lacking in virtue, selfish people looking out only for their personal needs, "cripple the common good of the Christian congregation and the reform of holy Church."[48] Gregory's leniency allowed the weeds of impurity, avarice, and pride to flourish in the garden of holy Church.[49] No wonder his subjects rose up against him! They suffered such injustice, inequity, and unfairness that Catherine declared they had no alternative but to revolt.[50] Like Justice in chains in the *Allegory of Bad Government,* justice could not prevail where vice was permitted to dominate the intentions of administrators. Injustice bred discord and war; bad leaders provoked rebellion.[51]

---

[46] Ibid., II, T258, 193.
[47] Ibid., II, T206, 61.
[48] Ibid., II, T239, 244.
[49] Ibid., II, T206, 61.
[50] Ibid., II, T169, 20.
[51] Ibid., I, T185, 245.

Continuing this theme, Catherine interpreted justice according to the understanding of her day. As a ruler, Gregory could not allow the misdeeds of his subjects to go unpunished; strict justice required that he "punish the criminal and exact whatever each can yield as far as possible, without war." She reminded him, however, that the justice of a spiritual leader must be tempered with mercy and charity; therefore, he should punish them "as a father must punish a child."[52] Calling Gregory to his role as pontiff, father, and good shepherd, she pleaded, "Use your kindness to conquer their malice," promising him that if he acted gently, "they would come and lay their heads in your lap in sorrow for what they have done."[53] They await a conciliatory sign, she told him.

As in the *Allegory of Good Government*, so in Catherine's exposition, the proper administration of justice would bring peace to Gregory's domain. Lorenzetti had pictured Sienese citizens paying just taxes and tributes, acknowledging proper dominion over lands and castles, all without war, because when justice prevailed, peace and concord followed. Catherine held out this prospect to Gregory. Peace was her overall objective. "Make peace with all of Tuscany," she pleaded, "Peace will follow true justice."[54] "Use your power and authority diligently," she urged, "and with a hungry longing for peace."[55] "I beg you," she wrote, "to invite those who have rebelled against you to a holy peace...."[56] And repeatedly, there is the refrain, "Peace, peace, peace" and "No more war."[57]

---

[52] Ibid., II, T255, 193.
[53] Ibid., II, T196, 20.
[54] Ibid., II, T255, 193.
[55] Ibid., II, T206, 61.
[56] Ibid., I, T185, 249.
[57] Ibid., II, T270, 346; T252, 273; T209, 300.

- 5 -
Catherine at Avignon

On June 18, 1376, St. Catherine, having offered her services as mediator between the republic of Florence and
the papacy, entered Avignon, and was honorably received by Gregory, who assigned as her dwelling the
palace of La Motte. Within two days of her arrival,
Catherine was ushered into the pope's presence.

Thomas Okey[58]

[Gregory XI] was far too well acquainted with the tor-
tuous policy of the Florentines to entrust peace negotiations to a humble religious, whose orthodoxy must
have been in some doubt, since a commission of bishops subjected her to an exacting interrogation.

Guillaume Mollat[59]

Historians frequently generalize the efforts of holy women
like Catherine and Birgitta of Sweden as self-appointed attempts
to influence popes according to their own perceptions of right
and wrong. In reality, medieval people, including the simplest,
the most powerful and the well educated were anxious for the
company of those who appeared to have penetrated the mystery of God. Holy persons, men and women, lay and religious,
were seen as divine gifts to the community, a mediating presence before God. Much like the ancient Greeks who sought the
wisdom of the oracle at Delphi, medievals came from neighbor-
ing cities and towns to seek the advice and counsel of saints and

---

[58] *The Story of Avignon*, 173.
[59] *The Popes at Avignon, 1305-1378*, 167.

mystics. In this way, their circles of influence widened and some, including Catherine of Siena, were drawn into the larger religious/ political questions of the day. Therefore, Catherine's reference to Gregory's early overture to her is significant, because it indicated the papal initiative in their relationship and Gregory's medieval penchant to be associated with "holy persons."

One should not assume, however, that Gregory would see Catherine as an astute political advisor. Rather, appreciating the stature she enjoyed in the broader Christian community, he would welcome her endorsement of his policies, her unwavering support and dedication to the church, and trust that her acknowledged sanctity would strengthen the unity of the church. On the other hand, the transformation of Catherine into a "public figure" did not stem from her personal desire for political recognition; rather, it was a profoundly obedient response to the need and entreaty of the church. Levasti's certitude regarding this point surfaces in his comment that, previous to this time, Catherine was never inclined to a political life, that her interests were in saving souls, reconciling differences, and "setting up a government of love" concerned with the "city of God" rather than the city of the world. This avowed concern for the "city of God" is what propelled her into the affairs of the church. She was "not an arbitrator," Levasti wrote, but "a friend of God."[60] Fiercely loyal to the church, Catherine stated clearly the priorities of her life mission in a letter to Gregory: "I have no other desire in this life than to see God's honor, your peace, and the reform of holy Church, and to see the life of grace in everyone."[61] For these goals Catherine would exert the full influence of her powers of persuasion.

Soon after the papal interdict had been imposed on Florence, on April 1, 1376, Catherine, rapt in prayer over the plight

---

[60] Levasti, 96-97.
[61] Noffke, *Letters*, II, T252, 272.

of the church, had a visionary experience. In it, she said that she came to an understanding of the mystery of the persecution of the church "and the renewal and exaltation to come." She saw herself entering into the side of Christ, who "placed the cross on my shoulder and put the olive branch in my hand," signs which she interpreted as a commission to bring the good news of peace to others. She was led to understand that from the sin of persecuting the church would come the full restoration of its former virtue and integrity. She became "so confident about the future," that she could give herself "completely to seeking God's honor, the salvation of souls, and the renewal and exaltation of holy church" and she promised that "by the grace and power of the Holy Spirit I intend to persevere until I die."[62] Motivated by this mystical experience, Catherine went to Florence to meet with several disciples, members of the Guelf aristocracy, who remained faithful to the papacy though it had meant the loss of their political power to the *gente nuova*.

Many questions have arisen regarding the official nature of Catherine's mission to Avignon. There is a strong possibility that it was her followers in the Guelf party who asked her to intercede with Gregory; however, since they would have had no legal authorization to do so, it would not have been an official request. If, on the other hand, the ruling Signoria of Florence had asked for her intercession, it would have been an insincere gesture since there was no desire for accommodation on their part. Since the Breton legions hired by the papacy were poised to enter Tuscany, however, they may have seen her presence at Avignon as a way of forestalling the threatened military action previously mentioned in her letter to Gregory.

Gregory welcomed Catherine as an honored and distinguished visitor to Avignon when she arrived on June 18, 1376,

---

[62] Ibid., II, T219, 91-92.

with her twenty-three followers, to join Raymond and his two companions already there. At her first papal audience, we are told that she addressed the Pope with commanding authority. On July 1 Gregory granted her permission to have a portable altar and to have daily Mass celebrated in any suitable place of her choice. Her Dominican followers were given extraordinary privileges of hearing confessions and ministering to all who presented themselves, a task which Raymond found exhausting, given the numbers who surrounded Catherine.[63]

After an official interrogation, conducted by three learned churchmen—in which Catherine responded with calm and intelligence—her official position was strengthened. Then, on August 17, 1376, Gregory issued a Papal Bull reiterating the decision of the Florence chapter two years earlier. Thus, the appointment of Raymond as confessor to Catherine and her followers as well as her direct obedience to the Master General of the Dominican Order, rather than to her superiors in Siena, was affirmed. The public acceptance of Catherine's authenticity became even clearer, as did the fact that her faithful support for the church and the papacy was a desirable consequence.

This explanation is important for the record since later historians, seeking to downplay her role in regard to the Avignon residence, will present Catherine in a less than favorable light. Mollat, for one, discounted Raymond of Capua's interpretation in the *Legenda* of Catherine's role as an official negotiator. He contended, "It is difficult to see how the Eight [in Florence], who were carefully guarded, could have had an interview with Catherine outside their city. If they did indeed entrust her with an official mission, how can one explain the silence of every contemporary source—narrative, diplomatic, documentary or epistolary." As evidence, he cites the fact that "the Saint makes no allusion

---

[63] Okey, 173-177.

to this occasion in a letter dated 28 June, in which she gives a short account of her interview with the pope." In addition, Mollat questions Raymond's recounting that Gregory said to Catherine at this first meeting, "In order that you may know clearly that I want peace, I leave it entirely in your hands; only remember that the honor of the church is in your hands."[64]

In the letter to which Mollat referred, sent June 28, 1376 to the "Eight of War" in Florence, Catherine made no reference to an official role as negotiator but related that she had spoken to Gregory, that he listened graciously, and was anxious for peace. She also stated carefully that the pontiff "thought he should give no other response until your ambassadors arrive here." But she does cite Gregory's statement "that if things were with you as I had been telling him, he was ready to receive you as his children and to do about the matter whatever seemed best to me."[65] This very diplomatic assertion, *"if things were with you as I had been telling him"* would be clearly understood by Catherine and by Gregory who, certainly more politically astute than Catherine, would be very cautious to yield concessions without proof of repentance. Levasti confirms that Gregory was disinclined to succumb to Catherine's pleading for peace and reconciliation with Florence; yet, he describes the papal reaction as one of great patience as Gregory explained to her the duplicity of the Florentines in using her.

Modern historians like Mollat are at pains to reassess the reputation of the Avignon popes who they feel were unfairly represented by their contemporaries, among whom they include Petrarch and Catherine. On the one hand, they assert that most of the popes at Avignon were men of personally devout life. Some of them seriously attempted reforms, both in the curia and in the

---

[64] Mollat, 166-167.
[65] Noffke, *Letters,* II, T230, 197.

church at large, and they built up an administrative and financial system that surpassed in efficiency those of all the other kingdoms of Europe. Scholars have even explained and defended papal taxation, the object of the fiercest criticism. At the same time, however, they acknowledge that "the spectacle of a rich, luxurious and powerful sovereign and his bureaucracy, living in their palace-fortress completely out of touch with the imperial city of the apostles, which had always been the center of the faith, was of itself a permanent scandal" and further declared that "during its prolonged stay the papacy and its court compromised with worldly standards and aims in an organic fashion which was more detrimental to the church than previous excesses of individuals."[66]

In regard to the role of Catherine of Siena in this political dilemma, what troubled some historians was the interpretation of Gregory that surfaced from the written record of Catherine's letters and from depositions of her followers. Multiple references to Gregory's weakness and indecisiveness in her letters to him as well as the inflated opinion of followers in regard to her role in papal politics and the return of the papal court to Rome, were two of the most common. In regard to the first issue, Catherine's letters continually call Gregory to courage. She begs him to return to Rome "like a courageous and fearless man." And "I long to see you a courageous man, free of any cowardice or selfish sensual love in regard to yourself or any of your relatives." She continued, "if you fail to act, you will be severely rebuked by God."[67] Catherine habitually appealed to her followers, both male and female, to act *virilimenti*, that is, manfully. This injunction implied throwing off all self concern, all indecision, all fear of consequences and to concentrate solely on furthering the will of

---

[66] David Knowles and Dimitri Obolensky, *The Christian Centuries: The Middle Ages*, II, 406.

[67] Noffke, *Letters*, I, T185, 249; II, T229, 191; II, T255, 192-193.

God, advancing God's glory, and becoming, as she was, totally given over to furthering the interests of God and his church in this world.

Some, however, feel compelled to criticize her use of the word in Gregory's regard. They cite translations that read: "Be manly and not fearful," and "come like a virile man who does not fear," noting "the view from Avignon was not so simple that a small dose of courage was all that was needed to rectify matters."[68] Indeed, what Gregory needed was immense courage to counteract the forces of his own family and a procession of politicians and clerics who, for their own personal gain, were determined to prevent him from dismantling the Court at Avignon. In addition, it becomes clear that Gregory, an intelligent and informed scholar, hesitated lest he make an erroneous decision, conscious more of its impact on the church than on himself personally. Fully aware of this aspect of Gregory's predicament, Catherine counseled him continually to courage in the strongest and most supportive terms. She wrote, "because your burden is greater, you need a more bold courageous heart, fearful of nothing that might happen."[69]

In regard to the second issue, Catherine's role in papal politics, once the duplicity of the Florentine leadership had been made clear to her, she no longer concerned herself in promoting their interests. She turned all her attention to the three issues that were paramount to her: the return to Rome, the call for a crusade, and the reform of church leadership. Even among these, the issue of Rome was primary. For example, she conversed at length with the Duke of Anjou, brother to the King of France, about leading the crusade. When invited by him to visit his brother the King to confer about this question, she demurred, lest in her absence from

---

[68] Thibault, Appendix C, 211.
[69] Noffke, *Letters*, II, T252, 271.

Avignon, some issue would arise to further delay the return to Rome.

As every hindrance to Gregory's departure arose, both real and fallacious, Catherine wrote to encourage the Pontiff to remain committed. For example, when a letter purported to be from a "holy person" warned Gregory that he would be poisoned on arrival in Rome, Catherine wrote, "I'll close by saying I do not believe the letter sent to you came from the servant of God who was named to you. Nor was it written from very far away; no, I think it came from quite near by, from the servants of the devil, who have little fear of God."[70] Even Mollat, though he stated that one cannot conclude "that St. Catherine's intervention was of overwhelming importance" conceded that because of the obstacles that faced Gregory, "St. Catherine of Siena's words of encouragement may well have been needed."[71]

Levasti reported Gregory's final request for Catherine's presence just days before the scheduled departure. Bartolomeo Dominici's personal record of the event stated that the pope called Catherine into his presence and asked her if he was right in his decision to return to Rome. Catherine was hesitant at first to reply until the pope stated he was not asking for advice, but for a revelation of the will of God. Catherine then reminded Gregory of a private vow he had taken on his elevation to the papal throne that he would accomplish the return to Rome. Considering her knowledge of this well kept secret a revelation, Gregory took her answer as an expression of the will of God.[72] The departure, so long in preparation, took place on September 13, 1376.

---

[70] Ibid., II, T239, 247.
[71] Mollat, 170-171.
[72] Levasti, 232-233.

- 6 -
The Return to Rome

The exodus was not as reposeful as Catherine would have wished. Omens darkly thronged about them and were hailed as divine warnings to turn back. The date was very inauspicious. The Pope's father, Count William de Beaufort, an old man, came running to the door, imploring his son not to go. Being firmly repulsed, he flung himself across the threshold, saying Gregory could not leave save over his grey hairs. It was an unpleasant scene. Quoting the verse: "Thou shalt trample upon the asp and the basilisk," the Pope stepped across the prostrate body of his father. Then his mule shied, backed, and could not be made to move. Another mule had to be brought, while murmurs arose from the mournful knot of people gathered to watch. Six cardinals remained in Avignon. All the others accompanied the Pope, who proceeded in easy stages to Marseilles. Catherine left Avignon the same day, with her company, taking another route by land.

Alice Curtayne[73]

This leave taking was but a prelude to the vexations that would accompany Gregory's journey: first a river voyage down the Rhône, then overland to Marseilles where on October second the party boarded galleys for the open sea. Storm after storm waylaid the papal fleet over sixteen days, forcing it to seek shelter several times until finally weighing anchor at Genoa on the eighteenth of October. Ten days later, the fleet sailed again, only

---

[73] *Saint Catherine of Siena*, 112.

to be afflicted once again by severe weather—one of the galleys sank. After putting in at several ports for safety, the flotilla reached Corneto in the Papal States on December sixth. The papal party remained there for five weeks while negotiating with the Romans to enter the city.

Catherine wrote to Gregory at Corneto, "I beg you for the love of Christ crucified, go as soon as you can to your own place, the place of the glorious apostles Peter and Paul. Also regarding yourself: try to go confidently; God for his part will provide you with everything you need for yourself and for his bride's well being."[74] She added, "Find encouragement and confidence in the true servants of God—I mean, in their prayers." Finally, on January sixteenth the papal party sailed on to Ostia, up the Tiber, and disembarked at the Church of Saint Paul, outside the walls of the city. The next day, Gregory and the Cardinals of the Curia processed triumphantly into the holy city of Rome.

Catherine set out from Avignon with her eyes to the future. Her initial concern for peace between Florence and the Pope had been overshadowed by the greater significance of the restoration of Rome as the center of Christianity. Traveling overland, the journey funded by Gregory, she and her companions passed through areas still suffering from the plague. Several of Catherine's followers became ill; consequently, their passage through Genoa stretched into a month's stay. The fact that Catherine was in Genoa when the papal party arrived there has led to stories that Gregory spoke privately to Catherine, receiving encouragement from her to continue on his journey despite the setbacks. According to Levasti, this story is not well substantiated historically, but not improbable.

Catherine's party left Genoa by sea, traveling to Pisa where

---

[74] Noffke, *Letters*, II, T252, 272.

she was heartened to hear of the warm reception given Gregory by Piero Gambacorta and the Pisans. Another month passed before her group returned to Siena after an absence of eight months. The Catherine who returned to Siena had become a seasoned apostle of peace. Her sphere of influence now narrowed, but the goal remained expansive: to bring God's love to everyone in need, to restore peace in Italy and in individual hearts, to support a crusade, and to do her share to effect reform in the leadership of the church.

The year 1374 marked a watershed in the life of Catherine of Siena. Every public event of her life can be dated as preceding or following the Dominican Chapter in Florence. Her validation by the order, the transfer of obedience from the local Sienese authorities directly to the leadership of the order, and the personal guidance and friendship of Raymond of Capua affirmed in the reality of daily life what Catherine had long known from mystical contemplation. She could acknowledge to herself, because others had seen it clearly, that she was especially called to do God's work in the world, to be an instrument of God's glory in the church. How this would be carried out, she trusted to God's revelation.

Everywhere she had traveled—Pisa, Lucca, Florence, Avignon—her circle had grown. Disciples joined her, drawn by her holiness, her prayerfulness, her single-minded commitment to God, to the church, to virtue, to the salvation of all whom she would encounter. How did this affect her? She grew stronger each day, more self confident, more committed, more secure in her personal union with God; she moved beyond all self concern, all measured response, totally open to anything that would bring about the renewal of God's church and its restoration to virtue and high principle. Avignon brought disappointment; yet being manipulated by the Florentines did not deter her. Her only desire was a thirst—she said she was dying of desire—to establish peace among Christians, to restore a sense of stability, order and dedication in Christ's church, in His vicar, and charity among all God's people.

What enabled her commitment, her totally generous service? First, her sense of complete union with God, a union which caused her to become one with the intense fire of God's love for all people. Second, the gift of human friendship, the circles of relationship that continually expanded around her. As these circles widened and intensified, so did Catherine's sense of self, a self which could address every need, give totally to whatever was at hand, negotiate with any and all as if Christ himself were present. In contemporary terms, she had demonstrated to herself and to others her capacity to produce change, to empower others, to increase their personal resources, their effectiveness, and ability to act. She had exerted influence in the broader religious, social, and political arenas.[75] She had, at last, assumed her true Dominican calling; she had become an influential preacher and teacher.

In this period, the expansive growth of Catherine's tree of virtue is evident. She has spiraled outward while the core of self has grown deeper; narrow interests have expanded to encompass broader issues of human existence and behavior.[76] The roots have settled deeply into the circle of self-knowledge in the knowledge of God. The marrow of patience has been exercised and matured in her efforts to influence political leaders and leaders of her church. Finally, the graft of discernment has enhanced her gifts as negotiator and counselor and will profoundly affect the future fruits and blossoms of the crown.

---

[75] Miller, "Women and Power," 198-199.
[76] Gordon Allport, *Pattern and Growth in Personality,* 287.

CHAPTER SIX

The Fruit of the Tree: Peacemaking

- 1 -
A Woman of Depth and Wisdom

As a rule we associate with very pure and spiritual women, even if not cloistered, a certain deficient sense of reality. We cherish them, and shield them from harsh contact with the world, lest the fine flower of their delicacy be withered. But no one seems to have felt this way about Catherine. Her "love for souls" was no cold electric illumination such as we sometimes feel the phrase to imply, but a warm understanding tenderness for actual men and women. It would be hard to exaggerate her knowledge of the world and of human hearts.

Vida D. Scudder[1]

The Catherine who returned to Siena in January of 1377 was a far different person from the seemingly shy, hesitant one who, in her first journey to Pisa three years earlier, remained secluded for two months in the house of a friend before allowing herself to be drawn into the political discussions that were shaping relations between Tuscan Italy and the papacy. This earlier act of

---

[1] *Saint Catherine of Siena as Seen in Her Letters,* 4.

spiritual submission to the Divine Will must also have contained some human elements of self-doubt and unease. Now, however, her experience at Pisa and Avignon, her acceptance by the mighty and powerful as a woman of depth and wisdom, has significantly expanded her self-possession and political instincts. We will see her demonstrating with new individuals in wider affiliations the mature qualities of a woman who has encountered first hand the political dynamics of her church and society.

Catherine's particularly turbulent era in history, was part of what has been described as the "calamitous fourteenth century."[2] The seventy-year papal residence in Avignon had seriously affected the relationship between the church and their Italian subjects, who, in obeying papal initiatives, often had the impression of submitting to a foreign power. In addition to the suspicion and distrust that continued to be played out in the anti-papal Tuscan League, family and political vendettas kept the Italian city-states in continuous turbulence and unrest. Working class artisans were organizing against the wealthy traditional ruling classes. Hired military bands roaming the countryside, often changing alliances in the middle of warfare, caused continuous physical and human destruction. Safety and security were seldom assured. This was the backdrop to the events that occupied Catherine's attention in the period following her return to Siena. Peace was always an issue for her, and the solidarity of God's church remained foremost in her mind. Levasti commented that she was a "totalitarian Catholic" for whom "there was no such thing as politics apart from religion—for she identified one with the other."[3]

Soon after her return, Guelf ambassadors from Florence arrived to seek a report about what had transpired in Avignon and to ask her to come to their city to personally brief those in power.

---

[2] Barbara Tuchman, *A Distant Mirror*, xiii.

[3] *My Servant Catherine*, 247.

Remembering the duplicitous behavior of the Florentines at Avignon, Catherine refused to go lest she compromise the dignity of the church by appearing to take sides against it in the question of the Tuscan League. She did allow Stephano Maconi to go in her place and, accompanied by her Florentine Guelf followers, Niccolò Soderini, Piero Canigiani, and Stoldo di Bindo Altoviti, he went to meet with the Eight of War. Following this meeting, a rumor spread throughout the city that "a certain Catherinated Siennese" was inducing the Eight to submit to the pope and an angry tumult engulfed the city. Stephano had to be spirited away to safety.[4] Florence was far from ready for peace.

Meanwhile, Catherine remained preoccupied with the concerns of Pope Gregory and the welfare of the church. She kept abreast of events in Rome and communicated with the pope whenever personal emissaries were available. Letters from this period continue to emphasize Catherine's original directive: to seek the reform of the church by the "appointment of good administrators."[5] She tied this issue to ending the violence on the Italian peninsula, reminding the pontiff that reform could not be achieved without peace.[6] Sienese ambassadors, whose access to the pope was made possible by her influence, carried Catherine's letter to Gregory. They arrived in Rome, charged to restore Siena's good relations with the papacy despite its half-hearted participation in the Tuscan League and the consequent penalty of the interdict. They had the added goal of regaining the Sienese port of Talamone on the Tyrrhenian Sea, which had been seized by military knights in service of the church. Catherine, too, urged Gregory to restore her city to his good graces. Her more mature political wisdom, however, led her to suggest, "Receive their apologies in such a way that they will not be involved in a war against

---

[4]   Gardner, *Saint Catherine*, 202-203.

[5]   Noffke, *Letters*, II, T285, 291; T209, 300; T270, 345.

[6]   Ibid., T209, 301; T270, 345.

Florence,"[7] that is, do not foolishly extend the conflict but contain it. Though calling Gregory to be a mediator and peacemaker, Catherine also counseled that, while extending forgiveness, he should not fail to correct those who had sinned, including both church administrators and civic authorities.[8] Gregory, for Catherine's sake, received the ambassadors kindly but failed to relinquish the seaport or remove the interdict.[9]

The same Florentine Guelf ambassadors who had come to Siena also traveled to Rome to welcome Gregory's return to Italy. The pontiff's demands remained unchanged, however. They must abandon the League and pay a huge indemnity. Unfortunately, this meeting coincided with a particularly violent attack on the people of the northern Italian town of Cesena on February 3, 1377 by forces led by Cardinal Robert of Geneva, later elected the first schismatic pope, Clement VII.[10] More than four thousand inhabitants of the town, men, women and children, were massacred sending "a thrill of horror" all through Italy and leading people to lose trust in popes and cardinals. The League was revitalized.[11] In a letter to Gregory in which she repeated over and over the need to end these military encounters and to restore peace, Catherine stated, "I don't see how, with these disastrous wars, you can have a single hour of good. What belongs to the poor is being eaten up to pay soldiers, who in turn devour people as if they were meat."[12] The promotion of a crusade, though not forgotten, became somewhat secondary. References appeared in her letters to those engaged in raising troops, collecting arms and

---

[7] Ibid., T285, 290; T252, 272.

[8] Ibid., T270, 345; T285, 289-290.

[9] Gardner, *Saint Catherine*, 203-204.

[10] Noffke, II, T209, 298; Brucker, 327.

[11] Gardner, *Saint Catherine*, 205.

[12] Noffke, II, T209, 300.

ships to take them to the East.[13] One letter to Gregory may indicate a less militant perception of the crusade as Catherine noted her own desire, together with that of Gregory to "win back the poor souls of the unbelievers who are not sharing in the blood of the slain, consumed lamb."[14]

Though there are indications that Gregory would have desired her supportive presence in Rome during these unsettling days, the horizons of Catherine's ministry narrowed geographically. Her daily activities returned to concerns and problems that she considered equally important to political ones: spiritual conversation, prayer, preaching, letter writing, care of the sick, advising those who came to her, and reconciling mutually hostile families.[15] The major events of this period include the founding of a monastery for women at Belcaro and a peace-making mission to the Salimbeni stronghold at Val d'Orcia outside the city. Eventually, at the behest of Gregory, she would journey to Florence to seek a peaceful end to the Tuscan anti-papal league.

- 2 -
Belcaro: A Monastery for Women

But Catherine was by nature not merely a contemplative; nor was she a nun in the strict sense of the word. She was continually communing with the divine, but she needed to work among men, to speak with them, warn and help them.... Not for her the strict timetable of the cloister, not a restricted circle in which her thoughts and actions must revolve.... 'The cell of self-

---

[13] Ibid., T256, T257.
[14] Ibid., T209, 301.
[15] Levasti, 239-240.

knowledge' was the refuge of the soul; but the cell
was not bounded by walls.... And as she was a real
apostle she did not think that others should come to
her, but that she should go to them.

Arrigo Levasti[16]

One of Catherine's first endeavors on her return to Siena
was to bring to conclusion a project that had been in the planning stage since before her journey to Avignon. To ensure the
continued spiritual well being of her many followers, she had
conceived the idea of founding a monastery for women. The property of Belcaro, originally a military installation about two miles
outside the city, had been given to her for this purpose by a
wealthy disciple, Nanni di Ser Vanni de' Savini, whose conversion, initiated through William Flete, had been accomplished
through Catherine's prayers and personal contact. While at
Avignon, this project remained in the forefront of her mind, and
she had presented her proposal to Gregory, receiving his authorization to found a convent of strict observance. The issue of a
papal bull to this effect and the grant of a dowry of up to two
thousand florins followed. Gregory appointed the Abbot of the
Monastery of Sant' Antimo, Giovanni di Gano, her good friend,
as his representative to oversee its implementation. On her return, Catherine sought the approval of the Commune of Siena to
utilize this former fortress site for her religious purpose, housing
"religious sisters, who will continually pray for the city and citizens and inhabitants of Siena and its contado."[17] Permission was
granted on January 25, 1377.

In the month that she remained at Belcaro, Catherine dedicated herself to financial arrangements, the construction of the

---

[16] *My Servant Catherine*, 244-245.
[17] Gardner, *Saint Catherine*, 208.

building and the formulation of a Rule of life. Planned as a contemplative monastery of strict observance and named by Catherine, the Convent of Santa Maria degli Angeli, it was geared to women of religious bent, often widows, for whom enclosure was a desired objective. Raymond's suggestion that the monastery was intended for ladies of the upper class,[18] those who came to Catherine for spiritual advice and counsel, but not inclined to follow her active and public path, is borne out in Catherine's communication with Benedetta, the Countess Salimbeni. She invited this wealthy young widow, daughter of the powerful Sienese family, to come to Belcaro "whenever the place is ready," adding, "If you come, you'll be coming to a land of promise."[19] Raymond records his presence at the formal dedication of the monastery "with Catherine's spiritual family, both sons and daughters."[20] The celebrant of the Mass of dedication was the initial instigator of Nanni's conversion, William Flete, in his first and only public appearance outside of his Lecceto hermitage.[21] Representing Gregory was the Abbot of Sant' Antimo, Giovanni di Gano. Catherine, however, had no intention of remaining at Belcaro herself. Within months, she would write to a disciple, "Don't be surprised that I am not there, for good children do more when their mother is away than when she is there, because they want to show their love for her and get more into her good graces."[22] Neither does Catherine propose that members of her own inner circle join the women at Belcaro.

Everywhere Catherine went, men and women alike flocked to her. The number and diversity of these followers spoke of the broad and dynamic appeal of her personality and spiritual cred-

---

[18] Raymond of Capua, 226.
[19] Noffke, II, T112, 337.
[20] Raymond of Capua, 226.
[21] Hackett, 91.
[22] Noffke, II, T294, 382.

ibility. Letters became the means of communication, offering advice, counsel, prayer, and often, political suggestions. Though these recipients might consider themselves her followers, perhaps even members of her family, they would be like distant relatives compared to the close knit team who traveled with her; were secretaries for her letters; participated in her works of mercy; lived the daily life that she did; and called her "Mamma." This family while functioning as a group united in their spiritual journeys, also remained individuals, free to seek God in his or her own way. They were not monastic but diverse; they lived apart—tertiaries, friars, laymen, and women—completely dedicated to Catherine and her mission.[23] Later, when the family gathered in Rome, they would reside communally and in poverty, ministering charitably to their neighbors in a cohesive manner due to the unique circumstance of their living outside their native city and environment over an extended period of time.

- 3 -
Val d'Orcia: Peacemaking and Conversion

The wild soldiery who gathered around the castles of these chieftains and formed their garrisons, were little better than banditti, and had spent their lives in murderous feuds, which scarcely deserved the name of civil wars. Among these warriors the holy maiden came to speak of peace and brotherly love.... Long habits of ruthless violence, long years spent without prayer or sacraments, had hardened their hearts and obscured

---

[23] Karen Scott, "Not Only With Words, But With Deeds: The Role of Speech in Catherine of Siena's Understanding of Mission," 196-198.

their understandings. The Evil One had indeed laid his
grasp on these poor souls, and seemed to claim their
wild and desolate region as his own; and he was to
be dispossessed, and rudely put to flight by her, whose
fragile form might have been seen one August evening
ascending the mountain path that led to the castle,
mounted on her little ass, and surrounded by her faithful disciples.

Augusta T. Drane[24]

Toward the end of the summer, Catherine responded to a
request from women of the Salimbeni clan to mediate differences
between two branches of this historically powerful Sienese family. At the time of the struggle for the survival of Siena in 1274,
achieved in the historic battle of Montaperti, the Salimbeni had
preserved the independence of the commune from Florentine
control by contributing a huge sum of money to pay mercenaries to assist in defending the city.[25] In return, the commune had
endowed the family with several castles in the hills of the *contada*
outside the city. A century later, in 1374, in one of the many power
struggles during the rule of the Riformatori, the Salimbeni descendants were exiled from the city and took up residence in
their castles high in the hills of the Val d'Orcia. It is possible that
the influence of the Salimbeni was of significance to the papacy
since Gerard du Puy, Gregory's nephew, and the Apostolic Nuncio, Berengario, attempted unsuccessfully to reconcile the family with the Sienese Republic in 1375, the same year that Siena
joined Florence in the anti-papal league.[26]

Ostensibly what brought Catherine to the Val d'Orcia, how-

---

[24] *The History of St. Catherine of Siena and Her Companions,* Vol. II, 60.

[25] Gardner, *Story of Siena,* 13.

[26] Noffke, I, T109, 264.

ever, was a family dispute between two cousins, Agnolino di Giovanni Salimbeni and Cione di Sandro Salimbeni, who lived in castles several miles from each other. Though the dispute was a family quarrel over the ownership of property, it was having a devastating effect on lives in the area as it played itself out in ambushes, skirmishes, looting, and pillaging. The whole area was living in siege. Little is revealed in Catherine's letters of the details of the family quarrel or its solution, but she does assure her mother, "I am staying to resolve a great scandal" and if you "knew the circumstances you yourself would be sending me here."[27]

In the summer of 1377, Catherine arrived at the Val d'Orcia accompanied by a band of her followers including the Dominicans Raymond, Tommaso, Bartolomeo, and Matteo Tolomei. Also included were laymen Neri, Malavolti, Gabriel Piccolomini and Pietro Ventura.[28] They came by way of the Monastery of Sant' Agnesa in Montepulciano where Monna Lapa and Cecca, whose daughter resided there as a novice, would stay while the others moved on. After attending to spiritual and reconciliation matters there,[29] the group traveled on to Castiglioncello di Trinoro, the residence of Cione di Sandro Salimbeni and his wife Stricca, a devotee of Catherine. After several days spent reviewing the history of the problem and devising a plan of action, the group journeyed to the Rocca residence of Agnolino di Giovanni Salimbeni whose mother, Biancina, offered Catherine gracious hospitality throughout her stay in the area. From her letters, it appeared that Catherine was as involved in the life choices of Biancina's two daughters, Benedetta and Elisabetta, as she was in the restoration of good will between her son and his cousin.[30] Biancina also encouraged Catherine to mediate the problems of the Belforte

---

[27] Noffke, II, T117, 442.
[28] Levasti, 245.
[29] Noffke, II, T123, 376.
[30] Ibid., T112, 333; T113, 368; T116, 620.

brothers of Volterra and her own brothers Trincio and Corrado de' Trinci of Foligno. Later, Trinci would be brutally murdered in a violent struggle to maintain his lordship over Foligno.[31]

Francesco Malavolti, who kept a record of this period, reported of the family dispute, "in a short space of time, she brought both of them to perfect concord, which many other barons and potent men had hitherto been unable to effect."[32] Nevertheless, Catherine remained in the valley for several months, seizing the opportunity to spread God's word in the *contada* area as she had done for so long within the city gates.[33] Her days were filled with cares and concerns brought to her for mediation and reconciliation. In addition, everywhere she went, she was besieged with hordes of people, streaming by the thousands down the hillsides to see her, to hear her words, to receive forgiveness and absolution from the group of priests who accompanied her day after day to the point of exhaustion. Accounts of these experiences tell of those possessed by devils being freed of their demons; of multitudes, separated from the church and the sacraments, some as long as forty years, falling to their knees at the sight of her.

Meanwhile, her followers in Siena were unsettled by her extended absence. She gently reminded them not to think of their own comfort or their desire for her presence. Rather, she recounted the great work being done in the Val. Using her symbolic expression "eating souls," she told them in a somewhat humorous manner "so many demons incarnate are being eaten up that Frate Tommaso says he has a stomach ache!" Even so, she says of her priests, "they aren't satisfied; they have an appetite for more, and are finding work here at good wages."[34] As unrest

---

[31] Ibid., T103, 418, T253, 422; Gardner, *Saint Catherine,* 222.

[32] Gardner, *Saint Catherine,* 213.

[33] Ibid., 212.

[34] Noffke, II, T118, 390.

among her own followers in Siena grew, so did rumors and suspicion among the general population. "The citizens of Siena are acting shamefully in believing or imagining that we are about to be contriving plots in the lands of the Salimbeni," she wrote to a follower. "It is God's will that I stay here," she stoutly proclaimed, and "I will do my best to use my life for God's honor and the salvation of souls throughout the whole world, and especially for my city."[35]

Missives began to arrive from a more troubling source, the Sienese authorities, protesting both her absence from Siena and her lengthy involvement with the Salimbeni. Siena's involvement in the anti-papal League and Catherine's known opposition to it contributed to this wariness and distrust. Levasti suggests that her sermons invoking peace and love may have been seen to imply her condemnation of their alliance with Florence and the League.[36] Given the temper of Riformatori politics, to be under suspicion could be a life threatening experience since "The government lived in daily apprehension of conspiracies; the prisons were full; executions were incessant."[37] Aware of these dangers from her experience with prisoners, Catherine's maturity and fearlessness were forcefully proclaimed as she responded to their complaints. After sermonizing, eloquently but in general, about those who do not see, or who live in darkness, or do not control themselves, she declared, "I see the devil is unhappy about the loss he has sustained and will continue to sustain by my coming here, by God's goodness. I came for nothing but to eat and savor souls, and to rescue them from the hands of the devils. I want to lay down my life for this.... I will go and stay as the Holy Spirit makes me."[38]

---

[35] Noffke, II, T122, 395-396.
[36] Levasti, 248.
[37] Gardner, *Saint Catherine*, 210.
[38] Noffke, II, T21, 417.

At this point in the Val d'Orcia sojourn, Catherine was visiting the Monastery of Sant' Antimo across the valley from the Rocca, another place where discord prevailed. The temporal and spiritual jurisdiction of the area had long been in dispute, a cause of long standing concern to Sienese officials. She defended her friend, the Abbot Giovanni di Gano, against their complaints declaring him "as great and perfect a servant of God who has lived in these parts for a long time" stating that, instead of complaining, they should reverence and assist him in his work. She reminded the rulers, "Every day you are complaining that priests and clerics are not being corrected and now when you find those who are willing to correct them, you stand in their way and complain." Finally, she declared her own independence, "Neither the ingratitude nor the foolishness of my fellow citizens will keep us from working even to the point of death for your welfare."[39]

Despite the strength of conviction and extraordinary intent pervading her writings, Catherine began to feel the toll on her physical and psychic well being from her labors, especially from the discordant reactions they induced. In addition, conscious that her connection to Gregory had become negligible, she had sent Raymond to Rome with suggestions and plans for promoting peace and the concord so important to her desire for the church. Raymond was never able to return as he was appointed by his superiors Prior of the Church of the Minerva, the Dominican center in Rome. The loss of this major source of support and encouragement was a devastating one. In addition, Gregory continued to ignore both Raymond and Catherine.

At Avignon, Gregory had interpreted Catherine's prayers and exhortations as prophecy. He had trusted that his return to Rome would restore the temporal power of the church; that the whole Christian world would rejoice and rally to support reform; and

---

[39] Ibid., 416.

that Rome itself would be revitalized and drawn to peace. Instead, after a short period of excitement, months of rioting, insurrections, and rebellions throughout the Italian peninsula had followed. Church finances were in disarray; his health deteriorating, Gregory felt misled and abandoned. He became distressed, despondent and angry.[40] He had come to rely on Catherine's supportive presence and anticipated her prayerful intervention in resolving the crises of the church; now, he became increasingly angry at her remaining in Val d'Orcia where conversions and family mediations meant nothing compared to the concerns of the church. She remarked in her letter to Raymond that the pope's displeasure could be due to "my being with all these people."[41]

Gregory's Curia, the predominantly French College of Cardinals, had never fully supported the return to Rome. Their unrest did little to alleviate his discouragement. There is also the strong possibility that under their influence, Gregory blamed Catherine personally for all the problems that had followed the move from Avignon. Instead of his return to Rome bringing about all those results that she had predicted—peace, reform, even a crusade—the situation had worsened beyond belief. Catherine may have inflamed this feeling further when, in her letter to Raymond, she speaks directly to Gregory calling for peace and kindness instead of war, adding, "Had you only done it the very day you got back to where you belong" and "You know (for you were told)."[42]

When Gregory moved south to the papal summer palace in Anagni in early May, anger on all sides continued to escalate and, unfortunately, dominated Gregory's decision making.[43] Military altercations became even more severe; both Florence and

---

[40] Gardner, *Saint Catherine*, 224.

[41] Noffke, II, T267, 474.

[42] Ibid., 475.

[43] Gardner, *Saint Catherine*, 224.

the church were increasingly bankrupted from the expense of keeping their forces engaged. Florentine ambassadors returned home convinced that no progress could be made and were emboldened to extend rather than mediate the confrontation. As the summer progressed, however, the peaceful environment of Anagni began to restore Gregory's health and with it, his peaceful intent. On his return to Rome in November, Gregory's attitude toward Catherine softened. He reestablished contact with Raymond and initiated plans to send Catherine to Florence in an effort to bring about the peace he now fully desired. At the same time, plans were set in motion for the commencement of full-scale negotiations among all the League members to take place at Sarzana on the northern borders of Tuscany.

Meanwhile, local criticism from Catherine's friends and enemies increased; her isolation from Gregory became more apparent; and the church continued to flounder in quarrels and conflict. Amid such controversy, it was only to her friend and sister Mantellate, Alessa, that she could unburden some of her suffering. Indicating her grief at being deprived of all creaturely consolation, Catherine wrote, "I want pain to be my food, and tears my drink, and sweat my anointing. I want pain to fatten me, pain to heal me, pain to give me light, pain to give me wisdom, pain to clothe my nakedness, pain to strip me clean of all selfish love, spiritual or material."[44] Unknown to her, however, rapprochement was under way; so, too, was a great gift of union with God.

When a letter from Raymond reached her with news of his visit with Gregory, followed by a missive from the pope himself, her heart exulted in joyous and prayerful contemplation. On the morning of October tenth, her prayer grew deeper and more intense as she found herself in direct communication with God.

---

[44] Noffke, II, T119, 791.

She wrote to Raymond to describe the four petitions she made and the divine response to each,[45] leading her to believe that good would come from all the evil that was dominating the world and the church. This contemplative experience would initiate the beginning of Catherine's primary written legacy, *The Dialogue.* The petitions she shared with Raymond at this time would later become the outline of her spiritual testament.

Catherine spent Advent in prayerful seclusion at the Rocca where the projecting terrace of the castle became like an island floating among the clouds. During this time, she "learned to write" her first letters, that is, notes of a personal nature by her own hand and in her own dialect. More than likely, she also penned ideas that would later appear in *The Dialogue.* She was back in Siena by the New Year, where she received notice from Gregory of his desire for her to go to Florence in the cause of peace.

- 4 -
Florence: Respect and Animosity

The position of the Eight had been strengthened by the collapse of peace negotiations and the consequent surge of anti-papal feeling in the city. But this did not deter the Guelf hierarchy from continuing to agitate for peace. Among the principal figures in this oligarchical campaign were three devotees of Catherine of Siena: Ristoro Canigiani, Stoldo Altoviti, and Niccolò Soderini, all from ancient patrician families. The Guelf sentiments of these men were intensified by their strong religious convictions. They persuaded the Sienese mystic to visit the Arno city for a second time

---

[45] Ibid., T272, 495-505.

on a peace mission, to convince the Florentines that they must return to papal obedience.... Thus intimately associated with the Parte leadership, she aroused both enthusiasm and hostility in the city.

Gene A. Brucker[46]

The Tuscan League had come into being during a violent and highly charged political period in Florence when a new ruling class of successful artisans with anti-papal leanings had replaced the old wealthy oligarchic Guelf leadership known for its support of the papacy. The French-influenced Avignon papacy had lost its position of primacy throughout Italy, and the new Florentine governors from the *gente nuova* built their new dominance on its ruins. Neither had the papal return to Rome done anything to alleviate difficulties or to end defiance. In fact, resolve to continue the struggle had increased over the summer. In October, the uniformly negative attitude of the commune appeared in a comment by an anonymous diarist. "The pope made so many varied and strange and burdensome demands upon the commune that all who heard them spoke in unison: 'We will sacrifice our property and our lives until nothing remains, rather than surrender to his will. Death to the rapacious wolf and cruel tyrant.'"[47] The unmistakable unanimity of this response emboldened the Florentine leadership.

After more than a year under the papal interdict, stress had heightened throughout the commune. Cries for peace became a daily prayer as citizens felt ever more deeply the deprivation of the spiritual resources of the daily office, the liturgy, and the sacraments. As commerce deteriorated, the once prosperous city-state was deprived of trade and industry, and the economic de-

---

[46] *Florentine Politics and Society, 1343-1378,* 332-333.
[47] *Diario d'anomimo fiorentino dall' anno 1358 al 1389,* 339-340, quoted in Brucker, 331.

spair of the city added to the spiritual desolation. Levasti described streets filled with endless processions accompanied by the singing of hymns of divine praise. Ascetic practices, almsgiving, and penance became fashionable. It was, he wrote, as if they wanted to prove that even in their excommunicated city they still practiced their faith with fervor.[48] Yet, many of those in power considered these activities a sinister device to turn public opinion against the Eight of War and toward peace.[49] After the return from Rome of their ambassadors and the failed attempt to restore peace, the Signoria, in a bold defensive move, decided to re-open the churches, to restore spiritual opportunities and, in doing so, defy the interdict. Clerics were forced to perform all the forbidden rites and services. Schism was on the horizon.

This was the situation in early March of 1378, when Catherine arrived on her peace-making mission to Florence to confront political and religious issues, equally intense in their significance. From Gregory's point of view, Catherine was sent, not as a political ambassador, but as a religious, as one whose presence might stir up consciences and create a peaceful and prayerful atmosphere in which the deep-seated differences might be resolved—and resolved in favor of the church. As a woman, it was expected that she would not be physically harmed. Also, the profound respect in which she was held would, it was hoped, mitigate violence and restore a harmonious relationship in which negotiations might ensue. When they met in Rome, Gregory had told Raymond, "They have written to me that if Catherine goes to Florence, I shall have peace." In deference to militant anti-clerical sentiment, there was caution, however, as by papal suggestion no priest accompanied her, only her Mantellate companions, Lisa and Cecca, the hermit Fra Santi and her two faithful scribes Neri and Stephano, later joined by Cristofano di Gano.

---

[48] Levasti, 259.
[49] Brucker, 320.

Catherine's Guelf supporters, who had long been seeking her intervention, welcomed her, providing housing and protection. Because of this affiliation, however, her reception was mixed. Gardner suggested that perhaps the only negative words regarding Catherine came from the historical records of this period. "By those of the [Guelf] Party she was reputed a prophetess, and by others a hypocrite and a bad woman; and many things were said of her, by some for treachery, and by others because they thought to speak well by speaking evil of her."[50]

Because of her singular devotion to the cause of the church and to restoring peaceful relations with the papacy, Catherine was either unaware of, or ignored the political motivation that accompanied the religious dedication of some of her Guelf associates. The record quoted above provides additional comment: "Either maliciously by her own will, or introduced by the instigation of these men, she was brought many times to the meetings of the Party, to declare that it was right to admonish, in order that they might take measures to stop the war." This is a reference to the practice of *ammonizione,* or political admonishment, an age-old privilege of the pro-papal *Parte Guelfa* to challenge the leadership of the pro-emperor Ghibbeline opposition. Reverting to these historic distinctions, the Party embarked on a wholesale proscription of political enemies by accusation as a Ghibbeline. Continued expansion of the meaning of Ghibbeline resulted in mass exclusions from office, initially to gain peace, but in reality to undermine the regime in power and regain control. For example, one man was convicted and removed from office on the basis that his ancestor had conspired to surrender Florentine territory to Emperor Henry VII (1308-1313).[51]

---

[50] Marchione di Coppo Stephani, *Istoria Fiorentina*, Book Nine, 788, quoted in Gardner, *Saint Catherine,* 230-231. At a later date, in a more peaceful era, the writer recanted this opinion.

[51] Brucker, 343.

In the *Legenda,* Raymond related a conversation with Niccolò Soderno in which he had suggested that a peaceful solution could be achieved in Florence with the removal of four or five members of the Signoria by this process. Once underway, however, hundreds of Florentines fell victim to this Guelf terror in the winter and spring of 1377-1378, a terror which, as time passed, was frequently utilized to exclude the rising artisan classes from political power, thus creating a new enemy. The most devastating effect was the accompanying loss of political, economic, and social status not only to the individuals but also to their families and descendants from generation to generation in perpetuity.[52] As Levasti commented, Catherine would never suspect that she had become, in the popular mind, a Party tool; nevertheless, she bore the brunt of the anger aroused by the unbridled Guelf use of admonitions. It does not seem possible, however, that she would support such a process once she understood its brutal harshness. In fact, Stephano Maconi left a testament to the fact that "she ordered me, as well as others, to speak against the scandals which arose out of the 'admonitions' in order that they might be remedied without delay. And I was actively occupied in this business, but without success."[53]

While political and social unrest continued in Florence, the peace conference set in motion by Gregory began in early March at Sarzana on the northeastern borders of Tuscany, presided over by Bernabò Visconti of Milan, earlier noted for waging war with the papacy. Representatives of Pope Gregory, the League, and the King of France were in the process of coming to agreeable terms when news arrived of the death of Gregory on March twenty-seventh. Much to the annoyance of Visconti, peace negotiations were abruptly terminated without results. On April

---

[52] Ibid., *passim,* 339-351.
[53] Drane, II, 96.

eighth, the Neapolitan Archbishop of Bari became Pope Urban VI, and when this news reached Florence on the twelfth, the city erupted in celebration of the election of an Italian Pope. Catherine too, on receiving reassuring news from Raymond, allowed herself to "rejoice and be glad" especially when Urban declared his determination to remain in Rome and proceed, as was the custom, with the appointment of new cardinals. The central issues of peace, reform of the church by the appointment of worthy leaders, and even of a crusade returned to the forefront of her thoughts and her letters. With the death of Gregory, she was instrumental in persuading the Florentine Signoria to return to observance of the interdict, news that she exultantly conveyed to Alessa in Siena. Using symbolism that conveyed the darkness of the Florentine experience, she called her to "continual vigil and prayer that the sun may soon rise; for the aurora has begun to dawn... the dusk of the great mortal sins" has been scattered and "the interdict is observed."[54]

Neither Catherine nor her Guelf supporters were willing to abandon the search for a peace settlement, and Catherine vowed to remain in Florence until it was achieved. But with the power of the Eight decreasing and the restoration of Guelf superiority—though not from among Catherine's followers—more vigorous admonitions followed, and angry ferment arose once again in the city. On June twenty-second, the fury of open insurrection was directed against the Guelf populace, including Catherine. As the unruly mob, "joined by ruffians from the other side of the Arno" destroyed and sacked homes of the Guelf leadership, Catherine's name surfaced, and they rushed to her residence. Thus occurred the famous incident when Catherine's life was threatened. She had eagerly offered her life in sacrifice, only to be disappointed when her assassin stepped back and the mob quickly

---

[54] Scudder, 270.

dispersed, somehow appalled at the iniquity of killing this holy woman. But it was clear that Catherine was no longer safe in the city, and few were willing or able to protect her. A pair of devoted followers from the lower classes, a tailor Francesco di Pippino and his wife Monna Agnesa secretly sheltered her until the city returned to a vestige of normalcy.

Even then, it was decided that Catherine should take refuge outside the city, but she refused to leave the confines of Florentine territory until peace was established with the papacy. Her destination, identified as a place where hermits gathered, is believed to be the Vallombrosa in the hills above the city, where she remained while the unrest continued. Several letters were written during this period of seclusion. To Raymond, she recounted the details of the threat to her person during the uprising, her great joy at the prospect of giving her life, and her tremendous disappointment when she survived. Her greatest fear was that the cause of peace would be deterred by this attack on her. Through Raymond, she begged Pope Urban, "not to delay the peace because of what has happened, but make it all the more promptly, so that then the other great deeds may be wrought which he has to do for the honor of God and the reformation of Holy Church." On a personal note, she added, "Ask him to release me soon out of my prison, for until peace is made it is impossible for me to leave this place, and yet I long to go [to Rome] and taste the blood of martyrs, and to visit his Holiness, and to see you once more... that we may all rejoice together."[55] In her own letter to Urban, she makes an equally revealing comment, "I do not wish to remain here any longer, nevertheless, do with me what you like."[56]

At the beginning of July, a semblance of calm was restored in Florence. As new leaders took office, the cause of peace came

---

[55] Drane, II, 100.

[56] Ibid., 103.

to the fore once again, and ambassadors were sent to Tivoli, on the northwest border of Rome, to meet with Urban and his small group of supporters. Both sides were under extreme duress to end hostilities. Money was an issue to both factions, but the cessation of the interdict and restoration of spiritual and commercial activity motivated the Florentines. Within the church, division over the validity of Urban's election was growing more serious. With internal opposition mounting, Urban could not afford, as Catherine put it, to carry on a war within and without.[57] Hence, negotiations moved swiftly; peace was restored; and Florence would soon be released from the interdict. Catherine entrusted this joyful news to Sano di Maco to share with her Sienese followers. "Oh, dearest sons, God has heard the cry of his servants, who for so long have cried aloud before his face," she wrote, and "the cloud has passed and fair weather has come." Then, "Saturday evening one olive came at one o'clock at night: and today at vespers came the other," and "I send you some of the olive of peace."[58]

Meanwhile, as these movements toward peace were taking place in Tivoli, another period of violence racked the city of Florence. On July nineteenth, a rumor spread through the city that an uprising was imminent. The next day, the whole populace was up in arms. This "Revolt of the Ciompi" centered on the equalization of rights to include those who had been traditionally barred, the unskilled workers who had no guilds and hence no representation in the government. In this outbreak of anarchy, sacking and burning were once again directed at the upper classes. On the twenty-second, these *populo minuto* took over the Palazzo Pubblico, and a new government, inclusive of all classes, was formed; all admonitions were overturned, and Florentines prepared for a new beginning of representative gov-

---

[57] *I, Catherine*, 180.
[58] Scudder, 272-273.

ernment. On August first, the city prepared to return to its normal activities as peace was restored. Then, in the evening, came the word from Tivoli of the greater peace: reinstatement with the church, the repeal of the interdict, the opening of the churches, and the restoration of religious services, of commerce and industry.

Catherine's work was done. Once the interdict was lifted, she gathered her followers to announce her imminent departure, not even waiting for the arrival of the formal absolutions planned for the tenth of August. She would, however, have the last word. Between her last hours in Florence and her arrival in Siena, she composed a powerful letter to the rulers of the city. In it, once again her political understanding of Justice and the Common Good emerged. "You are anxious to reform your city," she wrote, but "you will never succeed unless... you are concerned not only for yourselves but for the general good of the whole city." Turning to the issue of the treaty, she reminded them "show your gratitude by arranging as soon as possible for the prescribed Masses and Absolution (so that the Office can once again be said in praise to God) and for a procession held with due devotion." Becoming more personal, she informed them that she had hoped to celebrate the peace with them; however, "the devil had unjustly set people's hearts very much against me... so I have gone, with the grace of God." And then, "Sadly and sorrowfully I go, to leave the city in such bitterness."[59]

The resolution of the long-standing difficulties between the League and the papacy, which should have brought such blissful joy, was diminished by the knowledge that another, even greater, difficulty threatened the unity of Christendom. From the days when she remained hidden in the hills outside the city,

---

[59] *I, Catherine*, 198-200. It was a custom at this time that an olive branch of peace would actually be sent.

Catherine had begun to learn of the difficulties of dealing with Urban, of his tactless behavior and his unruly disposition that was often a cause of public scandal. There was a gradual withdrawal of support among the cardinals, many of whom left the city and gathered at the papal summer residence in Anagni, raising questions of the validity of Urban's election. When the Spanish Cardinal Pedro di Luna, a trusted confidant of Catherine and her followers, joined the opposition Catherine's prayerful hopes that a schism could be averted were demolished. Her letter to three Italian Cardinals, Orsini, Corsini, and Brossano, who were reluctant to support Urban, betrayed a forcefulness bordering on anger that is unique to this most distressful situation. "For you know what the truth is [the validity of the election of Urban]: it was you who announced it to us, and not we to you. Oh, how mad you are! For you told us the truth, and you want yourselves to taste a lie! Now you want to corrupt this truth, and make us see the opposite, saying that you chose Pope Urban from fear, which is not so; but anyone who says it—speaking to you without reverence, because you have deprived yourselves of reverence—lies up to his eyes."[60]

Catherine would be aware of the unruly conditions in the streets of Rome as the papal voting proceeded, of Urban's selection by all but four of the sixteen cardinals present, and of his solemn public enthronement accompanied by pledges of obedience from the cardinals participating in the ceremony. She would never for a minute doubt the validity of Urban's election. In this opinion, she would be influenced not only by her own prayerful perception but also by Raymond who had been present in Rome during the election and formal consecration of Urban, and who was an intimate of his inner circle, and a staunch supporter of an Italian Pope.

---

[60] Scudder, 279.

- 5 -
A Contemplative Critic

We have now reached the stage when every form of organized religious life that could be successfully developed within the social and religious framework of medieval society—every possible form, that is to say, with regard to purpose, organization, material support, and the relationship to the world at large—had been explored. The Benedictines, the Cistercians, the Augustinian Canons, and the Orders of friars between them had filled all the main areas open for development.... There was only one further step to be taken, and that was in the direction of greater freedom from social and hierarchical pressures and a greater diversity of individual effort.... The solitary religious figure, never indeed wholly submerged in the organizational zeal of the intervening centuries, once more emerged as a force in society. He (or, still more significantly, she) no longer appeared in the form of a St. Guthlac fighting a lonely battle to purify the land from evil spirits, but in the form of a St. Catherine of Siena, a Julian of Norwich, or a Gerhard Groote of Deventer: contemplatives and mystics, critics and reformers, who stood somewhat apart from the organized religious society around them. The spiritual warrior was out; the critic and contemplative came in.... In the place of the warrior, the new hope of Christendom lay in the individual prophet.

R.W. Southern[61]

---

[61] *Western Society and the Church in the Middle Ages*, 300-301.

The three principal episodes in which Catherine engaged, following her return from Avignon, required efforts unique from one another and evoked dissimilar responses and results. Each experience took place in a different setting, had an unrelated purpose, and offered challenges of increasing difficulty. Underlying all, however, were the critical issues that had drawn her out of seclusion to become a public personage: peace, unity, and the purification of the church. On one level, Catherine grew in maturity and worldly wisdom; on another more profound level, this period revealed her ever deepening and pervasive spirituality as her tree of virtue blossomed and bore visible fruit seasoned with discernment despite painful conflict and the ever present possibility of failure. Jean Baker Miller asserts the importance of the reassurance of a "community of like minded persons" when a woman "attempts to oppose the prevailing culture."[62] Throughout her public life, Catherine's devoted family of followers, both male and female members, provided this supportive environment to empower her to be a critic in a society in turmoil.

The establishment of the convent of Santa Maria degli Angeli at Belcaro, a project directed to her own followers, required significant advance preparation: obtaining the land, authorization from the Holy Father at Avignon, and legal permission from the Sienese authorities. Planning the buildings, preparing a Rule of life, making contact with women called to an enclosed religious life and selecting a superior to leave in charge comprised a second layer of significant tasks. Finally, taking leave of the project with complete trust in the individuals involved to fulfill their obligations to each other and to the commune required not only deep spiritual trust but remarkable human conviction and confidence in others. In allowing others to nurture their own tree of virtue, to nourish its circle of soil with humility as they grew

---

[62] Miller, *Toward a New Psychology of Women*, 132-133.

in knowledge of self and of God, Catherine permitted them to give root to a place of prayer and contemplation that would give birth to new plants of faith, hope, and love. While not a personally painful experience, this venture developed in Catherine a mature and accepting mode of conduct for the future: to strive to the best of one's ability and then, entrust the fruits to others.

Catherine's extended period of peacemaking in the Salimbeni territory of the Val d' Orcia provided deeper experiences of life's realities, both ordinary and remarkable. These included lengthy discussions to dispel anger and restore harmony to relationships as well as exhaustive daily meetings with repentant sinners flowing down from the hills to be in her presence and receive her blessing. Add to this demanding physical challenge the dimension of pervasive criticism and distrust on a political and personal level, the loss of the supportive presence of Raymond and seeming abandonment by Gregory. In the midst of this human anguish came intense spiritual communion with the Divine to nurture the sap of discernment. This period saw the initiation of the plan of her spiritual treatise, *The Dialogue*, a personal exchange of human questions and divine answers, a crowning achievement that eventually would cause her to be named a Doctor of the Church.

Finally, the months in Florence brought Catherine into close personal touch with the vicious realities of a political and religious experience gone totally awry. Perhaps, the optimism that carried her to Avignon and to the Val d'Orcia misled her to underestimate the complexity of the many levels of political incentive. The Guelfs were determined to restore their power, the Eight of War to defeat the papacy at any cost, the *gente nuova* zealous to retain their newly achieved political status, and the *populo minuto* to finally achieve political representation. However, it was the church and the papacy that dominated Catherine's thoughts. All else would fall into place if peace were secured, if the interdict were lifted, if religious harmony were restored. For the first time, she was faced with hatred and anger against her person; she was forced into hiding, maligned, and seriously threatened. Yet, in typical fashion, she continued God's work, reaching out in all directions: consoling, teaching, peacemaking, drawing disciples to herself, writing letters of support, and spreading God's words of love and forgiveness. This outreach was the difference between herself and the nuns she left at Belcaro to pray and intercede for others while she remained in the public sphere influencing events. Catherine continued to be the lay contemplative critic and reformer, producing fragrant blossoms of virtue and blessings for her neighbors.

If it is suffering that brings us face to face with the Divine, this was Catherine's experience in Florence, a personal and spiritually maturing one. She wrote parts of *The Dialogue* during those difficult days, leaving her notes behind in her haste to leave the city. Her developing mature interpretation of her tree of virtue will transform it into a tree of suffering as the roots, trunk, and crown become the feet of Christ nailed to the cross, the open wounded heart, and the mouth of the crucified one. This staircase of Christ's body will provide entrance to the final stages of her journey, the Bridge between heaven and earth.

PART FOUR

The Tree of the Cross

1378-1380

And I showed you three ordinary stairs
that are set up in the soul's three powers,
and how no one can have the life of grace without climbing all three stairs,
without gathering all three powers in my name.
Then I revealed to you how these stairs were, in a special way
a figure of the three spiritual stages,
symbolized in the body of my only-begotten Son.
I told you that he had made a stairway of his body, and showed it to you
in his nailed feet, in his open side,
and in his mouth where the soul tastes peace and calm.

THE DIALOGUE, 86:158

The Staircase of Christ's Body

Catherine's adult years, interpreted as a growing manifestation of the mature self in the world, could be read as a travelogue of journeys and a catalogue of aspirations. Pisa, Florence, Avignon, and Rome were the main destinations with local visitations and journeys of a secondary nature. Reform of the church, the return of the papal court to Rome, peace in Italy, support of a crusade, and the healing of the Great Schism would head the list of goals. Letters of exhortation to the pope, to religious and political leaders, to warring families, to ordinary people who sought her guidance; mediation of political and family disputes; the founding of a monastery for women and the preparation of her spiritual testament, *The Dialogue,* might highlight the list of related accomplishments. The intense spiritual development that generated and supported these endeavors is revealed in her symbolic ascent of the staircase of the body of Christ crucified. Like the roots, trunk, and crown of her tree of virtue, the three stairs of the feet, heart, and mouth of Christ portray the tree of the cross providing entry into depths of the mystery of Godhead.

Her letters offer clues to the increasing spiritual depth of her metaphorical images of the spiritual journey. Before her visit to Avignon, she wrote to Gregory XI, "I long to see you a productive tree planted in fertile soil and laden with sweet mellow fruit. For a tree uprooted from the soil (I mean the soil of true self-knowledge) would dry up and bear no fruit."[1] A later letter to him revealed further insight as she wrote, "I want you to be a tree of love, engrafted into the Word who is love, Christ crucified —a tree with its roots in deep humility."[2]

---

[1] Noffke, I, T185, 244.
[2] Ibid., II, T252,271-172.

181

Reaching ever deeper into mystery, the tree of nature, of life, of virtue, of love became the tree of the cross. In a letter to Frate Girolino at the Olivetan Monastery outside Siena, she wrote, "Let us, then, climb the tree of the most holy cross, for then we shall see and touch God and find the fire of his inestimable charity... and if you say: 'I can't climb this tree: it's too high,' I answer that he has hollowed out steps for you in his body. First raise yourself, heart and soul, to the feet of God's Son: then climb up to the heart, which is open and utterly spent for us, and so arrive at the peace of the mouth where you will learn to savor souls and make them your food."[3]

In a revealing statement written to the Dominican, Frate Niccolo da Montalcino, Catherine indicated Christ's personal revelation of this final stage of the tree image. "This was the rule he taught on one occasion to a servant of his. He said, Get up, daughter, rise above yourself and climb up onto me. And to enable you to climb up I have made the stairway for you by being nailed to the cross."[4] Similarly, a progressively explicit development of the three steps carved in Christ's crucified body emerges in the profound conversation of The Dialogue. God the Father clarifies the role of this staircase in giving access to the Bridge, the crucified body of Christ, providing final entrance to the kingdom of heaven.

Consonant with this developing imagery, Catherine's personal life entered into a painful and distressing period as all that she had accomplished for God and for the church seemed to fade away into utter failure. The schism in church leadership threatened to undo all that she had accomplished and hope became a difficult virtue to believe in. Interacting with the realities of the turbulent, often violent, society of her world, her own "tree of virtue" will become for her the "tree of the cross" as she faces the opposition and denigration that allow her to enter ever deeper into the reality of Christ's own passion and death.

---

[3]   *I, Catherine*, Letter 31, 145-146.

[4]   Noffke, I, T74, 313-314.

CHAPTER SEVEN

The Fruit of Wisdom

- 1 -
Siena

In Siena Catherine passed some calmer days. She was able to review the results of her labours and rejoice in what had been won for God. Two of her dearest wishes had been fulfilled—at the cost of her tears and blood. She never doubted for a moment that the return of the Papacy to Rome was largely due to her own efforts, and she believed that the peace between Urban VI and the Florentines was God's answer to her insistent prayers. Two other grave tasks remained to be accomplished: ecclesiastical reform and the Crusade; but she had no fear of failure, trusting that Heaven would graciously accept the sighs and longings of her soul. Meanwhile she could permit herself a little time to rest, or rather to plunge deeper into the Precious Blood of Christ, source of all strength, that renews our energies, makes athletes of the weak, heroes of the timid, and reveals to all the secrets of this life on earth and of the life to come.

Arrigo Levasti[5]

---

[5] *My Servant Catherine*, 281.

Catherine's return to Siena was marred first by the sadness of her necessarily discreet and hasty retreat from Florence but even more so by the news, several days later, of the August ninth denunciation of Urban's election by the dissident cardinals gathered in Anagni. Her immediate expectations following Urban's election had been optimistic. He had been an experienced administrator in Gregory's Court, a curial official who had served long and faithfully at Avignon before his appointment as Chancellor of the Holy See in Rome. He was thoroughly conversant with the affairs and government of the church, was familiar with French manners and customs and therefore acceptable to the French cardinals. He was committed to reform and opposed to a luxurious lifestyle; in addition, he was adverse to simony and similar perversions that had become customary in papal life. Almost immediately, however, his brusque, demeaning and angry behavior, previously held in check by his comparatively inferior position, became manifest.[6] Even Catherine's disciple, Fra Bartolomeo, visiting the pope in the company of Raymond, received a harsh reception.[7]

One can only imagine the pain and grief that Catherine experienced as she received news of the disturbing events unfolding in Rome with greater frequency. The Prior of Gorgona informed her of reports from Andrea di Piero Gambacorta of Pisa who had traveled to Rome on behalf of his father to congratulate the new pope. "According to what he says, this Holy Father of ours is a terrible man, and frightens people fearfully with his conduct and his words. He seems to have a great trust in God, by reason of which he fears no man in the world, and he is manifestly striving to abolish the simony and great pomp that reigns in the church of God."[8] Curtayne records further that the Pontiff's

---

[6]   Gardner, *Saint Catherine*, 258.

[7]   Scudder, 262.

[8]   Gardner, *Saint Catherine*, 270-271.

brusqueness became domineering rudeness, for example, interrupting a cardinal's speech with "Stop that foolish chatter" or threatening to excommunicate prelates who accepted gifts, and refusing audiences to those suspected of this behavior. Even his reforming instinct led to extremes, for example, curbing luxury by reducing meals to one dish.[9] The historian Francis Oakley categorized his treatment of the cardinals as "violent, erratic, abusive, suggestive even of insanity."[10] Rather quickly, the cardinals, not necessarily humble or patient men, became resentful and embittered and proceeded with plans to undo the election.

Meanwhile Catherine, deeply troubled by these disturbing events, did not neglect the concerns that she considered equally important: the needs of those who relied on her advice and support in both their spiritual and temporal lives. Her letters to individuals spoke of spiritual matters while those to Urban offered support and gentle reminders of patience and humility. Uncharacteristically, she prepared and sent him candied oranges "to sweeten the bitterness of life with honey gathered from the love of Christ."[11]

- 2 -
Contemplative Conversation

She went to Fra Santi's solitary dwelling somewhere outside the gates of Siena, intending to remain there some days. She asked her secretaries to listen intently when she was in ecstasy, which was more often now than ever before, and write down all she said. During

---

[9] Curtayne, 142.
[10] Oakley, 56.
[11] Levasti, 282.

these periods of ecstasy her body always became stiff
and without feeling, sight or hearing, but sometimes
words streamed from her lips, and she had on occasion dictated letters while in this condition. Now she
knew that the whole of the spiritual knowledge which
had been poured into her soul when, transported from
this world, she talked with her Lord, would be revealed
again to her in a concentrated form which she was
intended to give to her children as their inheritance.

Sigrid Undset[12]

Despite all that was going on around her when she returned
to Siena, Catherine was determined to dedicate herself to com-
pleting a full and permanent account of her personal testament.
Levasti speculates that her friends were constantly asking her to
teach them, to share with them the conversations with God that
took place while she was rapt in mystic prayer, and in response,
she may have conceived the idea to leave to them and to future
generations a permanent record of the words that she believed
that God had spoken directly to her.[13] Whether she felt an urgency to complete this task from a sense of failing health, or an
awareness of the necessity of committing it to writing while fresh
in her mind, she began almost immediately to set her plans in
motion.

Her obedient journey to Florence had delayed Catherine's
deep desire to concentrate on this undertaking. But, clearly, she
kept it in mind and heart, possibly dictating parts of it at quiet
times to one or more of her companions in Florence: Cecca and
Lisa, Neri and Stephano, and perhaps Cristofano di Gano and/or
Barduccio Canigniana, the Florentine who had become her de-

---

[12] *Catherine of Siena*, 229.
[13] Levasti, 294.

voted disciple.[14] In her haste in leaving that turbulent city, she left her manuscript behind, in the possession of the generous couple who had sheltered her during the violent days of revolt, but she would soon request its return. The Sienese hermitage of Fra Santi, with its small private oratory, was the place of uninterrupted solitude that she chose for this lengthy dictation. She directed her three scribes, Neri Landoccio, Stephano Maconi, and Barduccio Canigiani to record her every conversation, frequently conducted while in ecstasy.[15] It is believed that she herself wrote parts of her testament in her native Tuscan dialect at that time; subsequently, her scribes translated it into literate Italian.[16]

The name eventually given to Catherine's spiritual testament, *The Dialogue,* implies a conversation, an exchange of her questions, speaking in the third person, and God the Father, responding directly. The subject of these questions first appeared in Catherine's letter to Raymond from Rocca d'Orcia the previous October when she described for him an intense prayer experience in which she had expressed four petitions to "the most high and eternal Father." They appear at the opening of the *The Dialogue* with her first petition for herself. "The second was for the reform of holy Church. The third was for the whole world in general, and in particular for the peace of Christians who are rebelling against holy Church with great disrespect and persecution. In her fourth petition she asked divine providence to supply in general and in particular for a certain case which had arisen."[17]

As with all her writings, *The Dialogue* is replete with sym-

---

[14] Barduccio, the son of Pietro and the brother of Ristoro Canigiani, Florentine supporters of Catherine, had been drawn to Catherine during her stay in Florence. He returned to Siena as her disciple and scribe, remaining with her to the end of her life.

[15] Dictated in her Tuscan dialect, it was later translated into Latin by Cristofano di Gano. Drane, II, 122.

[16] Drane, II, 121.

[17] *The Dialogue,* #1, 26.

bolism, the language of mysticism. Catherine fashioned and re-fashioned images previously considered: the circle of soil, the roots, trunk, and crown with its virtues and blossoms, as symbols of her own human and spiritual development, both in *The Dialogue* and in her letters. Now, she moves them forward to encompass the journey from earth to heaven, leading to eternal salvation. As seen in her letters, the tree of virtue had become the tree of the cross. The inherent meaning of this characterization embodied not only personal suffering but intimate union with the suffering endured by Christ on the cross to redeem humankind, and open the gates of heaven closed since the sin of Adam and Eve. Again, as is customary in Catherine's writing, the staircase of Christ's body, the three steps carved in his feet, heart and mouth, assumed increased depth of meaning as she demonstrated its purpose: to provide entrance to the bridge that would lead to the gate of heaven.

In *The Dialogue,* it is God's voice that dominates the conversation. "My Son's nailed feet are a stair by which you can climb to his side, where you will see revealed his inmost heart. For when the soul has climbed up on the feet of affection and looked with her mind's eye into my Son's open heart, she begins to feel the love of her own heart in his consummate and unspeakable love…. Then the soul seeing how tremendously she is loved, is herself filled to overflowing with love. So, having climbed the second stair, she reaches the third. This is his mouth, where she finds peace from the terrible war she has had to wage because of her sins. At the first stair, lifting the feet of her affections from the earth, she stripped herself of sin. At the second she dressed herself in love for virtue. And at the third she tasted peace."[18]

A further interpretation integrates the image of the stairs with the three powers of the soul: memory, understanding, and will.

---

[18] Ibid., #26, 64-65.

Again, it is God speaking. "The memory holds on to my blessings and my goodness to the soul. Understanding contemplates the unspeakable love I have shown you through the mediation of my only-begotten Son.... The will, finally, is joined with them to know and desire me, the final goal. When these three powers are gathered together, I am in their midst by grace. And as soon as you are filled with my love and love of your neighbor, you will find yourself in the company of the multitude of solid virtues. Then the soul's appetite is ready to be thirsty, thirsty for virtue, my honor, and the salvation of souls.... You find that you have climbed the first step, that of desire.... Once desire is stripped of selfish love, you rise above yourself and above passing things. What you decide to keep, you love and hold not apart from me but with me, that is, with true holy fear and love of virtue. Then you will find that you have climbed the second stair. This is the enlightenment of the mind, which sees itself reflected in the warm hearted love I have shown you in Christ crucified, as in a mirror. Then you find peace and quiet, for memory is filled with my love and no longer empty... it is filled with me, and I am all good. After you have climbed you will find that you are gathered together. For once reason has taken possession of the three stairs, which are the three powers of the soul, they are gathered together in my name. When the two—that is, love for me and love for your neighbor—are gathered together, and the memory for holding and understanding for seeing and the will for loving are gathered together, you find that I am your companion, and I am your strength and your security. You discover the company of the virtues, and because I am in their midst you walk securely and are secure.... Then you are roused with eager longing, thirsty to follow the way of Truth.... So, walk on carrying your heart like a vessel emptied of every desire and every disordered earthly love.... When you have climbed the staircase, that is, when you are gathered together in my name, you move forward and cross over the bridge, following the teaching of my Truth who is that bridge. You run after his voice that calls out to you. (I told you earlier that he was inviting you when he cried out in the temple. 'Let whoever is thirsty come to me and drink, for I am the fountain of living water.')"[19]

- 3 -
The Bridge from Earth to Heaven

Catherine's style of writing is spontaneous, energetic and passionate. Much of its vitality comes from her superb use of imagery. Generally speaking, mystics like poets cannot express themselves without symbol or image. Catherine, the mystic, in attempting to communicate her experience of God, knows that the reality of that experience is inexpressible, and so she relies on some hint or parallel, contained in one image or another to stimulate the dormant intuition of her readers, and to convey to them something beyond the surface sense of her words. In her writings, metaphor trips over metaphor, and one image, barely formed gives way to another. It is as if her words cannot keep up with her desire to communicate what she knows and has experienced.

Mary O'Driscoll, O.P.[20]

One of Catherine's most complex symbols is that of the bridge, built on Christ's crucified body to remake the road from earth to heaven that was destroyed by the fall of Adam and Eve.

---

[19] Ibid., #54, 107-109.
[20] "Catherine the Theologian," 9.

This bridge, this new path leading to eternal life, is first mentioned in *The Dialogue* at the close of God's response to Catherine's prayers for Raymond, when he says, "he will rest along with the others, on the breast of my only begotten Son. And I will make of my Son a bridge by which you can all reach your goal and there receive the fruit of all the labors you have borne for my love."[21] Then followed, in God's voice, a lengthy description of the road, the stairs that gave entry to the bridge, and the river that ran below it.

A mighty river preventing anyone from reaching eternal life had overrun the road to salvation, broken up by Adam's sin. Its waves brought weariness and trouble, and all were drowning. No one, however righteous, could reach eternal life. But God, wishing to undo this situation, gave humans a bridge, his Son, so that they could cross over the river, the stormy sea of their darksome life, without drowning.[22] God made the bridge to join the earth of humanity with the greatness of Godhead. And it was necessary for everyone to keep to the bridge, following in the footsteps of the gentle loving Jesus because there was no other way.[23] Again, in God's own voice, we hear: "Your nature had to be joined with the height of mine, the eternal Godhead, before it could make atonement for all of humanity.... So the height stooped to the earth of your humanity, bridging the chasm between us and rebuilding the road."[24]

The bridge was entered by way of the three stairs of Christ's body, but the last stair was very high so that the flooding waters could not reach it; yet, it was still joined to earth because Christ, though lifted high on the wood of the most holy cross, never cut off his divinity from the lowly earth of his humanity. Thus, his

---

[21] *The Dialogue*, #20, 58.

[22] Ibid., #21, 58-59.

[23] Ibid., #23, 60.

[24] Ibid., #22, 59.

divinity was kneaded into the clay of humanity when its powers of memory, understanding, and will were harmoniously united.[25] The bridge had walls, made of stones of virtue to protect the traveler when it rained. These walls did not exist before Christ's passion because heaven was not yet unlocked with the key of the Son's blood, and the rains of justice prevented anyone from crossing over the river. The stones, hewn out of the body of Christ, were tempered with the mortar of his divinity and his blood, and fused with the heat of his burning love. Then, all the faithful could walk without hindrance, with no fear of the rain of divine justice because they were sheltered by the mercy that came down from heaven, through the incarnation. So the bridge had walls and a roof of mercy and the hostelry of Holy Church to serve the bread of life and the blood, lest pilgrims grow faint on the journey. The only way to enter into heaven was by means of a gate at the end of the bridge, which could be opened only with the key of Christ's blood. "And I, the Father, am one with the gate and the way that is my Son, eternal Truth, a sea of peace…. And once you have arrived there you pass through the gate, Christ crucified, to enjoy that living water—for now you find yourself in me, the sea of peace."[26]

While on earth, Christ had said that he was the Way, and now, the Father showed that indeed, his Son is the Way, in the image of a bridge. "When my only begotten Son returned to me forty days after his resurrection, the bridge was raised high above the earth. For he left your company and ascended to heaven by the power of my divine nature to sit at his eternal Father's right hand," then, "I sent the Teacher, the Holy Spirit. He came with my power and my Son's wisdom and his own mercy. He is one

---

[25] Ibid., #26, 65-66. Similarly, the cross was an anvil where Christ could be hammered into an instrument to release humankind from death and restore it to the life of grace.

[26] Ibid., #27, 67; #54, 109.

thing with me, the Father, and with my Son. He came to make even more firm the road my Truth had left in the world, his teaching. So though my Son's presence was no longer with you, his teaching—the way of which he made for you this lovely and glorious bridge—remained, as did his virtues, the solid stones of his teaching.... The Holy Spirit's mercy confirmed his teaching by strengthening his disciples' minds to testify to the truth and make known his way, the teaching of Christ crucified.... The way that he taught and about which I have told you has been verified by the apostles and proclaimed in the blood of martyrs. It has been lighted up by the doctors, attested to by the confessors, and committed to writing by the evangelists. All of these are living witnesses to the truth in the mystic body of holy church."[27]

"So first I made a bridge of my Son as he lived in your company. And though that living bridge has been taken from your sight, there remains the bridgeway of his teaching, which as I have told you, is held together by my power and my Son's wisdom and the mercy of the Holy Spirit. My power gives the virtue of courage to those who follow his way. Wisdom gives them light to know the truth along the way. And the Holy Spirit gives them a love that uproots all sensual love from the soul and leaves only virtuous love. So now as much as before, through his teaching as much as when he was among you, he is the way and truth and life—the way that is the bridge leading to the very height of heaven. That is what he meant when he said, 'I came from the Father and I am returning to the Father,'... and 'I will come back to you.'"[28]

"That roadway cannot be destroyed or stolen from anyone who wants to follow it, because it is solid and immovable and comes from me, the unchangeable one. So you must follow the

[27] Ibid., #29, 69.
[28] Ibid., #29, 70.

way courageously, not in the fog, but with the light of faith that I gave you as your most important adornment in holy baptism...."[29]

"But, those who do not keep to this way travel below through the river—a way not of stones but of water. And since there is no restraining the water, no one can cross through it without drowning.... How foolish and blind are those who choose to cross through the water when the road has been built for them.... Beneath the bridge, the going is wearisome and there is neither refreshment nor any benefit at all."[30]

"Now you have seen and heard what you asked of me, that is, how you should behave if you would not drown. I have told you that this is the way: to climb up onto the bridge. In this climbing you are all gathered together and united, loving each other, carrying your hearts and wills like vessels to me (who give anyone to drink who asks), keeping to the way of Christ crucified with perseverance even till death. This is the way you must all keep to no matter what your situation... because I have already told you that every state of life is pleasing and acceptable to me if it is held to with a good and holy will."[31]

In these selections, Catherine exhibits her deep familiarity both with Augustinian teaching and New Testament writings. Augustine traditionally underscored the basic significance of the unified love of God and of neighbor. From Augustine, she also derived the interplay of the three faculties of the soul: memory, understanding and will. As was her custom, however, she took this concept to deeper levels of meaning when she identified memory with the power of the Father, understanding with the wisdom of the Son, and the will with the love of the Holy Spirit.[32]

---

[29] Ibid., #29, 70.
[30] Ibid., #28, 67-68.
[31] Ibid., #55, 110.
[32] Hackett, *William Flete*, 114-115.

Similarly, her language echoes familiar words from the Gospel of John: "I am the way, the truth, and the life, no one goes to the Father except by me" (John 14:6). "I am the Light of the world. Whoever follows me shall have the light of life and will never walk in darkness" (John 18:12). "When I am lifted up from the earth, I will draw everyone to me" (John 12:32). "I have told you this while I am still with you. The Helper, the Holy Spirit, whom the Father will send in my name, will teach you everything and make you remember all I have told you" (John 14:26).

Commentators trace the imagery of the bridge to the sixth century *Dialogues* of Pope Gregory the Great whose impact on medieval spirituality was profound. Popularized in Catherine's day by Dominic Caval, O.P. (c. 1270-1342), a famous preacher and spiritual writer in Pisa, his writings would have been orally familiar to her from sermons and conversations with her Dominican followers.[33] In a manner customary in early medieval times, Gregory's *Dialogues* took place in response to queries by his disciple Peter, just as Catherine's conversation positioned her as the questioner and God as the responder. In keeping with his teaching methodology, Gregory prefaced his description of the bridge with the words, "We arrive at true understanding through images." And he gives as an example, "the just were seen passing over a bridge to a beautiful meadow, because the road that leads to eternal life is narrow."[34] His account is rich in contrasting images that convey essences of good and evil: the dark waters and the glowing meadows, the fetid river and the scented flowers. "He saw a river whose dark waters were covered by a mist of vapors that gave off an unbearable stench. Over the river was a bridge. It led to pleasant meadows beyond, covered by green

---

[33] D'Urso, *Il Pensiero,* 336; Benedict Ashley, "A Guide to St. Catherine's Dialogue," 242; Ashley attributes this connection to the contemporary research of D'Urso.

[34] Saint Gregory the Great, *The Dialogues,* 242.

grass and dotted with richly scented flowers. The fragrant odors pervading the region were a delight to all who lived there. Everyone had his own dwelling, which gleamed with brilliant light.... On this bridge saint and sinner underwent a final test. The unjust would slip off and fall back into the dark, foul waters. The just, unhampered by sin, could walk over it, freely and without difficulty, to the beautiful meadows on the other side."[35]

Unlike Gregory's account, Catherine's emphasizes the role of Christ in the story of salvation as God the Father relates how his Son, in giving his life, established a bridge connecting earth and heaven. Her description of the bridge is also rich with detail totally her own, more than likely influenced by her experience in Florence from whence she had just returned. Catherine's bridge bears a strong resemblance to the covered bridges of Tuscany, arched over the rapid and dangerous Arno River and lined with shops and eating-places. Later, in a letter to one of her followers, Catherine will chastise him with words from her description of the walls of the bridge, telling him he could have made rocks for this bridge with his blood.

- *4* -

Impending Disaster

The impudence of the reasons alleged by the cardinals for their action is well pointed out by Catherine. But Europe became divided in its allegiance, and war of words was soon followed by war of swords. Catherine rose to the occasion. The rest of her tempestuous life was spent in the desperate defense of the cause

---

[35] Ibid., 239.

of Urban, a man whom she rightly believed to be the lawful successor of Peter, yet concerning his unlovely character she was… under no illusions. The many letters which she wrote with the aim of convincing important personages of the validity of Urban's claims, are historical documents of high value. One feels in them all the amazement with which a woman whose native air was the mystical conception of an infallible Church, faced the realities of the ecclesiastical machine. But loyalty stood the test, and while never leaving the highest ground, Catherine proved herself capable of a statesmanlike treatment of the actual situation.

Vida D. Scudder[36]

While Catherine maintained the peaceful calm required to complete her spiritual text, papal events were moving rapidly to a fateful conclusion. By June, the eleven French cardinals in Rome [six had remained in Avignon to supervise the functioning of the curial apparatus], were in residence at Anagni accompanied by court officials, one of whom had taken the papal tiara from the Castel Sant'Angelo.[37] Spanish Cardinal Pedro de Luna, to whom Catherine and all concerned about the papacy looked for leadership, had joined the group at Anagni. He was quoted as saying, "if the pope or some other Romans found out that I or some other member of the Sacred College had doubts about his election, none of us would escape."[38] The three Italian cardinals remained uncommitted to either side, and Urban was left with only

---

[36] *Letters of Saint Catherine of Siena*, 274-275.

[37] Curtayne, 141; John Farrow, *Pageant of the Popes,* 171; On his deathbed, Gregory had committed to the care of the Governor of the Castel Sant'Angelo a large portion of the papal treasures, forbidding him to give up the keys of the fortress to anyone without the permission of the cardinals at Avignon. Gardner, *St. Catherine*, 253.

[38] Oakley, 58.

one faithful supporter, Cardinal Tebaldeschi of Rome, who died on September seventh, having affirmed the validity of the election with his last breath. In an encyclical letter on August ninth, sent to all the rulers of Europe, the dissident cardinals portrayed the character of Urban, the context of fear in which his election had taken place, and their decision "for the good of the Church" to annul his election and choose another pope. This encyclical initiated the schism that would last almost forty years.

The reforms for which Catherine had so faithfully labored were now out of the question; dissension and discord had multiplied beyond belief or expectation. The one success of all her efforts for the church had been the return of the papacy to Rome, and that achievement had now devolved into total disorder. Curtayne suggests that many looked to Catherine as the cause of this debacle for disrupting the harmony of the Avignon leadership. To them, the change of location had provoked the schism. And which was the greater evil, one pope living in exile or two contending popes? All but Catherine's faithful followers looked at her curiously and a veil of silence seemed to fall on the good things of the past.[39] Failure was a painful burden.

When Urban demanded that the cardinals join him at Tivoli, where the peace negotiations ending the anti-papal league had been completed, they refused. On August twenty-seventh, they moved out of the Papal States over the border to Fondi, an independent principality in the Kingdom of Naples, outside the jurisdiction of the pope. Within the month, on September eighteenth, Urban created twenty-nine new cardinals; six refused the honor.[40] At Fondi, the dissidents responded by electing an anti-pope on the twentieth. It has been suggested that each of the three Italian

---

[39] Curtayne, 155-156; Oakley, 56.

[40] Levasti, 268. According to Gardner the new cardinals were "of small note."

cardinals had been led to believe that he would be the next pope, and thus each had refrained from voting. The choice of the French warrior cardinal, Count Robert of Geneva, as Clement VII was a hapless one for Italians who remembered him for many unpleasant military intrusions throughout Italy, but primarily for the massacre at Cesena during the reign of Gregory XI that had taken thousands of innocent lives.

For the first time in over half a century, a non-French pope had been chosen; but never before in the history of the papacy had two claimants to the throne been elected within three months, by the same group, to serve at the same time. The Archbishop of Bari, who became Urban VI, was not Roman, but he had the triple advantage of being Italian, a subject of Giovanna, the Angevin ruler of Naples, and a long-standing curial official at Avignon. Clement VII was a good political choice. Young, active and energetic, he came from an eminent and powerful family, was related to the princes of Europe, and cousin to King Charles V of France. He, too, had served in the curia of the church and was ready to give his life for its safety. However, lacking in piety and known as a man of "liberal conscience," he was well suited to the designs of the dissident cardinals who sought to maintain the splendor and grandeur of a strong Church State, not a State Church, that could gather all of Catholic Europe around it.[41]

The two rival claimants to St. Peter's throne proceeded to clash on both spiritual and temporal matters. Each excommunicated the other and placed the supporters of his rival under interdict. Almost immediately both sides resorted to military protection to support their claims to the papacy. Although Clement would have taken Rome if he could, it was not necessarily a question of territory, since the Clementines had no desire to remain in Italy, nor did the Urbanites have designs on Avignon. Eventu-

---

[41] Ibid., 286-287.

ally, Clement made his way back to Avignon with his French
Curia, enlarged by nine new appointees,[42] while Urban, with his
new multinational Curia, remained in Italy. There were now two
popes, two papal administrations and two separate legal systems.
Clementines and Urbanites were each declaiming the other;
nations were choosing allegiances. The papacy became the pup-
pet of European politics, controlled by motivations extraneous
to its own purpose and welfare. Choosing which pope to obey
was an agonizing dilemma for some, but one made primarily
along political and dynastic lines.[43] England, Brittany, Portugal,
Germany, Hungary, Poland, Flanders, Sweden, Norway, Asian
churches,[44] and most of Italy supported the Roman obedience.
France, Aragon, Naples, Castile, Savoy, Scotland and Wales
confirmed the papacy of Clement. The outcome was the expansion of widespread disorder and an exceedingly grave constitu-
tional crisis. Religious orders were similarly affected. The prior-
general of the Carthusians and his followers opted for the
Clementine side and, more heartbreaking for Catherine, the Dominican Order was broken in two as the Master General, Elias of
Toulouse, sided with the Avignon papacy while large sections
of the Order were faithful to Urban.[45]

How did Catherine contend with all of this? She longed to
be in Rome, to be in the center of these most significant events,
to be a peacemaker, to bring the two sides together in one church,
one communion, one loving body of the faithful. Raymond was
her most dependable source of information but, as an insider and
committed Urbanite, the picture he presented was one-sided. He
did not admit extenuating circumstances; thus, neither did Cathe-

---

[42] Curtayne, 152.

[43] Duffy, 127. At times countries changed their loyalties, usually for political reasons.

[44] Under John XXII, missionary endeavors had been extended to Armenia, India, Ethio-
pia, and southern portions of East Africa. Ullmann, 291.

[45] Gardner, 284.

rine. The cardinals had rebelled against a pope that they themselves had elected and confirmed; therefore, they had sinned against God. Her communications from Raymond were informative, but in a sense, tantalizing. To be a bystander with no opportunity to respond, to impact events, was not a satisfactory role for her. When word finally came from Rome requesting her presence, she asked for a written commission, remembering the gossip that had followed her previous journeys outside the city; perhaps, too, she considered the negative attitude that implied her responsibility for schism. Nevertheless, her heart rejoiced. She had an indomitable belief that God would answer her entreaties; that her prayer could resolve the crisis. In *The Dialogue,* in the name of all his servants, she had implored God through the precious blood of his Son, "to be merciful to the world and make holy Church blossom again with the fragrant flowers of good holy shepherds whose perfume will dispel the stench of the putrid evil flowers."[46] This was her goal as she embarked on what would be her final journey to the city of her heart and soul.

- 5 -
The City of Saint Peter

The disarray, consternation and resultant conflict of loyalties through the length and breadth of Christendom is barely comprehensible to an observer in the twentieth century. There were now two popes fulminating against each other, and each claiming to be the sole vicar of Christ, and there were two Colleges of Cardinals. How was the ordinary Christian to decide who was the legitimate pope? ... Europe was split in two

---

[46] *The Dialogue,* #134, 275.

halves.... The church universal witnessed the nadir of the papacy which was to have been its authoritative guide. The resultant anguish besetting the conscience of so many contemporary Christians is hardly imaginable today. What deserves at least a passing remark is that the papacy itself—once more unwittingly—contributed to the sharpening of the individual and private judgment, thereby not inconsiderably fertilizing the ground for a particular strand of Reformation Christianity.

Walter Ullmann[47]

As Catherine waited impatiently for Urban's written confirmation of his request for her presence in Rome, excitement grew among her followers. Yet, there was tension, too, as a kind of finality, not apparent in previous journeys, invaded their enthusiasm; hence everyone wanted to accompany her. Catherine herself made the difficult selection in her customary manner: that is, to give equal significance to the women, priests, and laymen among her family of followers. Alessa, Cecca, Lisa and Giovanni di Capo would be joined by Fra Bartolomeo, Fra Santi, the Augustinian hermit Giovanni Tantucci, and Barduccio, Neri, and Gabriele Piccolomino. Stephano and Monna Lapa hoped to follow by Christmas.

When the commission from Urban arrived, the group rode out of Siena by the southern gate, passing within sight of Belcaro, into territory rife with mercenary troops. After a month, they reached the Holy City, so meaningful to their faith in God and to their church, on November 28, 1378, the first Sunday in Advent. How joyous was the reunion with Raymond, whose company they had been deprived of for well over a year. Imagine the awe

---

[47] *A Short History of the Papacy*, 295-296.

that each one felt to view the walls of a city so dear to each heart and the basilica that held the bones of Peter, the first pope.

This was not the sixteenth century basilica of Michelangelo with its great dome and the huge circular gathering space with the ancient obelisk in its center. The church at the heart of Catherine's fourteenth century had originally come into being to enshrine the bones of St. Peter, martyred in an adjacent amphitheater. Adapted from an early Roman law court, the basilica provided open interior gathering space for worshipers. Its simple frontage was triple arched with a central entry and a raised balcony from which a papal blessing could be bestowed. Within, an open atrium with a fountain in its center and bounded on three sides by a covered walkway, led to the worship area of the basilica beyond. Above the interior façade of the entranceway, the enormous mosaic, the *Navicella,* created by Giotto for the first holy year of 1300, portrayed in metaphor the church of that day, buffeted by storms of political conflict.[48] Based on the biblical account in Matthew 14:22-23 of Christ rescuing Peter from turbulent waters, it depicted the Apostles' storm-tossed ship in danger of sinking and Peter's reliance on Christ to save them. The effect of Catherine's initial view of this representation of the sinking bark of Peter so deeply stirred her anxiety regarding the church of her own time that references to Peter's bark began to appear frequently in her letters and prayers, continuing throughout this last period of her life. For example, in a recorded prayer of January 18, 1379, shortly after her arrival, she made the petition, "Peter, pilot of your ship… guide this ship into the port of peace."[49]

---

[48] Herbert L. Kessler and Johanna Zacharas, *Rome 1300: On the Path of the Pilgrim,* 217-218. This mosaic was later transferred to Michelangelo's basilica and placed in a similar location inside the new entrance façade.

[49] *The Prayers of Catherine of Siena,* #8, January 18, 1379, 64.

As the newcomers entered the city itself, reality quickly quenched their sense of elation when they heard and saw the clamor and destruction of war. The urban environment that awaited them bore no resemblance to the order and luster of their own Siena. During the seventy-year absence of the papal court, the declining economic structure and civic unrest had reduced the city to the status of little more than an overgrown village with a population that had declined to about 30,000, most of whom lived in a state of abject poverty.[50] The once proud and historic landscape had lost its grandeur as most of the famous monuments were broken and the majority of the basilicas were in disrepair. "The streets were torn and dirty and the great edifices of ancient majesty and beauty were victims of a riotous and unopposed decay."[51]

Danger lurked in those streets and byways as military forces threatened the gates of Rome. Armed galleys of the Clementines guarded the mouth of the Tiber River to intercept any communication from the sea, while in adjacent areas, such as the Kingdom of Naples, troops were being organized to settle the dispute by force of arms. Inside Rome, the battle to possess the Castel Sant'Angelo raged on. From the first days of trouble when French troops had taken possession of it, Roman militias repeatedly attacked its walls. In the noise and uproar of the street fighting, Urban was marooned outside the Vatican residence, lodged temporarily at Santa Maria in Trastevere.

The group took up residence in a house provided by the pope in the Rione della Colonne near the Church of the Minerva, the Dominican center in Rome, where Raymond was Prior. Here, they adopted a lifestyle of simplicity and voluntary poverty, trusting to alms or begging for their daily sustenance when neces-

---

[50] Ullmann, 292.
[51] Farrow, 171.

sary. Catherine, too, participated in this humble endeavor and spent her time in prayer, in dictating letters, in meetings with Urban, and in any activity which would further his cause. By late December, her mother arrived with several companions from Siena, increasing their numbers to eight women and sixteen men with frequent visits of additional pilgrims from Siena, often increasing their numbers to thirty and even forty people.[52]

The Sienese ambassador in Rome, Lando di Francesco, wrote to the Signoria of Siena to report the arrival of Catherine and her followers and Urban's welcoming reception of her.[53] At this meeting, Urban greeted Catherine warmly. Invited to speak, she had no need for an interpreter since all were Italian. She encouraged Urban and his assembly of Cardinals to have courage and not to be frightened by the Schism. Urban commented to those present, "This poor little woman puts us to shame by her courage; what need the Vicar of Christ fear, although the world stand against him? Christ the Almighty is more powerful than the world, and He will never abandon His Church."[54] He chose the day following her arrival to issue the papal bull, previously mentioned, excommunicating Clement and those who adhered to his obedience, though he was still unwilling to move against Pedro de Luna or the three Italian cardinals.

At their arrival, Raymond confided to Catherine that he had been directed by the pope to travel to France to advance the cause of the Urbanist papacy. His departure was scheduled for early December, leaving little time for them to converse after such a long separation. Raymond's journey would bring him into ex-

---

[52] Curtayne, 163.

[53] The ambassador was still seeking the return of the port of Talamone, taken during the period of the anti-papal league. Also for some reason, at this time the interdict had not been lifted in Siena and Catherine's followers in the city were distressed. Catherine advised Stephano not to participate in the sacraments. Drane, 211-212.

[54] Gardner, *Saint Catherine,* 288-289.

ceedingly dangerous situations, into territory controlled by armed forces intent on weakening Urban's position and eliminating his adherents. Yet, Catherine, with her indomitable courage, despite her own disappointment, used the time to encourage him and to buoy up his spirits with the significance of his task: to bring the French King and his people back to the sheltering arms of the Roman obedience, the one true and legal church. On the day of his departure, they had a long conversation that Catherine instinctively realized would be their last. She accompanied him down to the Tiber where he boarded a galley to the port of Ostia and then sailed on to Pisa.[55]

In parting, she said to him, "We shall never speak like this to each other again."[56] As his ship glided slowly down the river toward the sea, she knelt on the shore, raised her hand in blessing and, through her tears, prayed from a broken and lonely heart. The little that she had seen of the city's devastation, together with her instant recognition of the difficulties of Urban's temperament and facing what, at a distance had seemed so possible, made her realize how much she had always depended on Raymond's integrity, charity, and counsel. Once again, in so short a space, joy had turned to sorrow.

- 6 -
Conclusions

Even Catherine in a moment of clarity knew reform could not come from within. "Do not weep now," she said to Father Raymond, when he burst into tears at

---

[55] Sources differ as to whether the parting took place at Ostia or in Rome.
[56] Gardner, 292.

some new scandal for the Church, "for you will have still more to weep for," when in the future not only laymen but clerics would rise against the church. As soon as the Pope attempted reform, she said, the prelates would resist, and the Church "will be divided, as it were by a heretical pestilence." Catherine herself was never heretical, never disillusioned, never disobedient. The Church, the papacy, the priesthood, the Dominican order were her home, and their sanctity her foundation. She scolded, but from within the fold.

Barbara Tuchman[57]

All the hopes and dreams of reform that Catherine had placed on the return of the papal court to Rome had been completely shattered. The outcome was unthinkably more disastrous than what had been. And now, Raymond had departed from her life. What he had been to her was, not so much a teacher but a voice of affirmation. Raymond received the knowledge that she appertained from God and reflected back to her the assurance that what she perceived was sound dogma securely within the body of knowledge that was the doctrine of the church.

A strong woman is not to be tamed with a heavy hand any more than a vibrant lively steed is to be held in tight rein. The wise rider knows when to give the animal its head and when to direct its course by pressure on the reins. So, too, Raymond seems to have known when to let Catherine have her head and when to tighten the reins. Over the years, a mutual trust had grown between the two so that a totally free exchange was possible. Deference to the will of the other was as natural as a pendulum swinging methodically to the seconds of a clock. This sense of mutuality was undoubtedly God-given, a pure gift conceived in

---

[57] *A Distant Mirror: The Calamitous Fourteenth Century*, 327-328.

the soul of each, that they might be to each other a path of salvific growth toward human perfection.

This growth of mutual trust and affection emerged out of painful encounter as each discovered in the other strengths and weaknesses that had to be accepted and refined in the purely human experience of relationship. To the very end, Catherine was critical of the weakness of will that she perceived in Raymond; such criticism is well documented in her letters. Raymond's reaction to her criticism is seen through her letters as well, where she frequently seeks pardon for the harshness and bitterness of her words. Such conflict may have been the most crucial and painful ground of difference between them and would continue to the end of her life.

The darkness that engulfed Catherine's spirit at their parting was heavily influenced by the circumstances of her world and of the church. It was the kind of darkness where one's life comes to a standstill, where one is faced with the temptation to despair and to give up, what John of the Cross would later portray as "impasse." But this is also a place where the person in touch with God finds growth and transformation when, in the darkness, the sun breaks through, sparkling with the hope it brings. God is found in the darkness. "Ultimately it is the mystic, the contemplative woman, who will be reassured, affirmed, and loved, who will see and love, and for whose sake the world will be given sight, language, reassurance, and love."[58] Catherine seemed already aware of this understanding, as she immediately engaged herself in her most sublime vocation, to "Purify the Church," thereby helping to return it to its pristine life and purpose.

---

[58] Constance Fitzgerald, O.C.D., "Impasse and the Dark Night," 288-308.

CHAPTER EIGHT

A Church in Turmoil

- 1 -
A Council of Holy Persons

According to Catherine only the saints, the ascetics and the mystics could thoroughly reform the Church. It never occurred to her that these men, humble, pure and powerful in the realm of the spirit, might prove to be mediocre or incapable administrators of public affairs. She did not distinguish between the religious and the political Church, because she judged politics solely as an expression of faith, and would willingly have renounced all temporal power if she had thought it was in any way harmful to the power of the spirit. As there had to be a Papal State she thought of it as a vast religious community in which human passions should have no power to hurt, and all men should love each other like brothers, with their thoughts fixed on God.

Arrigo Levasti[1]

In the weeks following Raymond's departure, Catherine was frequently in the company of the pope. At the end of December, the Sienese ambassador in Rome, Lando di Francesco, reporting

---

[1] *My Servant Catherine*, 320-321.

to the Signoria of his city, mentioned that the Holy Father had spoken to her many times, had sent for her frequently, and that she obtained whatever she desired.[2] Both Catherine and Urban were agreed on the need for radical reform. Indeed, Levasti asserts that it was this consensus that enabled her to overlook the violent and autocratic nature that had alienated even his own supporters. In a letter to Raymond, she shared her thoughts on reform. "We see this bride all dismembered. But I hope that in His supreme and eternal goodness God will make her members whole once more, of sweet odor and not putrid, and that these members will be refashioned on the bowed shoulders of God's faithful servants, lovers of truth, by their many labors, sweats and tears, and humble continual prayers. And in our labors we shall find refreshment, rejoicing in the reformation of this sweet Bride."[3]

Since Catherine herself saw no impediment that could not be overcome by prayer and petition to God, perhaps she was able to instill in Urban the capacity to trust in spiritual solutions to the overwhelming problems that engulfed the church. Her strong belief that good, prayerful people, rooted in holiness and prepared for sacrifice, could accomplish immeasurable good, convinced him to attempt to gather in Rome a Papal Council of holy persons, mystics, and ascetics from among those whom she most respected and trusted, for the purpose of restoring unity, reforming the church, and eliminating the schism. The potential of this plan awakened powerful emotions in her since the reform of the church had been her consuming goal from youth, and now, the terrible plight of the church seemed to offer an opportunity to finally accomplish her dream. If the church had holy men to guide it, she believed it would become holy, and enable the setting up of the Kingdom of God on earth.

---

[2] Ibid., 321.
[3] Ibid., 320.

On December thirteenth, Urban drew up a papal bull, whose language indicates Catherine's influence, to be sent to all the people she indicated. It read in part, "In this horrible tempest that threatens the Church with shipwreck, we believe and hope to be divinely helped by the prayers and tears of the just, rather than by the arms of soldiers and by human prudence. Therefore, with Peter who, when he was sinking in the sea besought aid from the Lord, and straightway merited to be delivered by His loving hand, earnestly and with devotion of heart, we summon to our assistance the devout tears and assiduous prayers of the just children of the Church, that we may humbly and devoutly assail the ears of the Lord, and he may the sooner bend to have compassion on us."[4] This reference to the church as the bark of Peter, sinking in the sea, suggests once again the impact of Giotto's mosaic, the *Navicella,* and Catherine's attraction to it.

Recipients of Urban's letter were instructed to have special prayers and sacrifices offered night and day in all the congregations and hermitages of men and women in Tuscany and elsewhere, and to seek out representatives of the different religious orders who would present themselves in Rome for a meeting with the pope on January 17, 1379, the second Sunday after the Epiphany. Fra Bartolomeo Serafini, the Prior of the Carthusian Monastery on the Isle of Gorgona, a friend of Catherine's, was charged with circulating the pope's message and bringing the project to conclusion. Catherine wrote to him, "Now is our time in which it will be seen who is a lover of truth. We must arise from slumber and place the blood of Christ before our eyes, in order that we may be more inspirited for the battle. Our sweet Holy Father, Pope Urban VI, true Supreme Pontiff, seems to mean to adopt that remedy which is necessary for the reformation of Holy Church; he wishes to have the servants of God by his side,

---

[4] Gardner, *Saint Catherine,* 294.

and to guide himself and Holy Church by their counsels. For this reason he sends you this bull, in which is contained that you have to summon all those who are written here."[5] Catherine did not go outside of her own circle to identify the reform minded when she provided the names of men she knew and trusted as rooted in holiness and ready to give their lives for God's church. The names that have survived are Fra Bartomeo Serafini of Ravenna, the Vallombrosan Giovanni of the Cells, the Augustinian William of Flete, the Augustinian Fra Antonio of Nice, Fra Paolino da Nola, and the Spoletan hermits Andrea da Lucca, Fra Baldo, and Fra Lando.[6]

In her eagerness to move quickly toward the accomplishment of this goal, Catherine dispensed her own letters to some of the hermits to encourage them to leave their solitude. To William Flete and Antonio of Nice at Lecceto she wrote, "I shall perceive whether we have in truth conceived love for the reformation of Holy Church; for if it is really so, you will follow the will of God and of His Vicar, will come out of your wood, and make haste to enter the battlefield. But if you do not do it, you will be in discord with the will of God.... And do not hesitate because of not having a wood, for there are woods and forests here."[7] A similar letter, dispatched to Brothers Andrea, Baldo, and Lando, read: "Therefore I beg and constrain you in Christ sweet Jesus, that you come swiftly, to fulfill the will of God, who wills thus, and the holy will of the vicar of Christ, that is calling you and the others. You need not be afraid of luxuries or of great consolations; for you are coming to endure, and not to enjoy yourselves, except with the joy of the Cross."[8]

Her close associate, William of Flete—both teacher and dis-

---

[5] Ibid.
[6] Hacket, 93.
[7] Scudder, *Letters,* 308-309.
[8] Ibid., 311.

ciple—declined to accept the papal invitation. Catherine's response to this development was delivered, not to Flete himself, but to his fellow hermit at Lecceto, Fra Antonio of Nice. Her disappointment echoes in the severity of her response. "The time has come to find out who God's servants are and whether or not they are only seeking themselves for their own sake, God for the private consolation they find in him, and their neighbor for their own satisfaction; also whether we think God is to be found only in one place and not in another.... True servants of God have always come out in the open in times of need and adversity, but fled away in times of prosperity."[9] She then refers to a letter she had received from Flete, informing her that neither of the two would be joining the holy company in Rome. "I do not intend to reply to that letter, but I am very grieved at his foolishness.... If it is out of humility and fear of losing his peace that he does not want to come, then let him practice the virtue of humility by meekly and humbly begging leave of Christ's vicar, beseeching his Holiness to allow him to remain in his wood for his greater peace."[10]

It seems that Flete had implied that the invitation, guided by a human rather than a divine inspiration, would succeed only in drawing the recipients away from their peace and consolation. One can sense the tenor of annoyance in Catherine's response, "Your spirit is easily detached if it can be lost by change of place! On this showing, God is partial to places and is to be found in the woods, but nowhere else in time of need."[11] She then refers to two hermits who have responded obediently to the call of Urban, Fra Andrea da Lucca and Fra Paolino da Nola, who, despite age and poor health, have sacrificed their own personal desires for silence and consolation to make the journey

---

[9] *I, Catherine*, L. 51, 226-227.
[10] Ibid., 227.
[11] Ibid., 228.

to Rome. A final remark reveals her realistic perception of Flete, "I hardly expected him to come, but I certainly did not expect him to react so disrespectfully to the obedience laid on him, and in such a foolish way."[12]

Her displeasure was somewhat appeased when word came that England had declared for the Urban pontificate, a decision credited, at least partially, to Flete's promotion of the cause with his contacts in his homeland. In a letter to his community, the Augustinian Friars of the Province of England, he had written, "I recommend to your charity Pope Urban VI, because he is the true pope, as is clear to the servants of God through revelations, through inspirations, and through prayers."[13] In a similar letter to the Signoria of Siena, he had declared the need to pray with great urgency for the reformation of the church of God that was in great danger and offered a similar solution to both audiences. "Know that if from the beginning litanies and prayers had been instituted throughout Christendom, as had been necessary, these tribulations which are now continuing, would not have continued so long. Our guilt, our negligence are the cause of all these adversities."[14] Joyfully, Catherine conveyed the news of England's declaration to Stephano and his friend Pietro di Giovanni Ventura in Siena, enclosing a letter for Flete. Her followers there informed her that Siena had unhesitatingly declared for Urban. Christofano wrote, "I do not believe that there is a single man in Siena who does not hold and believe that Pope Urban is the true pastor of Holy Church, and if any ambassadors of the anti-pope come here, they will not be heard."[15]

---

[12] Ibid., 229.

[13] Hackett, 145. Gardner records that Flete had a vision while celebrating Mass that Urban was the true Pope, and that he conveyed this information to England where it was instrumental in the decision to declare for the Urbanist papacy, 298.

[14] Hackett, 166.

[15] Gardner, *Saint Catherine*, 300-301.

Meanwhile, Raymond continued on the papal mission, sailing from Pisa to Genoa, with the intention of crossing over the border into France where the roads and passes were guarded by the Clementine forces. Warned of the certitude of death in an ambush, he abandoned the mission, and returned to Genoa. That the danger was real would become apparent in the experience of the others involved in the mission, Jacopo di Ceva, Marshal of the Roman Curia, and Guillaume de la Voulte, Bishop of Valence. Both were arrested at the border by soldiers of the Count of Geneva, Clement's brother, and kept prisoner until they defected to the side of Clement.[16] Urban's response to Raymond was temperate, directing him to remain in Genoa and preach the crusade against the anti-pope. But, once again, Catherine was stung with sadness; disappointed by another of her followers whose taste for suffering and death came nowhere near her own.

To Catherine, who saw martyrdom as a glorious achievement, Raymond's behavior was a betrayal and she wasted no words in informing him of this. "You were not yet worthy to stay upon the field of battle, but you were driven back like a child; and you fled away willingly, and were glad at the grace that God granted to your weakness. Naughty father mine, how blessed would your soul and mine have been, if with your blood you had built up a stone in Holy Church for love of the Blood!"[17] Not only is this a reference to her symbolism of the bridge, built with stones of virtue cemented with the blood of Christ, but Levasti suggests that, from Catherine's arrival in Rome, her frequent visits to shrines and churches was a constant reminder of the blood of martyrs and she was sure that that blood still had the power to heal the church.[18]

---

[16] Ibid., 291.
[17] Ibid., 293.
[18] Levasti, 320.

Meanwhile, throughout Europe, bitterness and apprehension grew. One letter from a Frenchman to an Italian declared, "I fear that this evil beginning will have a worse sequence and the worst end; for men's wills are so discordant that they do not let their intellects freely consider the truth, and every day the one side gets further from the other."[19] The hermit, Giovanni of the Cells, wrote to a friend describing a prophecy that was circulating about the end of the world, predicting that, after Urban VI would come a pope named Gregory, and then would come the anti-Christ, who would be the last pope.[20]

The three Italian Cardinals, since they had not formally declared for Clement, had remained members of both the Urban and Clementine College of Cardinals. In the latter part of January, 1379, they broke off negotiations with Urban, though still not officially joining with Clement. Catherine wrote them a fiery letter, "I have had the greatest sorrow for you three, and more wonder at your sin than at that of all the others who have committed it. For if all had departed from their father, you ought to have been those sons who strengthened him, by manifesting the truth. Even if your father had given you nothing but reproaches, you ought not to play the part of Judas by denying his Holiness in every way."[21] To these Italian cardinals, the only solution to the problem lay in a decision by a general council of the church. Indeed, when Cardinal Orsini died in August, his dying confession acknowledged as Pope "whoever shall be approved by the Church and the Council," and he expressed contrition if he had ever done or said anything against the one who would be declared the lawful pope.[22] The idea of a Council festered for years and finally resolved the Schism at Constance in 1417.

---

[19] Gardner, *Saint Catherine*, 299.
[20] Ibid., 300.
[21] Ibid., 304-305.
[22] Ibid., 306.

- 2 -
Military Engagements

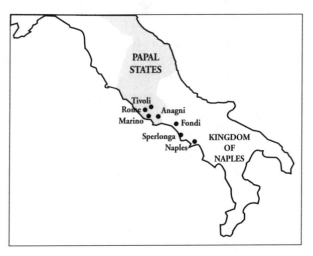

At the beginning of 1379, both sides resorted to raising armies of mercenary soldiers. In February, Clement, well supplied with financial means and political support, collected an army of Bretons and Gascons, including those who had participated with him in the destruction of Cesena, and put them under the command of his nephew, Louis de Montjoie, with orders to march upon Rome, where the French defenders of Castel Sant'Angelo were barely holding out. Montjoie set up his headquarters south of Rome, at Marino, where he ravaged the countryside without making any attempt to aid the defenders of Sant'Angelo. Early in March, Clement, suffering from fever, moved the short distance from Fondi to Sperlonga, taking up residence in a heavily fortified castle. In early April, in violation of the temporal power of the church in Italy, he issued a papal bull granting the Kingdom of Adria, part of the Papal States, to Louis of Anjou, the brother of the King of France. Levasti interpreted this as an indication that Clement, aware that his position in Italy was hopeless, was willing to spoil the church of its possessions in the faint hope of gaining an ally who could establish him as pope in Rome.[23]

Meanwhile Urban, proceeding along similar lines, was in dire need of money and military support. He took advantage of the longstanding Italian antipathy to their French oppressors to foster national pride, in order to turn the situation to his advantage. The allegiance of a united Italy of Rome, Tuscany, and Umbria, would promote his legitimacy among the reigning monarchs of Europe, who were hesitant to declare allegiance to either side. To accomplish this, he was willing to use the presence and support of Catherine as an intermediary within and without Italy; but his most urgent need was to find soldiers to support his cause and answer force with force, in what became known as the "*via facti.*" He succeeded in winning over the military Company of San Giorgio, Italian mercenaries led by the Count of Cenci, Alberigo da Barbiano, who successfully routed the French defenders of Sant'Angelo on April twenty-seventh. In response to this achievement, a warlike enthusiasm spread over central Italy.

On the heels of this victory, the Italian forces under Cenci marched out of the city on April thirtieth, north toward Tivoli, turning south to Marino where they would win a complete victory over the Clementine forces under Montjoie, who lost one third of his army, either killed or taken prisoner, as he was himself. This second victory assumed tremendous significance. On the one hand, to Italians, it was a remarkable reversal of fortune, since for so long a time they had been accustomed to being overrun by foreign mercenaries; on the other hand, it gave powerful impetus to the cause of Urban against the Clementines. However, when Urban moved to assume papal control of the Castel Sant'Angelo, the Roman civic authorities, fearing his intention to dominate the city and curtail their liberties, refused to relinquish

---

[23] Levasti, 334.

it, since Roman forces had liberated it. Accepting this defeat as best he could, and with Catherine's encouragement, amid a display of great pomp, Urban walked barefoot from his temporary quarters in Trastevere to Saint Peter's to offer thanks to God for the double victory at Marino and Sant'Angelo, and to formally take up residence in the Vatican.

Catherine wrote to him, "I rejoice with all my heart, most holy Father, that my eyes have seen God's will accomplished in you in that humble gesture—so long in abeyance—of the holy procession. Oh, how pleasing it was to God—and so displeasing to the devils that they tried to bring scandal out of it, both within and without, but the angels held them in check.... I remind you that Truth now desires you to devote all your care and concern to progressively establishing rule and order in God's Church, so far as you can in the time available. He will be working through you, giving you strength to accomplish and light to know whatever is required, together with wisdom and prudence in steering his Ship, and the will to do it.... And so you will overthrow tyrants and dispel the darkness of heresy by his power, for it is he who proclaims, and will proclaim, his truth."[24]

From a heart filled with gratitude at the developments at Castel Sant'Angelo, Catherine wrote to the Bandaresi, "the Maintainers of the Republic of Rome," on May sixth, unequivocally accepting them as the temporal rulers of the Eternal City. She first encouraged them to demonstrate their gratitude to God for their success by the purity of their lives, by abstaining from rash judgments, by fidelity to the church and to the Vicar of Christ. Then, aware of the insecurity of dealing with mercenary troops, she suggested that they show more gratitude to the Company of San Giorgio that had achieved the military successes for the Roman people and for the cause of Urban. "Bear yourselves chari-

---

[24] *I, Catherine*, 244-245.

tably and peacefully with them, in order that you may preserve them to your aid, and not let them have any cause for turning against you."[25] She also sent words of gratitude and encouragement to the Count of Cenci, and the members of his Company, still fighting in the area of Marino, perhaps conscious of a prevailing suspicion that they were being solicited to accept money from the Clementine forces to change their allegiance. "Keep in the field with the standard of the most holy Cross; think that the blood of these glorious martyrs is ever crying out in the sight of God, invoking his aid upon you. Think that this city is the garden of the blessed Christ and the very beginning of our faith, and, therefore, every one of his own accord should be filled with valor here.... We will do like Moses: for the people fought, and Moses prayed; and whilst he prayed, the people conquered. So shall we do, if only our prayer be pleasing and acceptable to God."[26]

Meanwhile, on May ninth, following the battle of Marino, convinced that no plan for war or resistance could succeed in Italy, Clement took refuge in the Kingdom of Naples, under the protection of Queen Giovanna. While Giovanna was entertaining the anti-pope royally, the Neapolitan populace, supportive of their fellow citizen, Urban, a native of Bari on the Adriatic coast of Naples, took to the streets surrounding the Queen's residence with cries of "Long Live Pope Urban." In fear for his life, Clement and his court left hastily to return to Sperlonga, where on May twenty-second, they embarked by ship for the journey to Avignon, arriving there on June twentieth.

In order to preserve peace in her kingdom, Giovanna, on May eighteenth, published a decree declaring the legitimacy of the Urbanist Papacy, together with her intention to dispatch am-

---

[25] Gardner, *Saint Catherine*, 309-310.
[26] Ibid., 310-311.

bassadors to Rome to complete her submission to Urban. Catherine was ecstatic with joy. She had long desired and encouraged the conversion of the Queen, perhaps because she was a strong woman in a position of power. But her jubilation was short lived. Within the month, fresh troops arrived to support Giovanna; her ambassadors were recalled from Rome; those who had rebelled against Clement's presence in the Kingdom were punished; and the Queen recanted her declaration for Urban. But her fate remained hanging in the balance, when another army, led by Charles of Durazzo, soon would make its way to Naples. Married to Giovanna's niece, Margherita, Durazzo had been promised title to the throne of Naples by Urban and would not hesitate to assume it. Indeed, when he finally arrived to do battle in Naples, his victory was stained by his imprisonment and murder by strangulation of the once powerful Giovanna, to whom Catherine had shown such fondness. Fortunately, Giovanna's death occurred when Catherine, herself, was far removed from worldly battles and more than likely unaware of this conclusion to her long struggle to win Giovanna's support for the cause of Urban. Gardner comments, "It is heartrending to find Catherine involved in this deplorable affair; but it is clear from her letters that she was merely Urban's tool, acting in good faith, without the slightest realization of the extent to which he and Charles were prepared to carry out the scheme."[27]

Meanwhile, the two popes settled into their separate jurisdictions, each seemingly strong enough to stand up to the other. From the well-organized grandeur of Avignon, Clement increased his activities to gain political and military support. From Rome, Urban initiated similar endeavors, still savoring the sweet taste of military victory, and in full expectation of final success. Unaware that Clement had received favorable support and backing

---

[27] Ibid., 324.

from the French Court, on June twelfth Urban issued an encyclical that assumed his position as true head of the church had been confirmed.[28] Then, for the second time, with Catherine's support, he tapped Raymond, still in Genoa, as his ambassador to approach King Charles of France, in the hope of gaining his affirmation and assistance. Since access overland from the east remained impossible, it was decided that Raymond's journey would take a circuitous route by way of Barcelona. Urban dispatched a message to the King of Barcelona introducing Raymond as his emissary in the hope that he would provide him safe passage over the border to France.[29]

Raymond was instructed to describe in detail the events of Urban's election, enthronement, and coronation, the Cardinals' public proclamations, their submission to all papal protocols for three months, and each specific situation that had occurred. Included also, were his recognition by Charles, the recently deceased Roman Emperor, as well as a lengthy list of those rulers and princes who acknowledged him as the true vicar of Christ and legitimate successor of St. Peter. Unfortunately, for a second time, Raymond's mission was unsuccessful. Cardinal Pedro de Luna,[30] once Raymond's close friend and supporter, now as deeply committed to the Clementine cause as he had been previously reluctant to commit to it, had been sent as Clement's legate to the King of Aragon. In this role, he had been instrumental in having several of Urban's apostolic appointees imprisoned and now used his influence to bar Raymond from access to the King of France by way of the Spanish Kingdom, just as surely as he had been deterred previously from the eastern borders of France.

---

[28] Levasti, 353-354.

[29] Gardner reports that the transcripts of these directives remain in the Vatican Archives, 316.

[30] He would become the second pope of the Avignon Papacy following the death of Clement.

Raymond remained in Genoa as Provincial of the Lombardy Province of a divided Dominican Order whose Master General, Elias of Toulouse, had transferred his allegiance to Clement.[31] He informed Catherine by letter of the failure of this second mission, begging her not to judge his courage by her standards and not to love him less because he had failed her. Her reply encouraged him that her love for him remained strong, but did not conceal her disappointment. Comparing human love to faith that is general, applying to all people, and particular "in the case of those bound together by a closer love," she spoke of "the very close and special love between" them, continuing, "It would seem, from what I have understood by your letter, that you have been struggling with conflicts and thoughts of all kinds occasioned by the devil's wiles and your own hyper-sensitiveness, for you thought the burden was too heavy for you and also that you were not big enough to be measured by my standards. And so you began to wonder whether I loved and cared for you as much as before.... I love you with the love with which I love myself, and so I firmly believe that what is lacking on your part, God in his goodness will provide! But it did not turn out like that, for you found ways of laying down your burden. And then so many scraps of excuses to cover over your faithless frailty—but not enough to keep me from seeing a good deal of it, and I can only hope it will be seen by no one else."[32]

Once again, Catherine raised a standard of strength and courage not attainable by the ordinary human. "Had you been faithful, you would not have been so vacillating, nor would you have become so mistrustful of God, and of myself; instead, like a faithful and readily obedient son you would have set about doing whatever you could manage to do. And if you could not go upright,

---

[31] Levasti, 364.
[32] *I, Catherine,* L. 57, 248-249. This someone else has been interpreted to be Urban.

you might have gone on all fours; if not as a friar, then as a pilgrim or, if you had no money, as a beggar. Faithful obedience like this would have achieved more in God's sight and in men's hearts than all our human prudence." As she continued, it became apparent that Catherine's disappointment with Raymond was part of a larger frustration, for she confessed, "Day and night I was being constrained by God concerning many other things too; all of which have come to nothing through lack of earnestness on the part of those who were to accomplish them, but most of all through my own sins which bar the way to all good. And so, alas, we see ourselves drowning, and offenses against God increasing with countless torments, while I am in torment. May God soon take me out of this dark life."[33] What is also revealed in this letter, is the influence that Catherine had exercised with Urban, when she suggests that she "did what she could to get someone sent to the King of France" and that Urban welcomed her idea of making direct contact with the King of Hungary, a task for which Raymond had also been considered. "Now," she continued, "it's up to the graciousness of the Holy Spirit to bring it about. On our own we do a shoddy job."

Further insight is given to the climate of Catherine's own life, as she encouraged Raymond not to listen to the "worldly-minded mockery, treachery and reproach the persecutors of holy Church have in store for you." And then, "You ask me to pray for our Order, and I you, for when I hear how things are, I feel my heart break within me. Generally speaking, our Province is still faithful to Pope Urban and to the Vicar of the Order who, I must say in all honesty, is conducting himself very well and being very prudent—for such times as ours—in his dealings within the Order, and with those who wickedly deny the truth.... Our most holy Father has ordered him and given him full authority,

---

[33] Ibid., 250.

to absolve all those Provincials who deny the truth about him." Then, she mentions Dominic, "our sweet Spaniard" and his "Order that has always proclaimed the faith, but is now contaminating it. This grieves me to death. All I can do is to end my life in weeping and great affliction." The Vicar to whom Catherine referred was Fra Tommaso Pozzalosco, who previously served as Provincial of Upper Lombardy. He would convene a General Chapter to meet in Bologna in 1380, but not live to see it. Raymond replaced him as Provincial and would be elected Master of the Order when the Chapter convened.[34]

Part of Catherine's grief is disappointment in her friends: in Raymond, for example, and in the holy circle she had gathered with such optimism, and who contributed so little to the lessening of conflict. Finally, Levasti suggests further cause for discouragement, "because the political ideas she defended no longer aroused a lively interest in her circle," and in the general atmosphere of strife, "the morality of the clergy became corrupt, and the faithful, bewildered and disgusted, grew indifferent or skeptical. Such great fissures appeared in the fabric of the Church that men feared it might crash to the ground."[35] More and more often, as the weeks passed, words of sorrow and heartache surfaced, but never despair. To Catherine, God's church was not merely a human institution and, no matter how distressing or discouraging the situation became, her faith in God would remain unshaken.

---

[34] Raymond of Capua, Introduction, xxiii.
[35] Levasti, 363-364.

- 3 -
The Family: Rome, Siena, Naples

It is not every heart that is able to share its love with
many friends, and yet to love them all with any degree of intensity. The common verdict of mankind is
in favor of the theory that affection, to be worth anything, must be limited to few, if not to one; and that
what it gains by diffusion, it loses in force. Those,
however, who hold that the perfection of love on earth
must be found in its resemblance to the charity which
reigns in heaven, will not readily yield the point that
in the heart of man, as in the house of God, there are
"many mansions"; and that if one such a heart be
purified from selfishness, there is absolutely no limit
to its power of loving. Such a heart was St. Catherine's.

Augusta T. Drane[36]

Catherine's daily activities in Rome, in addition to confer-
ences with the pope and his advisors, brought her frequently to
the Vatican offices seeking indulgences for friends, especially
those living in areas under interdict. In this way, the pope's secretary, Tommaso Petra, became a friend and follower. The family entertained multitudes of visitors: disciples, friends, foreign-
ers, and admirers, who came to her door seeking counsel and/
or consolation, or simply desirous to meet and pray with the renowned holy woman. All were received with hospitality, often
sharing in a meal provided by alms, sought in the streets of the
city by her fellow tertiaries, and often by Catherine herself. Each
day she attended Mass, received Communion, and spent long intervals in prayer, in charitable works, in dictating letters to pro-

---

[36] *The History of Saint Catherine and Her Companions*, 226.

mote the cause of Urban's papacy, and countless other endeavors dedicated to a similar purpose.[37]

These consuming activities limited her correspondence with her devoted family remaining in Siena. However, letters exchanged among Catherine's followers there, and those in Rome, kept members of the family informed about each other. Stephano was still unable to join them in Rome, ostensibly because of the illness of his brother, but more likely because of his mother's unwillingness to part with him, as well as Catherine's reluctance to give her reason for complaint. "You must not irritate or trouble your parents more than can be helped," she told him.[38] How deeply he felt the separation can be seen in his message, "Remember me to all our poor family, each one in order, bearing in mind that the head and every member is fixed in the very centre of my heart."[39] Barduccio and Stephano, in particular, felt mutually deprived of the other's company; their lives were dull without this companionship. Those in Rome kept Stephano busy delivering messages and resolving personal situations that arose in Siena, such as taking care of Monna Lapa's home. He was charged with the responsibility of looking after all the family members remaining in Siena and all the local needs that arose in their absence.

For some reason the interdict, the consequence of Siena's participation in the anti-papal league with Florence, had not yet been lifted nor had the port of Talamone been returned. Many religious Sienese were distressed by this and evaded the consequences by enrolling themselves as members of the house of a visiting Bishop and participating in the Mass and sacraments with him. Stephano consulted Catherine on this matter, and she re-

---

[37] Levasti, 371.
[38] Drane, II, 208.
[39] Ibid., 216.

plied that he had made a proper choice not to do this, advising him to wait patiently for the official end. Whenever she could, Catherine procured indulgences and privileges from Urban for her followers and did what she could to hasten the final settlement of the problem.

Catherine's major concern was the role of Siena in the question of the schism. She charged her disciples to keep her informed of public opinion in the city. From Siena, Christofano tried to assure her that all was well in that regard; however, as the military engagements proceeded, the question turned to money. The battle of Marino had been a tremendous success for Urban's cause, but financial expenditures had significantly drained the Vatican resources. At Urban's behest, Catherine encouraged her associates in Siena to pressure those in authority to support the pope in this need. She wrote directly to the ruling Defenders of the Republic urging them to demonstrate their gratitude to the pope for addressing the problems of the interdict and the port of Talamone.[40] She also appealed to her disciples in the La Scala confraternity, the Company of the Blessed Virgin, to show their gratitude both spiritually, by their prayers, and temporally, by pressuring the Magistrates of the Republic to come to the monetary aid of their pontiff. Stephano, who would deliver these missives, was directed to make this need known to whomever he met, "Try not to be tepid, but stir up the brethren and chiefs of the Company that they may do their utmost. If you and your brethren were what you ought to be, you would kindle all Italy."[41] Christofano wrote to Neri, in Rome, expressing the reality of the situation. In spiritual matters the Sienese would obey the Holy Father; however, the republic was financially strained from the necessity of providing large monthly sums for the defense of the

---

[40] Ibid., 217.
[41] Ibid., 218.

city from mercenary fighters ravaging the area. Eventually, a band of troops was sent to Rome to assist in the protection of the pope.

Christofano expressed his desire to join the others in Rome for Easter if his colleagues would allow it, and then posed a request, "Tell Mamma we are rather falling to pieces; I wish she would give us some sort of a rule, which for her sake we would obey, and meet together at certain times in her name; and beg her to write to her wandering sheep, though we are all well assured she does not forget us in her prayers."[42] Catherine's response suggested a spiritual society, common to the times, having regular meetings with "all serving Him without measure, not in your own way, but His; not choosing times and places, or seeking consolation, or refusing trials, but embracing suffering for the honor of God. Follow Christ crucified, macerating your bodies by watching, fasting and prayer. Resign your wills to the sweet will of God, and let your Society be a society of His servants." She then counseled them against idle conversation and criticism of others, recommending detachment and perseverance. She closed, "If I do not write to you, I nevertheless always love you, and occupy myself about your salvation in the presence of God. Have courage then, and love one another."[43] From this exchange, it is clear that Catherine had no intention or desire that these followers form any type of permanent religious or monastic association. Rather her expectation was that of a spiritually bonded group that would energize and guide its members to live good, holy, and purposeful lives. Supporting this proposal, in one of her recorded prayers from this period we find, "I pray also for those you have put into my desire with a special love: set their hearts so afire that they may be coals not dead but alight and ablaze with charity for you and for their neighbors. Thus in time of need they will have their

---

[42] Ibid.
[43] Ibid., 213-214.

ships well equipped for themselves as well as for others."[44]

With the situation in Naples still in flux, Neri, accompanied by the Abbot of Lislo, had been dispatched there as Catherine's emissary, in an effort to win back Queen Giovanna to Urban's cause. Fra Bartolomeo, in a letter dated September first, sent to comfort Neri, separated from the others, updated him on events within the family, about their daily life, about Catherine's activities with Urban, and about the alms they were receiving from friends. His closing comment, "Our mother has several times thought she was coming [to Naples]; but it does not seem to be the will of God, and the Pope does not consent, though at first he said that he wished it. I fancy now we must think no more about it," suggests that Neri still had expectations of being joined in Naples by Catherine, and once again, was disappointed.[45] Catherine, herself, wrote to him often, aware that he was miserable, especially in witnessing so many offenses against God.[46]

Appearances also suggest that Urban's reliance on Catherine as an advisor was waning, and that Catherine, herself, was aware of it. In one of her final letters to him she stated, "I should have come instead of writing, but did not wish to weary you by coming so often. Have patience with me; for I shall never cease urging you, by prayer, and by word of mouth or letter, as long as I live, until I see in you and in Holy Church what I desire, for which I know you desire, much more than I, to give your life."[47]

---

[44] *The Prayers of Catherine of Siena*, #18, March 25, 1379, 163-164.

[45] Drane, II, 221.

[46] Curtayne, 188.

[47] Gardner, *Saint Catherine*, 330.

- 4 -
The Final Months

Her death-agony began when the Romans at the beginning of January rebelled against the Pope and threatened to take his life. Broken with sorrow at this new horror, Catherine could do nothing but pray her Bridegroom not to allow such a terrible crime to occur. While she prayed, she saw with her inner sight how the whole town was flooded with devils who tried to incite the people to patricide. They screamed at the virgin: "Damned woman, do you dare to stand up against us? Do not doubt we shall see to it that you die a terrible death." She never replied, only continued to pray, for the people and for the Pope.

Sigrid Undset[48]

Toward the close of 1379, Catherine and her followers moved from the Rione della Colonna to a house nearer to the Church of the Minerva. On December fourth, she informed Neri, still in Naples, "We have taken a house near San Biaggio, between the Campo de' Fiori and Sant' Eustacio, and we think to return [to Siena] before Easter, by the grace of God."[49] It was this house, in the present Via Chiara, where her last illness occurred. Here, from January thirtieth to April twenty-ninth, she endured a prolonged torment of body and soul, and offered herself as a willing victim for the church.

Soon after the opening of the new year, Rome experienced fierce internal turbulence, an episode that plays a significant role in Catherine's story, since it coincided with her physical decline.

---

[48] *Catherine of Siena*, 264.
[49] Gardner, *Saint Catherine*, 329.

A Roman Prefect, Francesco di Vico, had unlawfully usurped control of the city of Viterbo and, when approached by Roman authorities, had reacted insolently and rudely. In response, the Magistrates of the Republic assembled a Council General to deal with the offender, planning to report their decisions to Urban, in deference to him as ruler of the Papal States. Aware of Urban's volatile temperament and the tenuous relationship between the papacy and the citizenry, Catherine was concerned that he would not receive these Magistrates with respect. In what is believed to be her final letter to Urban, she urged him to follow the example set by the sixth century pope, Gregory the Great, in governing the Republic with prudence "so that your firmness grounded in truth may be evident in the sight of God and men" and to receive the ambassadors "with as much gentleness as you can" reminding him of the necessity for himself and for the church to preserve "this people in obedience and reverence to your Holiness... so that loss, shame, and confusion may not follow later." Revealing her awareness of events transpiring in the city, of the "violence of wrath and irreverence toward the Roman ambassadors" shown by the Prefect, she asked Urban to continue to meet with the Magistrates frequently, and to "bind them prudently with the bands of love."[50] One can sense that Catherine, already aware that her advice was no longer as welcome as before, was cautious in her language. Referring to God as the "Ruler and Helper of the ship of Holy Church, and of your Holiness," she continued, "Be manful for me, in the holy fear of God; wholly exemplary in your words, your habits and all your deeds. Let all shine clear in the sight of God and men; as a light placed in the candlestick of Holy Church, to which looks and should look all the Christian people."[51]

---

[50] Scudder, 335.
[51] Ibid., 334 -335.

This last letter to Urban was dictated to Barduccio on the evening of Monday, January 30, 1380, the day following the first of several strokes that would continue to afflict her. "After we had written a letter," Barduccio wrote to a Florentine religious, "she had another stroke, so much more terrible that we all mourned for her as dead, and she remained for a long space of time, in such a state that no sign of life appeared in her; then, after several hours she rose up, and it did not seem that she was herself."[52] Her experience takes on new and mystical meaning in Catherine's letter to Raymond, when she describes the city, filled with demons, urging the citizenry to anger and frustration, so as to attack and destroy the Vicar of Christ.

"After a while, the demons began terrorizing me," she wrote, "to such an extent that I was absolutely stunned; they seemed to be raging against me as if a worm like me had been responsible for snatching from them what had long been theirs in Holy Church. Such was the terror, and the physical pain, that I wanted to flee from the study and take refuge in the chapel, almost as if the study itself was responsible for my agony. So I rose up and, being unable to move on my own, leaned on my son Barduccio. But I was immediately thrown down and, once down, my soul seemed to have left the body.... I saw that I could not move its tongue or any other part of it in any way, except as one would move a lifeless corpse. So I left the body alone, just as it was, while my understanding remained fixed in the abyss of the Trinity. My memory was filled with the thought of the needs of holy Church and of all Christians, and I cried out in God's presence, asking with confidence for divine help, offering him my desires and constraining him by the blood of the Lamb and by all the suffering that had been endured.... Then I was filled with wonder, while there remained such a pain in my heart that I have it

---

[52] Gardner, *Saint Catherine*, 332.

still. From that moment, every delight, every respite, every food, was taken from me and when, later, they carried me upstairs, the room seemed full of devils who launched into a fresh attack, the most terrible I have ever endured, in an attempt to make me believe and see that it was not I myself in my body, but an unclean spirit.... For two days and nights these storms went on.... Then on the feast of Mary's Purification [February second] I wanted to hear Mass. All the mysteries were then renewed, as God revealed the great need that there was—as later became apparent, for Rome had been on the verge of revolt, buzzing with slanderous and irreverent talk, but God put ointment on their hearts and I believe all will end well."[53]

Indeed, shortly after, as the unrest among the citizens developed into open confrontation, they stormed the Vatican. Urban ordered the gates thrown open, allowed the citizens to enter, and received them, seated on his throne in full ceremonial dress. That the confrontation ended peacefully was generally attributed to Catherine's prayers, but how much her pleas for patience and prudence in dealing with the Roman officials influenced Urban's behavior cannot be know. Gardner considered the respect in which she was held by the leader of the Roman republicans, Giovanni Cenci, to have been of pivotal influence in what he identifies as "her last political work, and surely not the least noble of her achievements."[54]

From this time forward, Catherine's experience of pain was as continuous as was her prayer for the resolution of the Roman situation and of the church in general. She revealed to Raymond that God had required that, throughout Lent, she should hear Mass every morning at sunrise for the intention of holy church. Then, "When it is time for Terce, and I get up from Mass, you would

---

[53] I, Catherine, L. 60, 267-269.
[54] Gardner, Saint Catherine, 332.

see a dead woman going to St. Peter's, where I take up again my toil in the barque of holy Church. And there I remain until it is nearly time for Vespers, nor would I ever wish to leave that place, night or day, until I see this people a little more firmly established [in peace] with their father."[55] Thus began her routine for the season of Lent.

Barduccio described her daily morning prayer as "of such intensity, that one hour of prayer more consumed that poor little body than two days on the rack would have done another. Therefore, every morning with tears we lifted her up after communion, in such a state that who saw her deemed her dead, and carried her to her couch. And, after an hour or two, she would rise up, and we went to San Pietro, which is a long mile from us, and she set herself to prayer, and she remained there until nearly vespers, after which she returned home, so exhausted that she seemed a dead woman; and acting thus she continued, every day in the same way, until the third Sunday of Lent."[56] It was then, as she prayed before Giotto's mosaic of the *Navicella*, she felt that Christ laid the crushing weight of the ship of his church on her shoulders. Her disciples carried her home and placed her on her couch, from which she rose only once more. "She lay in this way for eight weeks" recorded Barduccio, "without raising her head, full of such intolerable torments from head to foot, that she ofttimes said, 'these are not bodily natural pains, but I seem to have given leave to the demons to torment this body at their pleasure.'"[57]

Tommaso Petra, the papal secretary who was devoted to Catherine, visited her when he heard of her illness. Seeing the gravity of her condition, he urged her to call together her fol-

---

[55] *I, Catherine*, L. 60, 269.

[56] Gardner, *Saint Catherine*, 332-333.

[57] Ibid., 344.

lowers and counsel them for the future. On his advice, she gathered all her spiritual sons and daughters who were in Rome and spoke lovingly to them. First, she spoke in general of the spiritual life: that the heart could not be given completely to God unless it was free, open, pure and single; the need to acquire a love and a readiness for holy obedience to the commands of God and of superiors; the necessity of humble, faithful and continuous prayer to nourish virtue in the soul; to attain purity of mind by withholding judgment of one's neighbor and empty talk about his doings; to have a great confidence in divine providence, and lastly to love one another.

Then she commanded them never to lessen their desire for the reformation of holy church and to pray continually for the Holy Father, the Vicar of Christ. Of herself she declared, "Long while I have borne this desire; but especially, now more than seven years ago, it seemed that God put this exercise and inflamed desire into my soul. And, from then until now, no time has ever passed without my offering it up before the Divine Goodness, with mournful and painful and sweet desires; and it has pleased His Goodness for this to lay upon this weak body and make it bear diverse and varied infirmities and sufferings. But, especially at the present time, it seems that my sweet Creator, as he did with Job, has given leave to the demons to torment and smite as they please.... And now, at the last, it seems to me that my most sweet Bridegroom, after so much inflamed and panting desire, so many sufferings and bodily infirmities, wills that my soul should utterly leave this dark prison and return to her source. I speak not as though I saw the certainty of His will in this, but it seems to me so."[58]

Catherine reminded them that she had given her life in the church and for the church and consoled them that she was leav-

---

[58] Ibid., 346-347.

ing a place of great suffering to rest in the peaceful sea of God to be united with her sweet Bridegroom and that she would always be with them even more perfectly. Then, she called each one by name, telling them what she wished them to do to serve God in the future. Alessa should be the mother and head of her daughters who were Mantellate; her sons should have Raymond[59] as their father and leader. One by one, she called her disciples to her side and gave them advice; some should go to monastic orders, some should be priests, and others should be hermits. Then, as she begged their pardon if she had failed them in any way and for any pain or sorrow that she had been to them, one by one, the weeping disciples came forward and she blessed each one individually in Christ.[60]

On the eve of Holy Saturday, March twenty-fourth, when Fra Bartolomeo who had been called back to Siena to serve as Prior of the Monastery of San Domenico, visited the family in Rome, he was shocked at her appearance. On Easter Sunday, her thirty-third birthday, he offered Mass in her room. She rose to receive Holy Communion from his hands, collapsed back into her couch, but recovered her speech enough to talk coherently with him during the few days he remained in Rome. She revealed to him that Raymond would soon be chosen as Master General of their order and told Bartolomeo that he must always help him and be obedient to him.[61] Since he had to return to Siena, he implored her to give some sign of her restoration to health. Next morning before he left, she was joyful and talkative, embraced him and bade him to depart. Perhaps at Bartolomeo's urging,

---

[59] "Shortly before she left this world at noon on Sunday, April twenty-ninth, she named William Flete director of the famiglia." Hackett, 98. This is believed to be due to her foreknowledge that Raymond would become Master General of the Dominicans.

[60] Undset, 277-278.

[61] Ibid., 275.

Stephano arrived in Rome a few days later, though he is said to have heard a voice interrupt his prayer at the La Scala alerting him to her condition. It was he who, at Catherine's direction, wrote what would be her last letter to Bartolomeo and his companions at San Domenico, asking their prayers to the "Bridegroom Jesus to suffer me to offer up my life, even to the shedding of my blood for His glory, to illumine the face of the Church."[62] To Neri, still obediently in Naples, she sent a special message.

In her final letter to Raymond, she placed him, Bartolomeo, Tommaso and Giovanni Tantucci in charge of her book, and all her writings that they could find, to "do with them what you see will be most to the honor of God." To this list, she also added Tommaso Petra, the papal secretary. Then, to Raymond, she added another request, "be a shepherd and ruler to this Family, as a father, keeping them in the joy of charity and in perfect union; that they be not scattered as a sheep without a shepherd." Her final words were a request for forgiveness, "Pardon me, that I have written you words of bitterness. I do not write them, however, to cause you bitterness, but because I am in doubt, and do not know what the Goodness of God will do with me. I wish to have done my duty. And do not feel regret because we are separated one from the other in the body; although you would have been the very greatest consolation to me, greater are my consolation and gladness to see the fruit that you are bearing in Holy Church. And now I beg you to labor more zealously, for she never had so great a need: and do you never depart for any persecution without permission from our lord the Pope. Comfort you in Christ sweet Jesus, without any bitterness. I say no more to you."[63]

Her death came on April twenty-ninth, the Sunday before the Ascension, after long and continuous suffering. A few hours

---

[62] Gardner, *Saint Catherine*, 349.
[63] Scudder, 352.

before dawn, the spiritual family was called together. Fra Giovanni Tantucci gave her absolution; she received the indulgence for the hour of death granted by the pope, and Extreme Unction was administered by the Abbot of Sant'Antimo. Her struggle with the demons continued to the end and, as if in response to an accusation, once she said aloud, "Never vainglory, but always the true glory and praise of Jesus Christ crucified." She spoke to those of her spiritual family who had not been present for her previous final blessing, and she told each one, as she had done the others, what she wanted them to do after she was gone. To Stephano, in particular, she spoke forcefully, "And you, in virtue of holy obedience, I command in the name of God to go by all means to the Carthusian order, for God has called and chosen you to that."[64]

As the end was drawing near, Catherine prayed especially for the church and for Urban, whom she declared to be the true pontiff and Vicar of Christ on earth. She prayed for all her children whom God had given her, saying, "Father, they are Thine, and Thou gavest them to me, and now I give them back to Thee. Eternal Father, do Thou keep and guard them; and I pray that none of them may be snatched out of Thy hands."[65] Then she signed and blessed them and those who were not able to be present. Barduccio wrote that she spoke "with such tenderness that we thought our hearts would cleave asunder."[66] She continued praying with her followers until her last breath, held in the loving arms of Alessa and in the presence of her elderly mother, Lapa. At the end, she exclaimed several times, "Blood, Blood"; then softly said, "Father, into Thy hands I commend my spirit." And bowing her head, she breathed her last.[67] In Levasti's words,

---

[64] Gardner, *Saint Catherine*, 350.

[65] Drane, II, 270.

[66] Ibid., n. 2.

[67] Ibid., 271.

"Only a few minutes before her death did she finally cease from every desire and invocation for others, and turn to God alone, with a long sigh of surrender, and with unspeakable joy."[68]

Though Raymond was far away in Pisa, he was in her thoughts. He wrote in the *Legenda* that, at the very moment of her death, he heard a voice speaking "not to the ear of my body, but to that of my soul" saying, "Fear absolutely nothing. I am here for you. I am in heaven for you. I will protect and defend you. Do not be anxious; do not be afraid; I stand here for you."[69] At that point in time, Raymond, not yet aware of her death, was preparing to leave for the Dominican Chapter in Bologna, which would, as Catherine had predicted, elect him Master General of the Urbanist portion of the Dominican Order. It was then that he understood who had been speaking to him, and the import of the message. Her words would comfort him as he undertook the daunting task of reforming the Dominican Order under his jurisdiction, to return it to its original ideals, observances, and way of life.

In the moments following Catherine's death, the family locked the doors and windows of the house to keep out all but the intimate family and gave themselves up to their grief, taking consolation in being alone together. The secrecy continued until arrangements were made to bring her body to the Dominican Church of Santa Maria Sopra Minerva on Tuesday evening. Stephano reported that her body "remained fresh, of devout and angelic beauty, and emitting a sweet fragrance; her arms, hands, fingers, feet, and neck, and all her other members, being as flexible as though her holy soul had not departed from the body."[70] It was Stephano, accompanied by Barduccio, who carried her body to the Minerva, where they placed it behind an

---

[68] Levasti, 313.

[69] Raymond of Capua, #368, 341-342.

[70] Ibid.

iron grille, to safeguard it from people's devotion.[71] Both stood guard over the body as long as it was exposed. As the news circulated in the city, people flocked to the Minerva to venerate the still figure in the white dress and black cloak. They thronged the grille, bringing their sick in unending processions; many cures occurred, strengthening their devotion and excitement. At one point, Fra Giovanni Tantucci went up into the pulpit to address the assembly, but the crowd was such that no one was prepared to listen. He said, "She speaks better for herself," and gave up the effort.

Urban presided over a magnificent requiem carried out with impressive solemnity, and Giovanni Cenci, the Senator of Rome, had a second requiem of equal solemnity offered in the name of the Roman people. Gardner commented, "Thus, for one brief moment, did the Papacy and the Republic of Rome seem to meet in harmony and unity by the side of Catherine's tomb."[72]

On the second anniversary of Catherine's death, her teacher and disciple, William Flete, the hermit of Lecceto, to whom she had given charge of her family on her deathbed, composed a sermon to honor her memory. This lengthy testimony of praise, probably not delivered publicly, but spoken from Flete's heart, would anticipate the later honors that the church would bestow upon her. "In her letters and writings, in her knowledge and teaching, she was not Paul, but a Paula: a teacher of teachers, a pastor of pastors, an abyss of wisdom... an untiring preacher of the truth. She deserves to be called teacher of teachers, for she was a teacher both in her way of life and her knowledge, for her teaching is not earthly but heavenly: hence it ought to be especially guaranteed by Christ and approved of by the Church of God.... She deserves the title of teacher of teachers because she brought light to every point, every doubt: she saw the truth in the eternal Word.

---

[71] Curtayne, 202.

[72] Gardner, *Saint Catherine*, 352.

It was not the same with other teachers, for it was not she who spoke but the Holy Spirit spoke in her, and she was the instrument of the Holy Spirit."[73]

It would be some time before Raymond, occupied with his new responsibilities, could return to Rome to visit Catherine's grave in the small cemetery attached to the Dominican Monastery of the Minerva. By his direction, on October 3, 1383, her remains were removed from the cypress coffin that had been her resting place, and interred in a marble tomb inside the church.[74] Many changes would take place in the process. With papal permission, her head was removed from her body and encased in a reliquary to be transported to Siena. Other parts of her body were removed and given as sacred relics to her closest disciples.

Less than a year later, on May 5, 1384, when Raymond was able to be present in Siena to participate, the whole city came together to celebrate their saintly daughter. A solemn, but joyful, procession wound its way through the streets carrying the splendid reliquary containing Catherine's head to its final resting place in the Church of San Domenico. In addition to the dignitaries of the Commune, her eighty-year-old mother Lapa, followed by her remaining disciples, Dominican friars, and Mantellate, were part of the procession. Neither Alessa nor Barduccio lived to see this great honor, but undoubtedly enjoyed looking down on it, with Catherine, from their heavenly abode.[75]

Catherine's formal canonization by the church was delayed by the continuing schism that came to an end at the Council of Constance in 1417, but the title "saint" or "*beatissima*" was applied to her, informally, by devotees far and wide. By the

---

[73] Hackett, 194-195.

[74] Lodovico Ferretti, O.P., *Saint Catherine of Siena*, 156.

[75] Curtayne, 205; Alessa died in Rome soon after Catherine's death and Barduccio died in Siena in December of 1382.

pontificate of the Sienese Pope Pius II, conditions were such that he could respond in 1461 to the thousands of petitions that had accumulated in the eighty-one years since her death, and she was formally awarded the title of saint. In 1637, the room where she died was dismantled and reconstructed in the sacristy of the Minerva. This church was rebuilt and rededicated in 1855, and Catherine's body was carried in procession throughout the city of Rome as it was taken to her new resting place under the main altar. In 1866, Pius IX declared Catherine the co-patron of Rome and in 1939 Pius XII proclaimed her, with Saint Francis of Assisi, co-patron of Italy.[76]

Her final honor came in 1970, when Pope Paul VI declared her a Doctor of the Church, opening his pronouncement with the words, "Spiritual exaltation bursts into our soul as we proclaim the humble and wise Dominican virgin a Doctor of the Church." Among the many facets of her life and work illustrated in his homily were the foundational role of the Beatitudes as a model of superlative truth and beauty in Catherine's life and exterior activity; how she hungered for justice and was filled with mercy; and her infused wisdom, the result of her charism of wisdom directly infused from the Holy Spirit, which Paul VI affirmed as "a mystic charism." Her letters were described as "like so many sparks from a mysterious fire, lit in her ardent heart by Infinite Love, that is, the Holy Spirit." Finally, his declaration avowed, "We may therefore say that Catherine was the *mystic of the mystical Body of Christ, that is, of the Church*," a church that she had declared to be "nothing else but Christ Himself," and to whom she always felt it her duty to give reverence and obedience and work for interior reform, always in communion and filial obedience to Christ's rightful representatives.[77]

---

[76] Ibid., 158-159.
[77] *L'Osservatore Romano,* October 15, 1970, 6-7, *passim.*

- 5 -
Conclusions

Now it remains to say how one can tell that a soul has attained perfect love. The sign is the same as that given to the holy disciples after they had received the Holy Spirit. They left the house and fearlessly preached my message by proclaiming the teaching of the Word, my only-begotten Son. They had no fear of suffering. No, they even gloried in suffering. It did not worry them to go before the tyrants of the world to proclaim the truth to them for the glory and praise of my name. So it is with the soul who has waited for me in self-knowledge: I come back to her with the fire of my charity. In that charity she conceived the virtues through perseverance when she stayed at home, sharing in my power.   Catherine of Siena[78]

Catherine was a woman of many simultaneous contradictions, yet a woman whom God could utilize as a human instrument of transformation, conversion, and even salvation for many. She was a young, single, laywoman living in a traditional male dominated medieval society; yet, having answered God's call, she entered courageously into the affairs of a church and world marked by strife, discord, and seemingly insoluble challenges. She was a public figure and, at the same time, a contemplative mystic who, following her Dominican charism, kept the two roles in balance, continually integrating love of God and neighbor, rooting this authentic love of God in the truth of gospel revelation, and going out among those in need both near and far.[79]

---

[78] *The Dialogue*, #74, 136.

[79] Benedict Ashley, "Saint Catherine and Contemplative Spirituality," 1-2.

She was singularly uneducated, yet acknowledged as a theologian and doctor of the church whose formative sources were the ordinary virtues of faith, hope, and charity, and the gifts of the Holy Spirit, available to all, but in Catherine to a higher degree of perfection.[80] She was a dedicated advocate of God's church, while remaining a fierce but loving critic whose purpose was "to speak the truth in love."[81] Finally, brilliantly successful in the eyes of many, she was, seemingly, a fruitless failure in accomplishing her overarching goal. She had taken upon herself the entire responsibility for the church; her aspirations were enormous; she thought she could accomplish all for God, for humanity, and especially for the church. Levasti called her "the prophet of the ideal," one who longed to take all humanity with her as she soared in spirit to the azure heavens; to spiritualize all humankind, to be an integrating part of the humanity she loved and wished to save.[82]

Although Catherine's own prayer life was often extraordinary, this was not the central significance of her teaching. Her mystic spirituality has relevance today primarily because it adheres so closely to the heart of gospel teaching. Her principal concern was to become an agent of service and transformation, to "gaze with the 'eye of faith' into the clear light of the gospel and, by this light to work ceaselessly for the renewal of the church, of the world, and of those dear friends who had need of her."[83] It is this "fidelity to daily life in faith, hope, and love" that exemplifies what the theologian Karl Rahner called the "mysticism of everyday life," a mysticism of infused contemplation, in which God gratuitously makes himself known to the individual.

---

[80] Conleth Kearns, "The Wisdom of Saint Catherine," 342.

[81] Mary Catherine Hilkert, O.P., *Speaking with Authority: Catherine of Siena and the Voices of Women Today,* 143 and *passim.*

[82] Levasti, 313.

[83] Benedict Ashley, "Guide to Saint Catherine's Dialogue," 248.

Going a step further, Rahner wrote, "The Christian of the future will be a mystic or will not be a Christian anymore"; that is, every Christian will undergo a "genuine experience of God emerging from the very heart of our existence."[84] Moving mysticism from the margins of Christian life to the very center of people's every day experience introduces a standard for the future already modeled by Catherine in a mysticism that was both ecclesial and directed to the service of her neighbor and the needs of the church and world.

In the text of *The Dialogue*, the most profound work of this "teacher of teachers," Catherine spoke these respectful yet persistent words of petition, relevant in every time, even in our own. "You said, eternal Father, that because of your love for your creatures, and through the prayers and innocent sufferings of your servants, you would be merciful to the world and reform Holy Church, and thus give us refreshment. Do not wait any longer then, to turn the eye of your mercy. Because if it is your will to answer before we call, answer now with the voice of your mercy."[85] Then, in God's voice, words of comfort and guidance, "Be as little sheep in the garden of holy Church, grazing there in holy longing and constant prayer. Offer these to me on their behalf [unworthy ministers] so that I may be merciful to the world. Do not let either assault or prosperity cause you to abandon this grazing. I mean, I do not want you to raise your heads either in impatience or inordinate gladness. Rather, be humbly attentive to my honor, the salvation of souls, and the reform of holy Church. This will be a sign to me that you and the others love me in truth."[86]

This simple directive is available to all people of good faith,

---

[84] Harvey D. Egan, S.J., *What Are They Saying About Mysticism?*, 100, 104.
[85] *The Dialogue*, #134, 275-276.
[86] Ibid., #133, 272.

though the twenty-first century offers a different world view from Catherine's fourteenth century. The church that she knew is no longer one, but now all followers of Christ might be seen as one people, one church, not necessarily in name but in spirit. Today, she would ask, who is doing God's work on earth, loving and serving their neighbor, attending to those in need, living their lives in such a way that God can speak through them? An active ministry need not necessarily be a public one, but one that, allowing the simplest acts of faith, hope, and love to permeate daily life, gives root to the paradigm of the future, a mysticism of everyday life. With Catherine, all may strive to integrate knowledge of self in the knowledge of God, to nourish the tree of the church with the requisite virtues of humility, patience, and charity, as well as the important graft of discernment, so that this tree can flourish with a vibrant crown of good works. Then, like the Weeping Beech in the springtime, the tree of the church will bloom again and again. New life brings new hope, hope that repeatedly comes to birth in the human heart. Through God's grace, there will always be holy people, dedicated people, and God will speak through them to nourish the church that God has promised to be with to the end of time.

Bibliography

Catherinian Sources: Primary

Catherine of Siena. *The Dialogue,* tr. by Suzanne Noffke, O.P., Paulist Press, New York, 1983.

I Necrologi di San Domenico in Camporegio (Epocha Cateriniana, October, 1336-December, 1430), a cura di M. H. Laurent. Vol. XX in *Fontes Vitae S. Catharinae Senensis Historici,* cura et studio M. Hyacinthi Laurent O.P. et Francisci Valli (Università di Siena, Cattedra Cateriniana), 1937.

I, Catherine: Selected Letters of Saint Catherine of Siena, Kenelm Foster, O.P. and Mary John Ronayne, O.P., eds. & trs., Collins, London, 1980.

Raymond of Capua. *Legenda Major,* tr. Conleth Kearns, O.P., under the title *The Life of Catherine of Siena,* Michael Glazier, Inc., Delaware, 1980.

The Letters of St. Catherine of Siena, Vol. I & II, ed. & tr. by Suzanne Noffke, O.P., Arizona Center for Renaissance Studies, Tempe, Arizona, 2000.

The Prayers of Catherine of Siena, ed. by Suzanne Noffke, O.P., Paulist Press, New York, 1983.

Catherinian Sources: Secondary

Ashley, Benedict. "A Guide to St. Catherine's Dialogue," 237-247, in *Cross and Crown,* 1977, Vol. 29, 237-249.

_____. "Saint Catherine and Contemporary Spirituality," from *exCHANGE,* Vol. 11, No. 4, Winter, 1979 (online).

Cavalini, Giuliana. *Things Visible and Invisible: Images in the*

Spirituality of St. Catherine of Siena, tr. by Sister Mary Jeremiah, OP, Alba House, New York, 1996.

Curtayne, Alice. *Saint Catherine of Siena,* Sheed and Ward, New York, 1933.

Drane, Augusta, T. *The History of St. Catherine of Siena and her Companions,* Vol. I & II, Longmans, Green & Co., 1915.

D'Urso, Giacinto, O.P. *"Il Pensiero di S. Caterina e le sue Fonti,"* 335-388, Sapienze, VII, 1954.

Ferretti, Ludovico. *Saint Catherine of Siena,* Edizioni Cantagalli, Siena, 1996.

Gardner, Edmund G. *St. Catherine of Siena: A Study in the Religion, Literature, and History of the Fourteenth Century in Italy,* New York: E. P. Dutton & Co., 1907.

Grottanelli, F. *Epistolari* II, V. Meattini, ed., Siena, 1966, *Albero della Famiglia Benincasa.*

Hackett, Benedict, O.S.A. *William Flete, O.S.A. and Catherine of Siena,* Augustinian Press, 1992.

Kearns, Conleth. "The Wisdom of Saint Catherine," 324-343, in *Angelicum,* Pontificia Universitas, a Sancto Thoma, Vol. 57, 1980.

Levasti, Arrigo. *My Servant Catherine,* tr. Dorothy White, Newman Press, Maryland, 1954, originally published as *Santa Caterina da Siena,* Unione Tipografic-Editrice, Turin, 1947.

Noffke, Suzanne, O.P. "The Physical in the Mystical Writings of Catherine of Siena," 109-128, in *Annali d'Italianistica: Italian Women Mystics,* ed. by Dino S. Cervigni, Vol.13, 1995.

O'Driscoll, Mary, O.P. "Catherine the Theologian," 4-7, in *Spirituality Today,* Vol. 40, Spring, 1988.

Scott, Karen. "Not Only With Words, But With Deeds: The Role of Speech in Catherine of Siena's Understanding of Mission," Unpublished Doctoral Dissertation, University of California at Berkeley, 1989.

_____. "The Imagery of Conversion in the Letters of
Caterina da Siena," 91-108 in *Annali d'Italianistica:
Women Mystic Writers,* ed. by Dino S. Cervigni, Vol.
13, 1995.

_____. "Urban Spaces, Women's Networks, and the Lay
Apostolate in the Siena of Catherine Benincasa," 103-
119, in *Creative Women in Medieval and Early Modern
Italy: A Religious and Artistic Renaissance,* ed. by E.
Ann Matter and John Coakley, University of Pennsylva-
nia Press, Philadelphia, 1994.

Scudder, Vida D. *Saint Catherine of Siena as Seen in Her
Letters,* E. P. Dutton & Co., New York, 1927.

Undset, Sigrid. *Catherine of Siena,* tr. by Kate Austin-Lund,
Sheed and Ward, New York, 1954.

Secondary Sources

A. *Books*

Allport, Gordon. *Pattern and Growth in Personality,* New York,
Holt, Rinehart and Winston, 1961.

Barraclough, Geoffrey. *The Medieval Papacy,* Harcourt, Brace
& World, Inc., 1968.

Bellucci, Gualtiero and Piero Torriti. *Il Santa Maria della Scala
in Siena: l'Ospedale dai Mille Anni,* Sagep Editrice,
Genova, 1991.

Belting, Hans. *Likeness and Presence: A History of the Image
before the Era of Art,* tr. by Edmund Jephcott, University of Chicago Press, Chicago, 1994.

Bergmann, Martin S. and Milton E. Jucovy, eds. *Generations of
the Holocaust,* Basic Books, New York, 1982.

Bigelow, Brian, Geoffrey Tesson & John Lewko. *Learning the
Rules: The Anatomy of Children's Relationships,*
Guilford Press, New York, 1996.

Bosma, Harke, Tobi Graafsma, Harold Grotevant and David
deLevita, eds. *Identity and Development: An Interdisci-
plinary Approach,* Sage Publications, California, 1994.

Bowsky, William. *A Medieval Commune: Siena under the Nine,* *1287-1355,* University of California Press, Berkeley, 1981.

_____, ed. *The Black Death: A Turning Point in History?* Kreiger Publishing Co., New York, 1978.

Brucker, Gene A. *Florentine Politics and Society, 1343-1378,* Princeton University Press, Princeton, New Jersey, 1962.

Burckhardt, Jacob. *Siena,* Oxford University Press, London, 1960.

Burnham, Philip E. Jr. "Cultural Life at Papal Avignon, 1309-1376," Unpublished Doctoral Thesis, Tufts University, 1972.

Bynum, Carol Walker. *Holy Feast and Holy Fast: The Religious Significance of Food to Medieval Women,* University of California Press, Berkeley, 1987.

Cavallero, Daniela Gallavotti. *Lo Spedale di Santa Maria delle Scala in Siena: Vicenda di una Committenza Artistica,* Pacina editrice Oisa, 1985.

Christiansen, Keith, Laurence Kanter, Carl Strehlke. *Painting in Renaissance Siena: 1420-1500,* The Metropolitan Museum of Art, New York, Harry N. Abrams, Inc., 1988.

Coakley, John. "The Representation of Sanctity in Late Medieval Hagiography: Evidence from the Lives of Saints of the Dominican Order," Unpublished Doctoral Thesis, Harvard Divinity School, Cambridge, 1980.

Cole, Bruce. *Sienese Painting: From Its Origins to the Fifteenth Century,* Harper & Row, New York, 1980.

_____. *Sienese Painting in the Age of the Renaissance,* Indiana University Press, 1985.

Conn, Joann Wolski, ed. *Women's Spirituality: Resources for Christian Development,* Paulist Press, New York, 1986.

Cook, William R. and Ronald B. Herzman. *The Medieval World View,* 2nd ed., Oxford University Press, 2004.

Corr, Charles and Joan McNeill, eds. *Adolescence and Death,* Springer Publishing, New York, 1986.

Des Pres, Terrence. *The Survivor: An Anatomy of Life in the Death Camps,* Oxford University Press, New York, 1976.

de Santis, Francesco. *History of Italian Literature,* 2 Vol., tr. by Joan Redfern, Harcourt, Brace, New York, 1931; I.

de Voragine, Jacobus, *The Golden Legends,* tr. by Granger Ryan & Helmut Ripperger, Longmans Green, New York, 1948.

Duffy, Eamon. *Saints and Sinners,* Yale University Press, 1997.

Egan, Harvey, S.J. *An Anthology of Christian Mysticism,* A Pueblo Book, The Liturgical Press, Collegeville, Minnesota, 1991.

_____. *What Are They Saying About Mysticism?,* Paulist Press, New York, 1982.

Epstein, Helen. *Children of the Holocaust: Conversations with Sons and Daughters of Survivors,* Bantam, New York, 1980.

Erikson, Erik. *Psychological Issues: Identity and the Life Cycle,* International University Press, New York, 1959.

_____. *The Life Cycle Completed,* Extended Version with New Chapters by Joan M. Erikson, W.W. Norton, New York, 1997.

_____ ed. *Adulthood,* W.W. Norton & Company, New York, 2nd ed., 1978.

Farrow, John. *Pageant of the Popes,* Sheed and Ward, New York, 1950.

Gardner, Edmund G. *The Story of Siena and San Gimignano,* New York: E.P. Dutton & Co., 1913.

Gilligan, Carol. *In a Different Voice: Psychological Theory and Women's Development,* Cambridge, MA: Harvard University Press, 1982.

Hall, C. Margaret. *Women and Identity: Value Choices in a Changing World,* Hemisphere Publishing Corporation, New York, 1990.

Hammarskjöld, Dag. *Markings,* tr. from the Swedish by Leif Sjöberg, New York, Knopf, 1964.

Herlihy, David. *Pisa in the Early Renaissance: A Study of Urban Growth,* Yale University Press, New Haven, 1958.

————. *The Black Death and the Transformation of the West,* Samuel Cohn, Jr., ed., Harvard University Press, Cambridge, 1997.

Hilkert, Mary Catherine. *Speaking with Authority: Catherine of Siena and the Voices of Women Today,* Paulist Press, New Jersey, 2001.

Hook, Judith. *Siena: A City and Its History,* Hamish Hamilton, London, 1979.

Johnston, William, S.J. *The Inner Eye of Love: Mysticism and Religion,* San Francisco: Harper & Row, 1978.

Kessler, Herbert L. and Johanna Zacharas. *Rome 1300: On the Path of the Pilgrim,* Yale University Press, New Haven, 2000.

Knowles, David and Dimitri Obolensky. *The Christian Centuries: The Middle Ages,* 3 Vol., McGraw-Hill Book Company, New York, 1986, II.

Langer, Lawrence L. *Holocaust Testimonies: The Ruins of Memory,* Yale University Press, New Haven, 1991.

Levillain, Phillippe, ed. *The Papacy: An Encyclopedia,* Vol. III, Routledge, New York, 2002.

Martines, Lauro. *Power and Imagination: City States in Renaissance Italy,* Vintage, Random House, New York, 1980.

———— ed. *Violence and Civil Disorder in Italian Cities, 1200-1500,* University of California, Berkeley, 1972.

Maslow, Abraham A. *Toward a Psychology of Being,* Van Nostrand Reinhold Company, New York, 2nd ed., 1968.

McBrien, Richard P. *Lives of the Popes: The Pontiffs from St. Peter to John Paul II,* Harper, San Francisco, 1997.

Miller, Jean Baker. *Toward a New Psychology of Women,* Beacon Press, Boston, 1976.

Mills, Margaret R. *Image As Insight: Visual Understanding in Western Christianity and Secular Culture,* Beacon Press, Boston, 1985.

Mitchell, John J. *The Nature of Adolescence,* Detselig Enterprises, Calgary, Alberta, 1986.

Mollat, Guillaume. *The Popes at Avignon, 1305-1378,* tr. Janet Love, for Thomas Nelson & Sons, 1963, Harper Torchbooks, New York, 1965.

Newman, Barbara and Philip Newman. *Development through Life: A Psychological Approach,* The Dorsey Press, Illinois, 1975.

Norman, Diana, ed. *Siena, Florence and Padua: Art, Society and Religion 1280-1400,* Vol. I & II, Yale University Press, New Haven, 1995.

Oakley, Francis. *The Western Church in the Later Middle Ages,* Cornell University Press, Ithaca, New York, 1979.

O'Donohue, John. *Anam Cara: A Book of Celtic Wisdom,* Harper Collins, New York, 1997.

Okey, Thomas. *The Story of Avignon,* J.M. Dent & Sons, Ltd., London, 1926.

Petroff, Elizabeth Alvilda. *Body and Soul: Essays on Medieval Women and Mysticism,* Oxford University Press, New York, 1994.

Rotelle, John E., O.S.A., ed. *The Works of Saint Augustine: A Translation for the 21st Century,* Part III, Vol. 1, *Sermons* #1-19, tr. by Edmund Hill, O.P., New City Press, New York, 1991.

Saint Gregory the Great. *The Dialogues,* tr. by Odo John Zimmerman, O.S.B., New York, Fathers of the Church, Inc., 1959.

Saint Teresa of Avila. *Autobiography,* tr. E. Allison Peers, Doubleday Image, New York, 1960.

Schevill, Ferdinand. *Siena, The History of a Medieval Commune,* Harper & Row, New York, 1964.

Schimmelpfennig, Bernhard. *The Papacy,* tr. by James Sievet, Columbia University Press, New York, 1992.

Seppelt, Francis X., and Clement Löeffler. *A Short History of the Popes,* B. Herder Book Co., 1932.

Sheldrake, Phillip. *Images of Holiness: Explorations in Contemporary Spirituality,* Ave Maria Press, 1988.

Southern, R.W. *Western Society and the Church in the Middle Ages,* Penguin Books, Ltd., 1970.

Steindl-Rast, David. *Gratefulness, the Heart of Prayer: An Approach to Life in Fullness,* Paulist Press, New York, 1984.

Storr, Anthony. *Solitude: A Return to the Self,* Free Press, New York, 1988.

Straw, Carole. *Gregory the Great: Perfection in Imperfection,* University of California Press, Berkeley, 1988.

Thibault, Paul R. *Pope Gregory XI: The Failure of Tradition,* University Press of America, New York, 1986.

Tuchman, Barbara. *A Distant Mirror,* Ballantine Books, New York, 1978.

Tugwell, Simon, O.P., ed. *Early Dominicans: Selected Writings,* Paulist Press, New York, 1982.

Ullmann, Walter. *A Short History of the Papacy in the Middle Ages,* Methuen & Co. Ltd., 1972.

Van Os, Henk. *Sienese Altarpieces, 1214-1460,* Vol. I. tr. by Michael Hoyle, Bouma's Boekhuis BV, Groningen, 1984.

_____. *Sienese Altarpieces, 1214-1460: Form, Content, and Function,* Vol. II, Egbert Forsten Publishing, Groningen, 1990.

_____. *Vecchietta and the Sacristy of the Siena Hospital Church: A Study in Renaissance Religious Symbolism,* tr. by Eva Biesta, Kunsthistorische Studiën van het, Nederlands, 1974.

Waley, Daniel. *Siena and the Sienese in the Thirteenth Century,* Cambridge University Press, New York, 1991.

Weinstein, Donald and Rudolph Bell. *Saints and Society: The Two Worlds of Western Christendom, 1000-1700,* University of Chicago Press, Chicago, 1982.

Williman, Daniel, ed. *The Black Death: The Impact of the Fourteenth Century Plague,* Medieval & Renaissance Texts and Studies, Binghamton, New York, 1982.

B. Articles

Bowsky, William, "Anatomy of a Rebellion in Fourteenth Century Siena," 219-222, in Lauro Martines, ed., *Violence and Civil Disorder in Italian Cities, 1200-1500,* University of California, Berkeley, 1972.

Bryan, Elizabeth M. "The Death of a Twin," 187-192, in *Palliative Medicine,* Vol. 9 (#3, 1995) Cambridge University Press, New York.

————. "The Death of a Newborn Twin: How Can Support for Parents Be Improved?" 115-118, in *Acta Geneticae Medicae et Gemellologiae,* Vol. 35 (#1, 1986), The Mendel Institute, Rome.

Cannon, Joanna. "Pietro Lorenzetti and the History of the Carmelite Order," 18-28, in *Journal of the Warburg and Courtauld Institutes,* London, Vol. 50, 1987.

Conn, Joann Wolski. "A Discipleship of Equals," 1-34, in *Proceedings of the Theology Institute of Villanova University,* Villanova University Press, 1988.

Fitzgerald, Constance, O.C.D. "Impasse and the Dark Night," 287-311, in *Women's Spirituality: Resources for Christian Development,* ed. by Joann Wolski Conn, Paulist Press, New York, 1986.

Gilligan, Carol and Grant Wiggins. "The Origins of Morality in Early Childhood Relationships," 111-138, in Carol Gilligan, Janie Victoria Ward, Jill McLean Taylor, eds., *Mapping the Moral Domain: A Contribution of Women's Thinking to Psychological Theory and Education,* Harvard University Press, 1988.

_____. "Adolescent Development Reconsidered," viii, Ibid., Prologue.

Gordon, Audrey. "The Tattered Cloak of Immortality," 16-31, in Charles Corr and Joan McNeill, eds., *Adolescence and Death,* Springer Publishing, New York, 1986.

Johnston, Thomas J., O.P. "Franciscan and Dominican Influences on the Medieval Order of Penance: Origins of the Dominican Laity," 108-119, in *Spirituality Today,* 37 (Summer, 1985).

Lerner, Robert E. "The Black Death and Western European Eschatological Mentalities," 77-81, in *The Black Death: The Impact of the Fourteenth Century Plague,* Daniel Williman, ed., Medieval & Renaissance Texts and Studies, Binghamton, New York, 1982.

Maginnis, Hayden J. "The Lost Façade Frescoes from Siena's Ospedale di S. Maria della Scala," 180-194, in *Zeitschrift feur Kunstgeschichte,* Vol. 51, 1988, Berlin.

Martines, Lauro. "Political Violence in the Thirteenth Century," 331-353, in Lauro Martines, ed., *Violence and Civil Disorder in Italian Cities, 1200-1500,* University of California, Berkeley, 1972.

Miller, Jean Baker. "The Development of Women's Sense of Self," in *Women's Growth in Connection: Writings from the Stone Center,* ed. by Judith Jordan, Alexandra Kaplan, Jean Baker Miller, Irene Stiver, Janet Surrey, The Guilford Press, New York, 1991.

_____. "Women and Power," 197-205, Ibid.

Murphy, Lois. "Further Reflections on Resilience," 84-105, in *The Invulnerable Child,* E. James Anthony & Bertram Cohler, ed., The Guilford Press, New York, 1987.

Stegner, Wallace. "The Writer and the Concept of Adulthood," 227-236, in Erik Erikson, ed., *Adulthood,* W.W. Norton & Company, New York, 2nd ed., 1978.

Wainwright, Valerie. "The Testing of a Popular Sienese Regime: The *Riformatori* and the Insurrections of 1371,"

107-170, in *I Tatti Studies: Essays in the Renaissance* (Vol. 2, 1987), Florence.

Werner, Emmy. "Resilient Children," 68-72, in *Young Children* (November, 1984), Research in Review.

Woodward, Joan. "The Bereaved Twin," 173-180, in *Acta Geneticae Medicae et Gemellologiae,* Vol. 37 (#2, 1988), The Mendel Institute, Rome.

ST PAULS

This book was produced by ST PAULS/Alba House, the Society of St. Paul, an international religious congregation of priests and brothers dedicated to serving the Church through the communications media.

For information regarding this and associated ministries of the Pauline Family of Congregations, write to the Vocation Director, Society of St. Paul, 2187 Victory Blvd., Staten Island, New York 10314-6603. Phone (718) 982-5709; or E-mail: vocation@stpauls.us or check our internet site, www.vocationoffice.org